Units 5 & 8

Financial accounting: preparing accounts and returns

Study Pack

Intermediate (NVQ Level 3)

Published August 1995 by Financial Training, 136–142 Bramley Road, London W10 6SR

ISBN 1 85179 643 6

We are grateful to the Association of Accounting Technicians for their kind permission to reproduce tasks from the central assessments.

Printed in England by Communications In Print plc, Basildon, Essex.

41099

Contents

Review of Module Two

Answers to sessions

Practice simulations (Panther Alarms Ltd)

Practice central assessment

Index

Introduction

PREFACE

The assessment guidance given within this Study Pack is in line with the guidance issued by the AAT. You are advised to confirm the methods of assessment to be used for each unit by drawing up an *Assessment plan* with your Approved Assessment Centre (AAC).

Examples of assessment plans are only suggested formats. Other documents or planning methods are equally valid.

INTRODUCTION TO THE EDUCATION AND TRAINING SCHEME

Background to the scheme

The Association of Accounting Technicians (AAT) was founded in 1980 to provide a recognised qualification and membership body for accounting support staff. In 1991 it became the first and only professional accountancy body to adopt competence-led assessment. Each stage of the AAT's new Education and Training Scheme is graded as a National Vocational Qualification (NVQ) or, in Scotland, as a Scottish Vocational Qualification (SVQ) with levels 2 to 4. This means that, once you have completed each stage, you hold a nationally recognised qualification, which is recognised by employers. The scheme is open to anyone, regardless of previous experience or qualifications.

As well as being part of the AAT's membership process, the Education and Training Scheme offers a flexible opportunity for individuals to improve and gain recognition for their skills. In entering the scheme, you do not have to commit yourself to achieving AAT membership; in fact, each successfully completed stage is recognised with the issue of a separate certificate. The AAT will also issue (for an additional fee) certificates to record the successful completion of single or selected units.

If you decide to aim for membership, there are three requirements:

- proven competence

- a minimum period of relevant work experience (usually one year full-time or the part-time equivalent)

- evidence of suitability for membership and commitment to the AAT

This Study Pack deals exclusively with the requirement to prove competence. Further details of the other requirements are available direct from AAT.

Standards

Your aim is to prove your competence against a nationally agreed set of standards. These have been drawn up to reflect the skills, knowledge and understanding required by an accounting technician. They have been prepared to reflect the general types of skills required by any accounting technician rather than any specific job or industry, although some specialisation is possible at the Technician stage (NVQ/SVQ Level 4). You may specialise in accounting practice, industry and commerce or public sector. In addition, if you choose the public sector route, you may specialise in central government, local government or the NHS.

The AAT has decided that the key purpose of an accounting technician is:

To operate, maintain and improve systems to record, plan, monitor and report on the financial activities of an organisation

This key purpose is then broken down into key roles. These are the general areas in which an accounting technician should be competent:

- recording financial transactions
- preparing accounts
- reporting on organisational activities
- contributing to planning and controlling activities
- managing accounting systems
- contributing to assuring the quality of accounting systems
- establishing taxation liabilities
- processing accounting information by computer
- maintaining good office practice

Each role is sub-divided into *units of competence* which identify more specific areas of required competence. These units are arranged into three *stages* which are designed to show you what could normally be expected of accounting technicians as they progress and gain experience. It is important to realise that the stages are guidelines, but we will come back to this later (see *Flexibility* below). Each stage has a name (given by the AAT) and an NVQ/SVQ level. The units for Foundation stage (NVQ/SVQ Level 2) are as follows:

Recording financial transactions

4	Recording capital transactions
6	Recording cost information

Preparing accounts

5	Preparing financial accounts

Reporting on organisational activities

7	Preparing reports and returns

Establish taxation liabilities

8	Prepare VAT returns

Processing accounting information by computer

21	Information technology environment
22	Using spreadsheets

Maintaining good office practice

25	Monitor and maintain a healthy, safe and secure workplace *If not already completed at Foundation stage*

The arrangement of the units into stages gives the scheme structure and reflects typical patterns of development and progression. The scheme assumes that, if you are at the Foundation stage, an employer would expect you to be competent in a broad range of complex, technical or professional work activities, performed in a wide variety of contexts. Some of the activities could be complex or non-routine, and there could be some individual responsibility. Working with others – as part of a team, for example – might also be required.

Each unit is in turn divided into elements which are the specific activities within that particular area. Let us now look at one of the elements. You will now need to refer to Unit 5 Element 1 of your *Intermediate Student Record Book*. (**Note:** If you have not already registered with the AAT, you should do so as soon as possible. In fact this is vital otherwise you cannot sit any assessments until you have done so. In return they will send you a Student Record Book. You need this book to record your progress.)

Unit 5 Element 1 is a typical element within the standards.

At the top of the page you see the Unit number (in this case 5) followed by a list of *all* the elements for this unit (of which there are three).

The *performance criteria* given for this unit are essentially the things you must get right to be considered competent and are therefore very 'practical'. They also tend to be expressed in very general terms. Remember that the standards are trying to identify general skills rather than skills associated with a particular job or industry.

The *range statement* describes the range of situations in which you have to be able to carry out the performance criteria. The range statement essentially gives more detail, defines terms and gives examples as required.

In this case, the range statement explains that tax allowances are excluded, lists the methods of depreciation you must be able to apply and gives an example of a discrepancy, unusual feature or query.

The *knowledge and understanding* associated with this element is essentially a list of the background knowledge which you need to carry out the performance criteria competently. This will include legal aspects, accounting techniques required and other conventions.

Assessment

To establish your competence against the standards, you will be assessed by two methods:

- devolved assessment
- central assessment

The AAT decides which units are tested by devolved assessment and which by central assessment, although about half of the units in the whole scheme are tested by both.

Devolved assessment is carried out by an *Approved Assessment Centre* (approved by AAT). Subject to the arrangements of the AAC, devolved assessment is available at any time during the year. The central assessment is set by the AAT itself. It is only offered twice a year (on specified dates in June and December). We will look at the differences between the two types of assessment below. First of all let us look at the methods of assessment for the each unit of the Intermediate stage. To complete the Intermediate stage, you must gain a credit for *all of the following units*.

	Devolved assessment	Central assessment
Intermediate		
Unit 4 *Capital transactions*	•	
Unit 5 *Preparing accounts*	•	•
Unit 6 *Recording costs*	•	•
Unit 7 *Reports and returns*	•	•
Unit 8 *VAT*	•	
Units 21 & 22 *IT and spreadsheets*	•	
Unit 25 *Health and safety* (if not already completed at Foundation)	•	

(**Note:** To achieve a credit in a particular unit, you must be assessed as competent in both the devolved assessment and (if applicable) the central assessment. There is no weighting between the two types of assessment; you must be assessed as competent in both to achieve a credit.)

Flexibility

Before looking at assessment in more detail, you should be aware of the flexibility allowed by the AAT within the scheme.

You choose the units you attempt

At any one time, you may attempt a complete stage, individual units or a group of units (not necessarily all taken from the same stage).

For example, the following combinations of units would all be valid:

- complete Foundation stage

- Unit 4 *Recording capital transactions* and Unit 5 *Preparing financial accounts*

- a combination of units from both the Foundation and Intermediate stages (for example, units relating to recording financial transactions)

You can attempt the devolved and central assessments when it suits you

Subject to the arrangements agreed with your AAC, you may sit the devolved assessments to fit in with your own progress. You may sit the central assessments in any order and in any combination at any sitting. In fact, the central assessment timetable is arranged to make this possible.

In addition, you do not have to have attempted or passed the devolved assessment for a particular unit before attempting the related central assessment.

There are no time limits

There are no time limits to any part of the scheme and any devolved or central assessment passes are held indefinitely.

Devolved and central assessments

The main differences between the two methods of assessment can be summarised as follows:

	Devolved assessment	*Central assessment*
Assessment carried out by	Approved Assessment Centre (AAC)	AAT
Available	At any time during the year (subject to AAC's arrangements)	June and December only
Covers	All the performance criteria across the entire range statement and some aspects of knowledge and understanding	Selected aspects of knowledge and understanding and performance criteria
Methods of assessment	A variety of flexible methods, including accounting portfolios and projects	Using the same method (ie. written papers set and marked by the AAT)

PLANNING FOR DEVOLVED ASSESSMENT

Your objective

Remember that your objective at all times is to provide the assessor with evidence that you are competent in the performance criteria and have the necessary knowledge and understanding required for each unit. The assessment process is a method of collecting that evidence.

The devolved assessment must test all of the performance criteria across the whole of the range statement. It may also test parts of the knowledge and understanding. Since it concentrates mostly on the performance criteria, the devolved assessment tends to concentrate more on the practical aspects of the activities covered.

Devolved assessment is a very flexible form of assessment, although the AAT suggests the following two main methods at the Foundation stage:

- accounting portfolio
- project work

The *accounting portfolio* is a collection of evidence that you put together to prove that you are competent in each of the units you have chosen to attempt. Ideally, this would consist of examples of relevant tasks you have carried out as part of your work or work placement period.

If you have previous experience of the areas being assessed, either through work or by successfully completing another qualification, you may be able to include this evidence in your accounting portfolio. This process is known as *accreditation of prior learning*. We will look at this in more detail below.

The best source of evidence within your accounting portfolio would be *workplace evidence*, whether it arises from *prior learning* or from work which you undertake in the future. We will look at how you can identify workplace evidence below.

If you are unable to submit workplace evidence for some or all of the performance criteria for a particular element, then you may complete a *simulation*. Simulations are exercises or case studies set by your AAC which simulate completing tasks in the workplace. Most simulations contain facsimile documents which you are required to process as if they were real documents. The exact format of the simulation will depend upon the elements to be assessed.

In addition to submitting your accounting portfolio, your AAC will probably ask you additional questions which will also form part of the evidence for assessment.

Identifying prior learning

Your first task is to identify areas in which you have prior learning or experience.

You should use the following tables to identify the performance criteria in which you feel you could already demonstrate competence without further study, either because you have already completed another accounting or business studies qualification, or because you have previous or current work experience in these areas.

These tables list the performance criteria and range statements for each of the elements of Unit 5. You should complete the *Prior learning and experience* column with brief details of your specific experience. You should then record in the next column whether this experience is current or past. If your experience arises from another qualification, you should give the year of completion.

Note: Please note that completing this document is only part of the actual assessment process. You will still be required to prepare and submit an accounting portfolio.

Assessment plan for Unit 5: Preparing financial accounts

Element 1: Record income and expenditure

Performance criteria	Prior learning and experience	Timing	Assessment methods		Portfolio Ref.
			APL	Other	
(a) Income and expenditure is correctly recorded in the appropriate ledger accounts.					
(b) Any accrued or prepaid income and expenditure is correctly identified and adjustments made.					
(c) The organisation's policies, regulations, procedures and timescales are observed.					
(d) Income and expenditure is analysed in accordance with defined requirements and appropriate information is passed to management.					
(e) Discrepancies, unusual features or queries are identified and either resolved or referred to the appropriate person.					
Range statement					
• Items of income and expenditure for an organisation, including capital receipts and payments					

Knowledge and understanding	Prior learning and experience	Timing	Assessment methods		Portfolio Ref.
			APL	Other	
Unit 5 assumes competence in Units 1, 2 and 3 The business environment: – General function and status of SSAPs and FRSs Accounting techniques: – Accounting treatment of accruals and prepayments – Use of transfer journal – Methods of analysing income and expenditure Accounting principles and theory: – Principles of double-entry accounting – Basic accounting concepts and principles – matching of income and expenditure within an accounting period, historic cost, accruals, consistency, prudence, materiality – Function and form of accounts for income and expenditure The organisation: – Background and understanding that the accounting systems of an organisation are affected by its organisational structure, its administrative systems and procedures, and the nature of its business transactions					

Element 2: Prepare accounts from incomplete records

Performance criteria	Prior learning and experience	Timing	Assessment methods		Portfolio Ref.
			APL	Other	
(a) Essential accounts and reconciliations are correctly prepared.					
(b) Existing primary information is accurately summarised.					
(c) Other relevant information is correctly identified and recorded.					
(d) Investigations into the client's business transactions are conducted with tact and courtesy.					
(e) The organisation's policies, regulations, procedures and timescales are observed.					
(f) Discrepancies, unusual features or queries are identified and either resolved or referred to the appropriate person.					
Range statement					
• Reconstructing any accounts from data in an unusual or incomplete form					
• Discrepancies, unusual features or queries include situations where insufficient data has been provided, where there are inconsistencies within the data					

Knowledge and understanding	Prior learning and experience	Timing	Assessment methods		Portfolio Ref.
			APL	Other	
Unit 5 assumes competence in Units 1, 2 and 3					
The business environment:					
– General function and status of SSAPs and FRSs					
– Need to present accounts in the correct form					
– Legal, VAT and tax requirements					
– Main requirements of SSAPs 2, 5, 9, 12, 13, 21, or any relevant FRSs as they affect this element					
Accounting techniques:					
– Accounting treatment of accruals and prepayments					
– Use of transfer journal					
– Methods of restructuring accounts from incomplete evidence					
– Correction of different types of error					
– Making and adjusting provisions					
Accounting principles and theory:					
– Function and form of a trial balance					
– Basic principles of stock valuation: cost or NRV; what is included in cost					
– Objectives of making provisions for depreciation and other purposes					
The organisation:					
– Background understanding that the accounting systems of an organisation are affected by its organisational structure, its administrative systems and procedures, and the nature of its business transactions					

Element 3: Prepare the extended trial balance

Performance criteria	Timing	Assessment methods		Portfolio Ref.
Prior learning and experience		*APL*	*Other*	
(a) The trial balance is accurately extended and totalled.				
(b) Totals from the general ledger or other records are correctly entered on the extended trial balance.				
(c) Any errors disclosed by the trial balance are traced and corrected.				
(d) Any adjustments not dealt with in the ledger accounts are correctly entered on the extended trial balance.				
(e) An agreed valuation of closing stock is correctly entered on the extended trial balance.				
(f) The organisation's policies, regulations, procedures and timescales are observed.				
(g) Discrepancies, unusual features or queries are identified and either resolved or referred to the appropriate person.				
Range statement				
Relevant accounting policies include the treatment of depreciation and other provisions				

Knowledge and understanding	Prior learning and experience	Timing	Assessment methods		Portfolio Ref.
			APL	Other	
Unit 5 assumes competence in Units 1, 2 and 3 The business environment: – General function and status of SSAPs and FRSs – Main requirements of SSAPs 2, 5, 9, 12, 13, 21, as they affect this element and any relevant FRSs Accounting techniques: – Accounting treatment of accruals and prepayments – Use of transfer journal – Correction of different types of error – Making and adjusting provisions Accounting principles and theory: – Principles of double-entry accounting – Basic accounting concepts and principles – matching of income and expenditure within an accounting period, historic cost, accruals, consistency, prudence, materiality – Function and form of a trial balance – Basic principles of stock valuation: cost or NRV; what is included in cost – Objectives of making provisions for depreciation and other purposes The organisation: – Background understanding that the accounting systems of an organisation are affected by its organisational structure, its administrative systems and procedures and the nature of its business transactions					

Assessment plan for Unit 8: Preparing VAT returns

Element 1: Prepare VAT returns

Performance criteria	Prior learning and experience	Timing	Assessment methods		Portfolio Ref.
			APL	Other	
(a) VAT returns are correctly completed from the appropriate sources and submitted within the statutory time limits.					
(b) Relevant inputs and outputs are correctly identified and calculated.					
(c) VAT documentation is correctly filed.					
(d) Submissions are made in accordance with currently operative VAT laws and regulations.					
(e) Discussions with VAT inspectors are conducted openly and constructively to promote the efficiency of the VAT accounting system.					
Range statement					
• Exempt supplies, zero-rated supplies, imports and exports					

Knowledge and understanding	Prior learning and experience	Timing	Assessment methods		Portfolio Ref.
			APL	Other	
The business environment:					
– Basic law and practice relating to all issues covered in the range statement and referred to in the performance criteria. Specific issues include:					
– the classification of types of supply					
– registration requirements					
– the form of VAT invoices; tax points					
– Sources of information on VAT: Customs and Excise Guide					
– Administration of VAT; enforcement					
The organisation:					
– Background understanding that the accounting systems of an organisation are affected by its organisation structure, its administrative systems and procedures, and the nature of its business transactions					
– Background understanding that recording and accounting practices may vary in different parts of the organisation					

Deciding on assessment methods

Based upon your comments in the *Prior learning and experience* column, you should identify the method of assessment which is *most likely* to apply.

If you feel there is a sufficiently good match to offer your prior learning or experience as evidence of competence, you should tick the *APL* column. If you have no previous experience or your experience is not sufficiently relevant, you should put a cross in the *APL* column. You should consider each of the *performance criteria* individually, asking yourself the following questions. Where you feel that your answers to the all the questions relating to performance criteria are satisfactory, you should put a tick in the APL column.

- How closely does my experience match the performance criteria? For example, do I have experience across the whole range specified?

- Did I carry out this activity frequently enough to be considered competent?

- How much assistance, if any, did I require to complete this task?

- Where my experience was in the past, could I still carry out the same task to the same level of competence today?

- Where my experience was in the past, is this area of work subject to frequent changes? Have I kept up to date with those changes?

Other methods of assessment

For each of the performance criteria against which there is a cross, you must now decide the best method of collecting evidence. If there are only a few gaps, maybe this is an area in which you could arrange for further experience as part of your current work or work placement.

If there are only one or two gaps, your AAC may accept a piece of written evidence in which you describe what you *would do* in those circumstances. If you think you are unlikely to be able to submit any other form of evidence, then you will probably have to complete a simulation.

Complete the *Other methods* column with brief details of the most likely method.

(**Note:** Remember that what you have drawn up is simply a plan and you may alter this at any time during the assessment process, for example, if you gain further work experience against any of the performance criteria or as a result of discussions with your AAC.)

Assessment and study

Your next step is to agree your assessment plan with your AAC and to decide when assessment will take place as part of your broader study programme.

You should now start work on your *accounting portfolio*.

You may wish to use the planning document as the basis for your accounting portfolio by completing the final column *Portfolio reference*.

PREPARING AN ACCOUNTING PORTFOLIO

Objective

As we saw earlier, your accounting portfolio will be a collection of evidence which you have gathered together to demonstrate to the assessor that you are competent in your chosen elements.

As we saw above, your *accounting portfolio* will consist of:

- evidence of prior learning and experience
- current workplace evidence
- simulations

Using the assessment plan which you drew up above, we can now think about what might be included in the accounting portfolio. Once you have identified what might be included, the best approach is to gather evidence gradually over a period of time. Many people find it easiest to keep a file at work into which they put a copy of each piece of evidence as it arises. You will also need to allocate some time to actually compiling the portfolio.

The best approach is to complete one unit at a time. You should submit for assessment all the evidence relating to a single unit or group of units *at the same time*.

Essentially, your portfolio will be a collection of documents, selected by you which you feel are sufficient to demonstrate your competence in the performance criteria.

Most of these documents will probably be photocopies of actual pieces of work completed as part of your work or as part of a work placement. You may also wish to include evidence of other qualifications, including copies of certificates and syllabuses, accompanied by a short explanation of their relevance to the standards.

You may also find that you need to prepare short written descriptions, but we will look at specific examples of these below.

Each piece of evidence must be accompanied by a completed *commentary sheet* which you will find in your *Student Record Book*. Do not forget that the accounting portfolio also provides evidence of your communications skills which are seen as an important part of all assessments at all stages.

UNITS 5 AND 8

Contents

Let us now look at specific examples of evidence which you could include in a portfolio for Unit 5 *Preparing financial accounts*.

The following items might be found in a candidate's portfolio. Note that it might not be necessary to include all of these types of evidence, neither is this an all-inclusive list of possible evidence.

- Photocopies of the candidate's diary of accounting work undertaken, highlighting tasks relating to the recording and analysing of income and expenditure

- A description of the steps taken by the candidate to identify accruals and prepayments at the period-end

- A description of an unusual transaction (development expenditure) and the steps taken by the candidate to determine the correct accounting treatment

- A photocopy of an extended trial balance prepared by the candidate, accompanied by a short description of work undertaken

- A copy of a letter to a client, drafted by the candidate, requesting further information regarding the client's business transactions (preparation of accounts from incomplete records)

- Photocopies of stocksheets and other working papers supporting the period-end stock valuation, accompanied by a description of the candidate's involvement

- A signed statement prepared by the candidate and signed by a supervisor, detailing the work carried out in their employment

- A copy of a certificate from another accounting qualification (completed six months earlier) and a copy of the syllabus which includes the preparation of accounts from incomplete records, accompanied by a short description prepared by the candidate explaining the relevance to the standards

- A simulation covering Unit 5 Element 2

Notice how the candidate has made the relevance of each of the items to her experience clear, for example by including a description of her involvement or of the actual procedures carried out.

Similar documents relating to VAT would be included in a portfolio for Unit 8.

Note: Employer statements must give detailed descriptions of work carried out and its relevance to the standards. They are unlikely to be accepted in isolation. It is not acceptable for employers to submit a simple statement declaring an individual's competence in the place of an accounting portfolio. In addition, it is not acceptable for anyone other than a representative from your AAC to sign off your *Student Record Book*.

A note about confidentiality

You may have concerns about submitting copies of confidential documents as part of your accounting portfolio. In all cases, you are advised to seek permission from your employer and to remove as appropriate (with liquid paper) any sensitive information.

If there are further problems of confidentiality, you should consider submitting detailed descriptions of actual work undertaken, signed by your employer, or evidence generated by completing the activities within this Study Pack.

If in doubt, you should always discuss the best method of assessment for you with your AAC.

Format and presentation

You are advised to use a lever arch file as the volume of documentation may be considerable.

Presentation is an important part of your accounting portfolio. All documents should be neat and tidy, with careful indexing and cross-referencing. A checklist is given below which you may find useful to ensure that your accounting portfolio contains the basic information required for assessment.

The assessment process

Your accounting portfolio will be assessed, one unit at a time, against the standards. In most cases, the assessment process will involve a short interview.

There are two possible outcomes of the process: you will be assessed as either *competent* or *not yet competent*. In the case of the latter, you will receive feedback as to where improvements need to be made within your accounting portfolio and invited to re-submit it at a later date.

(**Note:** Grades are not awarded for accounting portfolios.)

Accounting portfolio completion checklist

Overall format and contents

Are your name, address, AAT registration number, AAC number and the identity of the units attempted clearly shown on the file?

Have all documents been numbered?

Have you included a list of all the documents within the portfolio?

Have you supplied a list of all the performance criteria for this unit, cross-referenced to the relevant evidence?

Have all the performance criteria been covered by the evidence included within the portfolio?

Does each piece of work have a completed commentary sheet attached?

Does the portfolio contain a signed statement (or statements) from your supervisor/manager that your contribution to each piece of work has been accurately recorded and that permission has been given to include certain documents?

Individual pieces of work

Does each piece of work have a clear title and show the date of its preparation (eg. extended trial balance as at 30 September 19X3 of A Ltd prepared November 19X3)?

Are the commentaries neatly and clearly presented?

Is it clear, in every case, exactly what your contribution was to the piece of work?

Is it clear how each piece of work demonstrates your competence in the particular performance criteria?

If you answer *No* to any of these questions, then you should not submit your portfolio without supplying this additional detail.

Financial Training

PREPARING FOR SIMULATION

What will the simulation cover?

Most simulations will cover either complete units or selected elements. Where you only require a simulation to cover certain performance criteria, you may find that your AAC still requires you to sit a simulation covering a complete element or unit as it may not be possible to assess those performance criteria out of context.

A typical simulation covering all the Unit 5 or Unit 8 elements would require you to carry out accounting tasks as well as prepare a short business communication, such as replying to a letter or preparing a memorandum.

How much preparation is required?

You must be confident that you are competent in all the relevant performance criteria before attempting the simulation. Attempt (or revise) the *practice simulation* within this Study Pack.

Remember that there is no pass mark for simulations; you are either assessed as competent or not yet competent. This means that you should aim to complete every task with complete accuracy. In fact, a few minor errors may be allowed, but this can only be decided by the assessor.

How long will it last?

There is no set time period for a simulation, although most take between three and four hours to complete. There is a time limit, but the aim is not to put you under unrealistic time-pressure, but to ensure that you can complete tasks in a reasonable period of time.

What is the assessor looking for?

While preparing for simulation, it is worth considering what the assessor is looking for. Remember that the assessor will assess you as either *competent* or *not yet competent*. To give you an indication of the general level required, ask yourself whether your supervisor/manager would be satisfied with a particular piece of work if you submitted it for review. Remember that the simulation is meant to simulate real work tasks, so the same standards must apply.

If we consider a typical simulation for Unit 5 or Unit 8, the assessor will be looking for evidence of good presentation skills, completeness, good communication skills, accuracy and technical knowledge.

Good presentation skills

All work should be neat and well presented, as if it were real work. You should use black ink or biro. Pencil is not acceptable, neither is correcting fluid (eg. Tipp-Ex). Cross out any errors neatly and clearly. Always use a ruler for underlining.

Completeness

All tasks should be complete (for example, columns totalled). Unlike in other forms of test, you cannot decide to leave out part of an exercise and still hope to be successful.

Good communication skills

Communication skills are fundamentally important in all the assessments for all stages. You are expected to show a good standard of English, including correct spelling and correct use of accounting terms.

Accuracy

All calculations must be completed accurately (for example, the calculation of the VAT element of cash sales or the calculation of discounts). All documents completed – such as cheques, etc. – must be accurate. All accounting entries must be correct.

All discrepancies and exceptions must be identified and dealt with correctly. At the Intermediate stage, this normally means referring them to someone at supervisor level.

Technical knowledge

Any explanations given – for example, how VAT works – must be accurate.

CENTRAL ASSESSMENT

Preparing financial accounts

There are three central assessments at Intermediate stage: one for each of Units 5, 6 and 7. The central assessment for Unit 5 is called *Preparing financial accounts*. Unit 8 is *not* tested by central assessment.

What format will the central assessment take?

You will be provided with a booklet in which you should write your answers. You are unlikely to need additional writing paper.

What will be covered?

At the Intermediate stage, the central assessment will mostly test the knowledge and understanding aspects of Unit 5, but it will inevitably test some of the performance criteria as well. The assessment lasts three hours. The format of the assessment has recently changed, but it is likely to be as follows. Please note that you must complete all tasks.

Section 1

This part of the assessment is based on a scenario and focuses on the extended trial balance. The scenario normally features a sole trader, but could feature a limited company.

You will be required to prepare journal entries, post them to the adjustments column of the extended trial balance and (normally) to extend the resulting figures into the appropriate columns for the profit and loss account and balance sheet. You may be asked to clear a balance on a suspense account or to adjust for errors. Other adjustments typically involve calculating depreciation, valuing stock, arriving at a provision for doubtful debts and calculating accruals and prepayments.

Section 2

This section will probably consist of several short answer questions and one or two longer 'communication' exercises which may be related to the scenario in Section 1.

The short answer questions will test your understanding of accounting treatments and principles.

The 'communication' exercises will require you to write memoranda, business letters or notes in reply to queries (often from the owner of the business). You will almost certainly be asked to relate proposed or actual accounting treatments to fundamental principles or to the requirements of accounting standards (eg. SSAP12, SSAP9).

Section 3

This part of the assessment tests your ability to prepare accounts from incomplete records. You will be given a separate scenario and information (eg. summary cash book, narrative points). From this you may be asked to calculate figures such as closing stock, profit for the period and the balance on the capital account. You could also be asked to reconstruct ledger accounts.

Common problems with central assessment

The assessor has made the following comments:

- Candidates must understand that, particularly in a computerised accounting system, the ability to enter transactions via the journal is a core skill.

- There is a serious weakness with most candidates' understanding of the conceptual nature of bookkeeping. Candidates tend to know how to deal with a particular transaction but not why it is dealt with in a particular way. Understanding the underlying bookkeeping concepts and principles is important so that unusual transactions which may not have been met before can be dealt with in a logically correct manner.

- Many candidates have serious problems in explaining conceptual and practical areas of bookkeeping. In some cases, it is difficult to know whether it is a weakness in understanding or communication. Candidates should appreciate that effective communication is essential and this aspect must be given more attention. There is no point in having the technical knowledge if it cannot be communicated.

- One overall weakness of a significant number of candidates is untidiness and poor presentation. Although neatness is of less importance in computerised accounting systems than with manual bookkeeping, neat and careful presentation often reflects neat and careful thought.

- It must be remembered that Intermediate level builds on Foundation level skills.

- There is a common failure to answer the question set.

- Practice in a variety of questions together with a clear understanding of the inter-relationship of the elements in an accounting system is needed to respond competently to non-routine situations.

What the assessor is looking for

The assessor is looking for the same standard of presentation and technical and communications skills described above as relevant for devolved assessment.

Once again, your objective is to prove that you are competent in the unit(s) being assessed. You must therefore aim for 100% accuracy and an extremely high standard of presentation.

How to tackle the central assessment

- Always read all the instructions carefully before starting.

  Assessment tasks vary from sitting to sitting. If you do more than you are required to do, you will waste valuable time.

- Work through the paper in the order set.

  You may discover that some of the tasks in section 2 relate to aspects of section 1.

- Allocate your time sensibly between the tasks, although time-pressure should not be a problem if you are well-prepared.

  The instructions give a suggested time allocation for each section.

- Work methodically through the bookkeeping exercise and the incomplete records exercise.

  You must aim to get all of this exercise correct if you are to be assessed as competent.

- If you have problems with one of the short answer questions, leave it and return to it later.

  Never leave a gap.

- Plan your approach to the communications exercises carefully.

  Read all the information carefully. Make sure you understand what you are required to do and what the aim of the communication is. Remember that in most cases you are writing to someone with limited or no knowledge of accounting, so you must explain any accounting terms.

THE ROLE OF STUDY

Studying for different reasons

Finally, we need to consider the role of study within the scheme. Whatever your previous experience, you will inevitably need to devote a considerable amount of time to studying, even if it is only to familiarise yourself with the coverage and likely content and format of the central assessment. This Study Pack contains study and practice material covering all the performance criteria and knowledge and understanding required for this unit.

The objective of this Study Pack is to provide you with:

- guidance on completing the assessments for this unit

- examples of best practice as a reference when preparing your *accounting portfolio*

- study and practice materials for simulations

- study and practice materials for central assessment

USING THIS STUDY PACK

Whatever your previous experience, you are therefore encouraged to work through this Study Pack, paying attention to the areas which are most relevant to you. Here is a short explanation of the aim of each aspect of this Study Pack and the areas in which they are relevant.

- *Sessions:* Contain study material and examples on a particular topic to help you learn the required techniques. The relevant performance criteria are identified at the start of each session. In addition, the knowledge and understanding required for that topic are included within that session.

- *Practice simulations:* Practice simulations covering all the Unit 5 elements and Unit 8. These simulations are designed to be as difficult as, if not more difficult than, the real simulations which you will have to sit.

- *Practice central assessment:* A practice central assessment in the style of the *Preparing financial accounts* central assessment.

FURTHER STUDY MATERIAL

The Financial Training Company also publishes a *Central Assessment Pack* designed to give you additional practice towards the *Preparing financial accounts* central assessment. As well as containing new exercises of the sort featured in the real central assessments, it also contains brief revision notes of all major topics and a mock central assessment in the style of the real Central Assessment.

Central Assessment Packs are available from your usual supplier of Financial Training Company study materials.

PUBLISHER'S NOTE

Financial Training study materials are distributed in the UK and overseas by Stanley Thornes (Publishers) Limited. They are another company within the Wolters Kluwer group. They can be contacted at: Stanley Thornes, Ellenborough House, Wellington Street, Cheltenham GL50 1YD. Telephone: (01242) 228888. Fax: (01242) 221914.

Your chances of success in the AAT assessments will be greatly improved by additional tuition, either at one of Financial Training's centres or by home study. For details of our open learning programmes please contact us at:

Open Learning Department
The Financial Training Company
136 – 142 Bramley Road
London W10 6SR

Tel: 0181–960 4421
Fax: 0181–960 9374

Introduction to final accounts

OBJECTIVES

By the end of this session you will be able to prepare a basic set of final accounts.

This session also addresses the following performance criteria:

- Income and expenditure is analysed in accordance with defined requirements and appropriate information is passed to management.

- The organisation's policies, regulations, procedures and timescales are observed.

- Discrepancies, unusual features or queries are identified and either resolved or referred to the appropriate person.

INTRODUCTION

This session will show you how to use the information contained in the trial balance to construct the **final accounts** of a business.

The final accounts of a business are concerned with providing the owners with two essential pieces of information. The trading and profit and loss accounts are used to calculate the business **profit or loss** of a trading period. The balance sheet is used to show the **financial position at a set date**.

This session also addresses some of the professional conduct issues which are relevant to your work as an accountant.

THE TRADING ACCOUNT

Purpose

The purpose of the trading account is to calculate the **gross profit** on the trading activity of a period. This profit is the amount left after the cost of goods sold has been deducted from the sales of that period.

We can therefore state that:

Gross profit is sales minus cost of goods sold.

Illustration

Reid received £2,500 from sales. The goods sold were bought for £1,750. What is his **gross profit**?

$$\begin{aligned} \text{Gross profit} \quad &= \quad \text{Sales} - \text{Cost of sales} \\ &= \quad \text{£2,500} - \text{£1,750} = \text{£750} \end{aligned}$$

The trading account may be presented in two formats:

(a)   as it is an account held in the general ledger, it may be presented as it appears in the ledger (although not every enterprise has a trading account in its general ledger);

(b)   for ease of interpretation by the businessman who is not an accountant and is not concerned with double-entry, it may be presented in a vertical format.

The vertical format for this example is shown below.

Mr Reid
Trading account for the year ended 31 December 19X6

		£
Sales		2,500
Less: Cost of goods sold		
Purchases		1,750
Gross profit		750

We shall develop this format as we introduce new elements to the example in this session.

Note: Should the final figure in the trading account be negative, it will be described as a gross loss and shown in brackets.

The trading account in the ledger

The trading account has debit and credit sides. The debit represents the expenses of selling; the cost of goods sold. The credit side represents the income from selling. The entries in the trading account are transferred or 'posted' from other ledger accounts.

The accounts to be cleared to the trading account at the end of an accounting period will become known to you as you practise constructing final accounts. You should, however, recall that a balance represents either of the following:

(a)   *A debit balance*

> (i)   An asset: record in the balance sheet.
> (ii)   An expense: record in the trading or profit and loss account.

(b)   *A credit balance*

> (i)   A liability: record in the balance sheet.
> (ii)   An item of income: record in the trading or profit and loss account.

Illustration

Extracts from the book of account of Mr Reid

Sales account

	£		£
		30 Nov 19X6 Bank	1,500
		31 Dec 19X6 Debtors	1,000

In order to 'post' or transfer the balance from the sales account to the trading account at the end of the trading period, it is necessary to go through the balancing process as before, but once we ascertain the balancing figure, we do not carry it down: we transfer it to the trading account.

Sales account (after posting to trading account)

	£		£
		30 Nov 19X6 Bank	1,500
31 Dec 19X6 Trading account	2,500	31 Dec 19X6 Debtors	1,000
	2,500		2,500

Trading account

	£		£
		31 Dec 19X6 Sales	2,500

Note: The credit entry to meet the double-entry requirement is found in the trading account, shown above. The balance transferred to the trading account closes the sales account as at 31 Dec 19X6. The purchases account is dealt with in a similar manner.

Purchases account

	£		£
31 Sep 19X6 Bank	750	31 Dec 19X6	
31 Oct 19X6 Creditors	1,000	Trading account	1,750
	1,750		1,750

Trading account

	£		£
31 Dec 19X6 Purchases	1,750	31 Dec 19X6 Sales	2,500

Note: The debit entry is found in the trading account shown above. The balance transferred to the trading account closes the purchases account as at 31 December 19X6.

Our trading account may now be closed off.

Trading account

	£		£
31 Dec 19X6 Purchases	1,750		
31 Dec 19X6 Gross profit			
(balancing figure)	750	31 Dec 19X6 Sales	2,500
	2,500		2,500

Compare this with the vertical format previously shown.

Note: At present we have a single entry in our ledger (£750 debit) with no corresponding credit – we shall deal with this again shortly and you will find that the credit is passed to the profit and loss account.

Closing stock

The only additional element which we require to deal with at this stage is stock. If Mr Reid had sold all his purchases, then the cost of goods sold would be the purchases figure. If, however, some of the goods purchased for resale had not been sold, then the cost of goods sold would have been the purchase price of those that were actually sold. The cost of goods sold therefore becomes:

Cost of goods sold = Purchases – Stock at end of period

The stock at the end of the period is found by a physical count of the number of goods still in store at the end of the trading period. These are then valued at cost. These goods were an asset of the business at 31 December 19X6 although they have been accounted for through an expense account (purchases).

Thus we should, at least overnight, give them their proper status as assets by opening an account for stock but, since stock is constantly changing, we shall close this account the following morning.

Suppose now that in Mr Reid's case, his stock at 31 December 19X6 was calculated to cost £250. The double-entry would then be:

	Dr £	Cr £
Stock account (asset)	250	
Trading account (to reduce purchases to cost of goods sold)		250

His ledger would then appear as follows.

Stock account

	£		£
31 Dec 19X6 Trading account	250	31 Dec 19X6 Balance c/f	250
1 Jan 19X7 Balance b/f	250		

Trading account

	£			£
31 Dec 19X6 Purchases	1,750			
31 Dec 19X6 Gross profit		31 Dec 19X6 Sales		2,500
(balancing figure)	1,000	31 Dec 19X6 Stock		250
	2,750			2,750

This balancing figure – the gross profit – again seems to be a single entry. We shall see in a moment that the double-entry is completed by a credit to the profit and loss account but let us stay with stock for a moment.

The trading account in its vertical presentation form, would now appear as:

Mr Reid
Trading account for the year to 31 December 19X6

		£	£
Sales			2,500
Less:	Cost of sales		
	Purchases	1,750	
	Less: Closing stock	250	
			1,500
			1,000

You will agree that this is a better presentation from Mr Reid's viewpoint but you must get the double-entry clear so let us continue.

Opening stock

We said earlier that the stock account was only held in the ledger overnight. As an opening entry in the next period of trading, the transfer between trading account and stock is reversed so that for the duration of the next period the ledger will contain the following:

Stock account

	£		£
1 Jan 19X7 Balance b/f	250	1 Jan 19X7 Trading account	250

Trading account

	£		£
1 Jan 19X7 Stock account	250		

In order to see how both opening and closing stocks are dealt with, let us look ahead to the 19X7 results of Mr Reid's business.

Let us say that in 19X7, Mr Reid has the following (summarised) transactions:

	£
Sales	3,500
Purchases	2,000
Closing stock (at cost)	400

Then, at the year-end, closing stock will be accounted for as before and the ledger will appear as follows:

Stock account

		£			£
1 Jan 19X7	Balance b/f	250	1 Jan 19X7	Trading account	250
31 Dec 19X7	Trading account	400	31 Dec 19X7	Balance c/f	400
		650			650
1 Jan 19X8	Balance b/f (asset)	400			

Trading account

		£			£
1 Jan 19X7	Stock account (opening)	250	31 Dec 19X7	Sales	3,500
31 Dec 19X7	Purchases	2,000	31 Dec 19X7	Stock account (closing)	400
	Profit and loss a/c	1,650			
		3,900			3,900

Mr Reid's trading account in vertical presentation will be as follows:

Mr Reid
Trading account for the year to 31 December 19X7

	£	£
Sales		3,500
Less: Cost of sales		
Opening stock	250	
Purchases	2,000	
	2,250	
Less: Closing stock	400	
		1,850
Gross profit		1,650

Note: At this stage it is important that you appreciate the overall effects of opening and closing stock on cost of sales and thus profit. The mechanics of their double-entry will be returned to in a later session.

THE PROFIT AND LOSS ACCOUNT

Purpose

The purpose of the profit and loss account is to calculate the **net** profit of the business. The net profit is found by deducting all trading expenses from the gross profit. The excess of gross profit over expenses is the net profit. Again, it may be negative, a net loss.

We can therefore state that:

Net profit = Gross profit after deducting all trading expenses incurred in the trading period.

Thus the double entry for gross profit is to debit trading account and to credit profit and loss account.

Illustration

Returning to 19X6, Mr Reid (from the previous example) had the following expenses:

Rent	£350
General expenses of	£200

By the use of our formula, we may find the net profit.

$$\text{Net profit} = \text{Gross profit} - \text{Expenses}$$

$$= 1,000 - (350 + 200) = 1,000 - 550$$

$$\text{Net profit} = £450$$

The profit and loss account in the ledger

This figure is also derived from the double-entry accounting system.

Relevant extracts from his (summarised) ledger are as follows:

Trading account

	£		£
Purchases	1,750	Sales	2,500
Profit and loss	1,000	Stock	250
	2,750		2,750

Rent

	£		£
Bank	350		

General expenses

	£		£
Bank	200		

Profit and loss account

	£		£
		Trading account	1,000

We now wish to charge the expenses against the gross profit and this is simply done by clearing the balances on the expense accounts to the profit and loss account as follows:

Rent

	£		£
Bank	350	Profit and loss	350

General expenses

	£		£
Bank	200	Profit and loss	200

Profit and loss account

	£		£
Rent	350	Trading account	1,000
General expenses	200		
Net profit	450		
	1,000		1,000

Again, we have inserted a single entry: net profit £450. Where is the credit to go to maintain the double-entry? Since the business has now increased its net assets by £450, Mr Reid's investment in the business has increased and the business owes a further £450 to Mr Reid. In other words, his capital has increased by £450. With the further information that Mr Reid originally brought £7,450 into the business at the beginning of 19X6, the double-entry is completed as follows:

Capital account – Mr Reid

		£			£
			1 Jan 19X6	Bank	7,450
31 Dec 19X6	Balance c/f	7,900	31 Dec 19X6	Profit and loss a/c	450
		7,900			7,900
				Balance b/f	7,900

A vertical presentation for the profit and loss account would appear as follows.

Mr Reid
Profit and loss account for the year ended 31 December 19X6

	£	£
Gross profit		1,000
Less: Expenses		
Rent	350	
General expenses	200	
	——	
		550
		——
Net profit		450
		——

Notes

(1)   The profit and loss account, like the trading account, is always dated for the year (or period) ended . . . . . It also has debit and credit sides just like any other account.

(2)   The gross profit is calculated in the trading account.

(3)   Expenses are simply posted from the ledger accounts to the debit side of the profit and loss account.

(4)   Net profit is the balance on the account. It may well be negative, showing a net loss.

Format

The trading and profit and loss accounts shown above form the basic introduction to **final accounts**. You should develop from this as you work through the following sessions.

You should be aware, however, that the trading and profit and loss accounts shown above are more normally presented jointly under one heading. This makes no difference to the double entry whatsoever. The following is the more acceptable layout for a trading and profit and loss account and you should use this layout for all examples from this point on.

Session 1

Mr Reid
Trading and profit and loss account for the year ended 31 December 19X6

		£	£
Sales			2,500
Less: Cost of goods sold			
Opening stock		Nil	
Add: Purchases		1,750	
		1,750	
Less: Closing stock		(250)	
			1,500
Gross profit			1,000
Less: Expenses			
Rent		350	
General expenses		200	
			(550)
Net profit			450

THE BALANCE SHEET

Nature and purpose

The final step in final accounts' preparation is the construction of the balance sheet. You should note however that the balance sheet, not being an account, is *not* a part of the double-entry system, but it is derived from the double-entry system and is a summary of the balances carried down on the ledger.

The balance sheet is simply a statement, listing a company's assets and liabilities as at a single point in time. This is usually at the end of the last day of trading in any trading period. It shows the financial position of the business as at that point in time.

Constructing the balance sheet

In an earlier session, you were introduced to the balance sheet layout. We are now going to use this layout to construct a balance sheet.

Example

Mr Reid: Trial balance after the trading and profit and loss accounts have been completed as at 31 December 19X6:

	Dr £	Cr £
Fixtures	5,000	
Debtors	1,000	
Stock – closing	250	
Cash at bank	2,500	
Cash in hand	150	
Capital		7,450
Creditors		1,000
Net profit		450
	8,900	8,900

The task is to place each of these balances into the appropriate section of the balance sheet. Draft your own before reviewing the answer below.

Solution

Mr Reid
Balance sheet as at 31 December 19X6

	£	£
Assets employed		
Fixed assets		
Fixtures at cost		5,000
Current assets		
Stock	250	
Debtors	1,000	
Cash at bank	2,500	
Cash in hand	150	
	3,900	
Less: Current liabilities		
Creditors	1,000	
Net working capital		2,900
		7,900

	£	£
Financed by		
Capital	7,450	
Add: Profit (loss)	450	
Less: Drawings	–	
		7,900

Note: Current assets are always listed in this order in the balance sheet with the least liquid items first (ie. stock) and most liquid last (ie. cash in hand).

OTHER ITEMS OF NOTE

Carriage

These items relate to the expense of transporting goods. Carriage outwards is the expense of transporting the goods sold to the buyer's premises. It is an expense which is debited to the profit and loss account.

Carriage inwards is the cost of transporting purchases made by the company to its place of storage. This expense increases the cost of purchases:

> Purchase price £95 and cost of carriage to the warehouse £5. The actual purchase cost of these goods is therefore £100. This is shown in the trading account where the total carriage inwards expense is added to the purchases figure.

Returns

These items relate to the reality that most business firms experience. Items sold may at some stage be returned, which may reflect errors in packaging, faulty goods or errors in postage. Whatever the reason, such returns are known as sales returns or returns inwards. The correct accounting treatment is to record these in a separate ledger account (debit returns inwards and credit the debtors account). Returns inwards is posted to the trading account to reduce the sales figure.

Returns outwards relates to the return of goods purchased to the supplier. Again a separate ledger account is maintained (purchases returns or returns outwards account) and the balance is posted to the trading account to reduce the purchases figure.

Trading account form

The trading account, after recording these two items would take the following format:

Trading account for the period ended 19X6

		£	£	£
Sales				X
Less:	Returns inwards			(X)
				X
Less:	Cost of goods sold			
	Opening stock		X	
	Purchases	X		
Less:	Returns outwards	(X)		
Add:	Carriage inwards	X		
			X	
			X	
Less:	Closing stock		(X)	
	Cost of goods sold			(X)
Gross profit				X

FULLY WORKED EXAMPLE

Scenario

The following trial balance was extracted from the books of account of A Whittaker on 30 September 19X6.

	Dr £	Cr £
Sales		37,200
Purchases	23,112	
Stock: 1 October 19X5	4,776	
Carriage outwards	752	
Carriage inwards	468	
Salaries and wages	4,894	
Motor expenses	1,326	
Returns inwards	880	
Returns outwards		710
Rent	580	
Motor vehicles at cost	4,400	
Fixtures and fittings at cost	600	
Sundry expenses	2,404	
Creditors		6,095
Debtors	8,977	
Cash at bank	12,124	
Cash in hand	200	
Drawings	4,200	
Capital		25,688
	69,693	69,693

Stock at 30 September 19X6 was valued at £5,950.

Method

Step 1: Mark each item on the trial balance with one of the following marks.

T   –   for trading account
P   –   for profit and loss account
B   –   for balance sheet

This may seem tedious, but until you have mastered the art it is a useful means of minimising errors.

Step 2: Construct the trading account, crossing off each T from the trial balance as you use each item on the trading account.

Step 3: Close off the balances in the relevant ledger accounts.

Step 4: Construct the profit and loss account, crossing off each P from the trial balance as you use each item on the profit and loss account.

Step 5: Close off the balances in the relevant ledger accounts.

Step 6: With the remaining balances on the trial balance (check that *all* of these are marked with a B) construct the balance sheet.

Step 7: Balance off all the asset and liability accounts and bring the balances down, dated the first trading day of the next trading period.

Solution

Step 1

A Whittaker
Trial balance at 30 September 19X6

	Dr £	Cr £	
Sales		37,200	T
Purchases	23,112		T
Stock: 1 October 19X5	4,776		T
Carriage outwards	752		P
Carriage inwards	468		T
Salaries and wages	4,894		P
Motor expenses	1,326		P
Returns inwards	880		T
Returns outwards		710	T
Rent	580		P
Motor vehicles at cost	4,400		B
Fixtures and fittings at cost	600		B
Sundry expenses	2,404		P
Creditors		6,095	B
Debtors	8,977		B
Cash at bank	12,124		B
Cash in hand	200		B
Drawings	4,200		B
Capital		25,688	B
	69,693	69,693	

Stock at 30 September 19X6 was valued at £5,950.   T/B *

*Note: The trial balance at this stage always contains the opening stock. The closing stock is given by note and, as it is not yet part of the double-entry, two references are required in the final column.

A Whittaker
Trading and profit and loss account for the year ended 30 September 19X6

		£	£	£
Sales				37,200
Less:	Returns inwards			(880)
				36,320
Less:	Cost of goods sold			
	Opening stock		4,776	
	Purchases	23,112		
Less:	Returns outwards	(710)		
Add:	Carriage inwards	468		
			22,870	
Less:	Closing stock		(5,950)	
	Cost of goods sold			(21,696)
Gross profit				14,624
Less:	Expenses			
	Carriage outwards		752	
	Salaries and wages		4,894	
	Motor expenses		1,326	
	Rent		580	
	Sundry expenses		2,404	
				(9,956)
Net profit				4,668

A Whittaker
Balance sheet as at 30 September 19X6

	Cost £	£	Net book value £
Assets employed			
Fixed assets			
Fixtures and fittings	600	–	600
Motor vehicles	4,400	–	4,400
	5,000	–	5,000
Current assets			
Stock		5,950	
Debtors		8,977	
Cash at bank		12,124	
Cash in hand		200	
		27,251	
Less: Current liabilities			
Creditors		6,095	
Net working capital			21,156
			26,156
Financed by			
Capital		25,688	
Net profit		4,668	
Drawings		(4,200)	
			26,156

A Whittaker: General ledger

Sales account

	£		£
September		September	
Trading account	37,200	Balance	37,200

Returns inwards account

	£		£
September		September	
Balance	880	Trading account	880

Purchases account

	£		£
September Balance	23,112	September Trading account	23,112

Returns outwards account

	£		£
September Trading account	710	September Balance	710

Carriage inwards account

	£		£
September Balance	468	Transfer to Trading account	468

Carriage outwards account

	£		£
September Balance	752	September Profit and loss account	752

Salaries and wages account

	£		£
September Balance	4,894	September Transfer to profit and loss a/c	4,894

Motor expenses account

	£		£
September Balance	1,326	September Profit and loss account	1,326

Rent account

	£		£
September Balance	580	September Profit and loss account	580

Sundry expenses account

	£		£
September Balance	2,404	September Profit and loss account	2,404

Trading account

	£			£
October		September		
Stock account	4,776	Sales		37,200
September		Returns out		710
Returns in	880	Stock		5,950
Purchases	23,112			
Carriage in	468			
Profit and loss	14,624			
	43,860			43,860

Stock account

	£			£
October		October		
Balance b/f	4,776	Trading account		4,776
September		September		
Trading account	5,950	Balance c/f		5,950
	10,726			10,726
October				
Balance b/f	5,950			

Fixtures and fittings account

	£			£
September		September		
Balance b/f	600	Balance c/f		600
October				
Balance b/f	600			

Motor vehicles account

	£			£
September		September		
Balance b/f	4,400	Balance c/f		4,400
October				
Balance b/f	4,400			

Debtors

	£		£
September Balance	8,977	September Balance C/F	8,977
October Balance b/f	8,977		

Bank account

	£		£
September Balance	12,124	September Balance c/f	12,124
October Balance b/f	12,124		

Cash account

	£		£
September Balance	200	September Balance c/f	200
October Balance b/f	200		

Creditors

	£		£
September Balance c/f	6,095	September Balance	6,095
		October Balance b/f	6,095

Capital account

	£		£
September Drawings	4,200	September Balance b/f	25,688
Balance c/f	26,156	Profit and loss account	4,668
	30,356		30,356
		October Balance b/f	26,156

Profit and loss account

	£		£
September		September	
Carriage out	752	Trading account	14,624
Wages and salaries	4,894		
Motor expenses	1,326		
Rent	580		
Sundry expenses	2,404		
Capital	4,668		
	———		———
	14,624		14,624
	———		———

Drawings account

	£		£
September		September	
Balance	4,200	Capital c/f	4,200

CAPITAL AND REVENUE EXPENDITURE

As you have seen before, only *revenue* expenditure (eg. the payment of rent) is charged to the profit and loss account whereas *capital* expenditure (eg. the purchase of a motor car) is not.

Revenue expenditure is expenditure incurred in:

(a)   the acquisition of assets required for conversion into cash (ie. goods for resale);

(b)   the manufacturing, selling and distribution of goods and the day-to-day administration of the business;

(c)   the maintenance of revenue-earning capacity of the fixed assets (ie. repairs, etc).

Remember, the amount of revenue expenditure charged against the profits for a year is the *amount incurred* for the period irrespective of whether or not cash has been paid. Similarly, all sales made during the period under review will be included in the trading account even though all the cash may not have been received. This is the *accruals concept*, covered later.

Capital expenditure is expenditure incurred in:

(a)   the acquisition of fixed assets required for use in the business and not for resale;

(b)   the alteration or improvement of assets for the purpose of increasing their revenue-earning capacity.

Since the benefit is spread over a considerable period of time, capital expenditure is not immediately charged to the profit and loss account.

ANALYSING INCOME AND EXPENDITURE

Many enterprises rely on their accounting systems to provide them with detailed information about the business.

Example

A company sells three categories of products. At present, the company operates a manual system of bookkeeping with sales ledger, purchase ledger, nominal ledger and cash book. If the company wished to analyse its gross profit between the three categories of products, how would the existing system of bookkeeping have to be amended? (Example based on a short answer question which appeared in an AAT Central Assessment)

Solution

Analysis of sales, purchases and stock within the three categories (ie. three sales accounts, etc.)

Most accounting systems can be adapted to provide additional analysis in this way. It is possible to set up several different accounts for sales, several different accounts for purchases and several different accounts for stock. This means that the day books must also be able to distinguish between purchases and sales relating to the different categories. Normally, the day book must contain separate columns for each product. If the business uses a computerised accounting system and the day books are integrated with the nominal ledger, it may be necessary to maintain separate day books.

Depending on the type of business, the number of products and the accounting system it may also be necessary to:

- train accounts staff to post items to the correct day book analysis column and account;

- analyse individual invoices (with the analysis normally being carried out on the face of the invoice before being posted to the day book and the debtors' or creditors' ledger);

- devise a system of coding (particularly if the accounting records have been computerised);

- physically segregate different categories of stocks within the warehouse;

- introduce timesheets so that the cost of labour can be analysed (in a manufacturing business);

- apportion the cost of overheads between the various product lines (in a manufacturing business).

PROFESSIONAL CONDUCT

This Study Pack concentrates upon the practical aspects of your work as an accountant; for example, it will teach you the mechanics of preparing an extended trial balance.

However, you should be aware that there are other aspects of the work of a professional accountant. In practice, these issues will affect you to some extent.

Policies and procedures

Most organisations are likely to have their own policies, regulations and procedures for preparing accounts and returns. These cover matters such as the type of accounting records used, authorisation procedures and accounting policies (such as the method of stock valuation to be used). Accounting procedures will vary according to the size and structure of the organisation and the nature of the business.

Timescales are likely to be important in most organisations. Limited company final accounts must be filed with the Registrar of Companies within ten months of the end of the financial year (or seven months if the company is a public company). Deadlines are likely to be particularly tight if the company has to report its results to the public and the financial press, or where it is owned by another company, particularly if that company is overseas.

Many businesses are required to produce accounts within a timescale in order to raise finance or as a condition of continued support from banks.

Dealing with discrepancies and unusual items

In the course of your work, you are likely to have to resolve matters such as discrepancies and the treatment of unusual items.

Examples:

- Control accounts do not agree to the list of balances.

- There is lack of agreement between physical assets and records.

- The trial balance does not balance.

- Purchases include items which are unusually large or of an unusual type.

- There are inconsistencies within the information that has been provided.

All discrepancies must be investigated and adjustments made for any errors found.

You may not necessarily have access to all the information that you need. This is particularly likely if you are preparing accounts from incomplete records. If you cannot resolve items yourself, you should refer them to the appropriate person.

There is another reason why it is important to identify discrepancies and unusual items. An accounting system which is not properly controlled increases the scope for errors in the financial statements and may be an invitation to fraud.

QUESTIONS

1   G Brown

The following is the trial balance of G Brown as at 31 May 19X6.

Required

Construct the appropriate final accounts for the year ended 31 May 19X6.

	Dr £	Cr £
Sales		96,450
Stock – 1 June 19X5	23,500	
Purchases	73,180	
Carriage inwards	560	
Carriage outwards	1,850	
Wages and salaries	11,250	
Rent and rates	6,050	
Returns outwards		1,105
Communication expenses	352	
Insurance	820	
Sundry expenses	318	
Buildings at cost	25,000	
Fixtures at cost	3,500	
Creditors		12,295
Debtors	14,320	
Cash at bank	3,500	
Cash in hand	150	
Drawings	8,500	
Loan from C Green		10,000
Motor vehicles at cost	12,000	
Capital		65,000
	184,850	184,850

Stock at 31 May 19X6 was valued at £25,350.

2   Jason Sarmiento   (AAT CA J94)

Jason Sarmiento, trading as Futon Enterprises, is a sole trader assembling and selling futons. A futon is a Japanese-style bed, consisting of a slatted wooden frame and a mattress. Jason buys in the pre-cut timber and the mattresses and assembles the futons for sale through his retail shop in Lincoln and by mail order.

The assembly takes place in a small workshop to the rear of the shop and is carried out by a full-time assembler. The business also employs a driver, a secretary and you, the accounts clerk. Jason spends most of his time in the shop and dealing with the mail order side of the business.

The business accounts are currently operated using a manual system, though Jason is actively engaged in investigating computerised accounting systems.

A very simple sales ledger is operated and the purchase ledger contains about 20 accounts. There are few cash transactions.

Purchases of raw materials are posted to a materials account. The assembler's wages are posted to the production wages account. No separate production overheads account is maintained.

Assessment task

You were present at a meeting with Jason last week over the possible diversification of the business into the assembly and sale of sofabeds. With two distinct products, Jason would be keen to assess the profitability of both futons and sofabeds. He has asked you to prepare an explanation as to how the company's accounting system will have to be amended to provide this additional analysis.

Use a memorandum to explain how the company's accounting system will have to be amended.

3   Abdul Mohim   (AAT CA D93)

Country Crafts Ltd is a small business which started in 1988. It buys craft items – such as pottery, hand-made clothes and wooden toys – from a large number of small craft producers and then sells them to craft shops throughout the country.

The rented premises consist of a warehouse containing racks and bins to hold the craft products along with an adjoining office and garage. The company owns two delivery vans, used for both collections and deliveries, and two company cars.

The company was started by two friends, Sandip Patel and Abdul Mohim, who met on a small business training course in Leicester. Sandip has responsibility for buying and selling and has built up a network of small craftworkers who make stock for him. Abdul is responsible for the running of the warehouse and the office together with the administration of the business.

In addition to the two owners, the business employs two drivers, a warehouseman, two accounts clerks and a secretary.

You are the senior of the two accounts clerks and you are responsible for the nominal ledger.

The company's accounts are currently operated using a manual system, but computerisation of the accounts should take place in the near future and some equipment has recently been purchased.

The sales ledger holds at present about 100 accounts; the company has no cash customers.

All purchases of craft products are on credit and the purchase ledger contains about 80 accounts.

You have received the following memorandum from Abdul Mohim:

> 'I am concerned about the amount of information our accounting system gives us about our business. It shows the profit we make for our total business, but does not compare the relative profitability of the different areas of our business. I think we

could divide our stock into four main categories: china, giftware, paperware and toys. It would be very informative, then, to know how profitable each line of business is. Can you let me know as soon as possible how we might go about changing our accounting system to provide us with such information?

Assessment task

Write a memorandum in reply to the above query.

SUMMARY

- Trading account is used to calculate **gross profit**.

- **Gross profit** = Sales – Cost of sales

- The trading account *may* be a separate account in the general ledger. In any case, it will always be presented in vertical format by any trading company as part of the **trading and profit and loss account**.

- Sales, purchases and stock accounts are closed off and the balance transferred to the trading account at period-end.

- The trading account and other expense and income accounts are closed off and the balance transferred to the profit and loss account at period-end.

Accruals and prepayments

OBJECTIVES

The performance criteria covered by this session are as follows:

■   Income and expenditure is correctly recorded in the appropriate ledger accounts.

■   Any accrued or prepaid income and expenditure is correctly identified and adjustments made.

■   Income and expenditure is analysed in accordance with defined requirements and appropriate information is passed to management.

INTRODUCTION

The simplest way of recording income received and expenses paid is to look at cash receipts and payments. The problem with this approach is that even in the simplest businesses this may give a misleading impression. Accounts prepared on this basis may not be **consistent** from one period to the next. For instance by encouraging debtors to pay early and delaying payments to creditors a very misleading picture of the profitability of a business could be achieved.

To correct this accounts are prepared on the basis of income earned and expenditure incurred rather than amounts received and paid. This is the **accruals concept**, as defined by SSAP2 as one of the fundamental accounting concepts.

Adjustments are therefore needed for:

●   expenses incurred during the period but paid or payable after the end of the period (**accruals**);

●   payments made in the period relating to benefits to be received in a subsequent period (**prepayments**).

At the period-end, each account must be examined in turn. Adjustments must then be made for accruals and prepayments so that when the charge for the period is made to the trading and profit and loss account, the correct amount is transferred.

WORKED EXAMPLES

Example

Ian's annual rent is £5,000 but he has paid only £3,000. Write up the rent account.

Rent

		£			£
30.6.X1	Cash	3,000	31.12.X1	Trading and profit and loss account	5,000
31.12.X1	Accrual c/f	2,000			
		5,000			5,000
			1.1.X2	Accrual b/f	2,000

Further example

Suppose that in 19X2 he pays £10,000.

Rent

		£			£
30.6.X2	Cash (ii)	10,000	1.1.X2	Accrual b/f (i)	2,000
			31.12.X2	Trading and profit and loss account (iii)	5,000
			31.12.X2	Prepayment c/f (iv)	3,000
		10,000			10,000
1.1.X3	Prepayment b/f	3,000			

The approach is therefore

- establish the opening balance (i);
- record the cash paid (ii);
- record the profit and loss account amount (iii); and
- determine the balance carried forward as a balancing figure (iv).

Alternative approach

An alternative approach would be as follows:

- establish the opening balance (a);
- record the cash paid (b);
- record the **balance carried forward** (c); and
- determine the **profit and loss account amount** as a balancing figure (d).

Rent

		£			£
30.6.X2	Cash (b)	10,000	1.1.X2	Accrual b/f (a)	2,000
			31.12.X2	Trading and profit and loss account (d)	5,000
			31.12.X2	Prepayment c/f (c)	3,000
		10,000			10,000
31.12.X2	Prepayment b/f	3,000			

Which method you use will be determined by the information available. Usually you will be able to use either method.

INCORRECT ESTIMATES OF ACCRUALS

So far, we have seen that it doesn't matter which approach you take to adjusting ledger accounts for accruals – using the profit and loss or the balance carried down as the 'balancing figure'.

However, a lot of accruals are only 'best estimates' of the liability, if the charge for the last period of the year is not known with certainty. This would be particularly true of accruals for expenses such as electricity, telephone, etc.

When the bill is received and paid in the following period, it may be found that the amount accrued was too large or small.

In this case, we do not go back and change the previous year's accounts (an expensive option if the accounts have already been printed and sent out to owners/shareholders!).

Instead, the previous period's under- or over-accrual will be absorbed into the current period's profit and loss charge. It will *not* be allowed to affect the balance carried down at the end of this period, which must be the best estimate of the current liability (or prepayment) if any.

Illustration

Barry started business on 1 December 19X1. During the year to 31 December 19X2, he made the following payments for telephone:

Bill period	£
1 month to 31.12.X1	40
Quarter to 31.3.X2	105
Quarter to 30.6.X2	120
Quarter to 30.9.X2	135

Write up the telephone account for the year to 30.11.X2.

The accrual for the two months unpaid will generally be estimated on the basis of the latest bill:

$2/3 \times £135 = £90$

Telephone

19X2		£	19X2		£
Jan	Cash	40	Nov	Trading and profit and loss account	490
April	Cash	105			
July	Cash	120			
Oct	Cash	135			
Nov	Accrual c/f	90			
		490			490
			Dec	Accrual b/f	90

Now suppose Barry's bill for the quarter to 31 December was in fact £150 – so the accrual should have been $2/3 \times £150 = £100$ – an under-accrual of £10.

This will be absorbed into the profit and loss charge for the year to 30.11.X3; there is in fact no need to work out the under- or over-accrual if the balance carried down is calculated first, leaving the profit and loss account transfer as the balancing figure – the 'alternative approach'.

Suppose Barry had paid bills totalling £420 in that year (including the bill to 31.12.X2), with an estimated accrual of £115 needed at the end of November.

The ledger account for that year would appear as follows:

Telephone

19X3		£			£
	Cash	420	Dec 19X2	b/f	90
Nov	Accrual c/f	115	Nov	Trading and profit and loss account	445
		535			535
			Dec	Accrual b/f	115

The profit and loss charge is calculated to balance the account and can be analysed as:

	£	£
Charge for year to 30.11.X3:		
1 month to 31.12.X2 ($1/3 \times 150$)	50	
Remaining cash paid (420 – 150)	270	
Accrual	115	
		435
Under-accrual for year to 30.11.X2		10
		445

INCOME ADJUSTMENTS

If a business has a source of sundry income, in respect of which it has actually received more or less cash than is attributable to the current period, accrual and prepayment type adjustments will also need to be made.

If *too much* cash has been received (eg. a business's tenant has paid some rent in advance) then a liability will arise, ie. the equivalent of an expense accrual.

If the payer is *behind with payments* (eg. the bank has not yet credited interest due) then an debtor asset will arise, ie. the equivalent of an expense prepayment.

IDENTIFYING ACCRUALS AND PREPAYMENTS IN PRACTICE

Most businesses need to carry out procedures to identify accruals and prepayments when preparing their year-end accounts.

The accountant should carry out the following checks:

- Review lists of accruals and prepayments prepared for the previous year-end. The list will probably contain similar items from year to year.

  The following are normally paid in advance (ie. give rise to prepayments):

  - rates (general rates and water rates)
  - insurance (motor vehicles, building, professional indemnity, other)
  - telephone *rental*
  - road fund licences
  - maintenance charges on photocopiers, etc.

  The following are normally paid in arrears (ie. give rise to accruals):

  - electricity
  - gas
  - telephone *usage*
  - wages
  - holiday pay
  - travelling expenses
  - interest (on bank accounts and on other loans)
  - audit and accountancy
  - cleaning

  The following may give rise to accruals *or* prepayments:

  - rent payable
  - hire charges
  - maintenance charges
  - income *receivable* (eg. rent, interest)

- Review all invoices received after the year-end. This will identify potential accruals, including any items which have arisen for the first time in the current year.

Look for:

- items payable for a period (eg. covering three months and received one month after the year-end);
- invoices received after the year-end dated before the year-end.

- Review all accounts for income and expenditure. Look for:

    - amounts which are significantly higher than for the previous year;
    - amounts which are significantly lower than for the previous year;
    - accounts for items payable monthly or quarterly.

Illustration

Rent payable for the year ended 31 December 19X4 was £12,000.

Rent payable account for the year ended 31 December 19X5:

		£
1.1.X5	Balance b/f	2,000
1.3.X5	Invoice	3,000
1.6.X5	Invoice	3,000
1.9.X5	Invoice	3,000
1.12.X5	Invoice	3,000
		14,000

The charge for rent is higher than for the previous year. Four quarterly invoices have been received during the year, but there appears to have been no increase in rent payable. Therefore the invoice received on 1 December almost certainly includes the charge for January and February 19X6.

In large organisations, it may be necessary to circularise managers and other persons responsible for authorising expenditure, particularly if accounts have to be prepared very shortly after the year-end. These persons may still be holding invoices which relate to the period before the year-end. Some organisations use a checklist; others may simply request information using a memorandum.

Managers should be requested to provide:

- details of the last invoices received before the year-end;
- details of the first invoices received after the year-end;
- photocopies of all relevant invoices;
- details of any other potential accruals or prepayments of which they are aware.

QUESTIONS

1   Neil commenced business on 1 May 19X0 and is charged rent at the rate of £6,000 per annum. During the period to 31 December 19X0, he actually paid £4,600.

What should his charge in the profit and loss account be in respect of rent?

2   Graham paid £1,200 insurance during the year to 31 March 19X0.

As at 1 April 19Y9, he had overpaid £400 and the correct charge in the profit and loss account for year to 31 March 19X0 is £1,300.

What is the amount of the prepayment at 31 March 19X0?

3   The following information relates to a company's rent and rates account:

	Closing balance £	Opening balance £
Rates prepayment	30	20
Rent accrual	120	100

Cash payments of £840 were made in respect of rent and rates during the period. What is the charge to the profit and loss account for the year?

4   A business makes up its accounts to 31 December. You are required to calculate the proportion of the following transactions which need to be included in the accounts for the year ended 31 December 19X5 and to prepare the rent receivable accounts for the same period.

(a)   Received £1,000 in July 19X5 being rent in advance for the 12 months to 30 June 19X6.

(b)   Received £800 in March 19X6 being rent in arrears for the six months ended 31 March 19X6.

5   If an organisation rented a field owned by your company for a car boot sale in January 1994 and had paid £250 in advance, how would that transaction be treated in the 1993 accounts? Briefly explain the effect in the 1994 accounts.

(AAT CA D93 – amended)

6   The last electricity bill received and included in the Light and Heat a/c had been for the period 1 December 1992 to 28 February 1993. This bill was for £336.

(a)   Should the electricity used between 1 March 1993 and 31 March 1993 be included in the accounts for the year ended 31 March 1993?

(b)   If not, why not or, if so, how should the value of electricity used be estimated?

(AAT CA J93)

7   An acquaintance wishes to use your shop to display and sell framed photographs. She will pay £40 per month for this service.

(a)   How would you account for this transaction each month?

(b)   If, at the end of the year, the acquaintance owed one month's rental, how would this be treated in the accounts?

(AAT CA J94)

8   Accruals and prepayments   **(AAT CA J93)**

Write a memorandum to your employer in answer to the following comment:

It seems to me that we have to do a lot of fiddling with the accounts at the year-end. For example, the rates bill is always paid for a full year in advance and we have to work out how much of the bill applies to our financial year. We also have to work out how much electricity, gas and telephone charges we have used before we even receive the bill. Would it not be much simpler and cheaper to work out the profit by subtracting the cash we pay out during the year from the cash we receive?

9   Wally

Wally rents premises at a rental of £6,000 per annum. He sublets part of the premises to Tony at £1,800 per annum and another part to Gregory at £1,200 per annum.

On 1 July 19X4 Wally had paid his own rent up to date, Tony's rent was three months in arrears and Gregory had paid his rent to 30 September 19X4.

During the year ended 30 June 19X5 the following transactions took place:

(a)   Wally paid his rent at the end of each quarter except the amount due at 30 June 19X5 which was outstanding.

(b)   Wally received the following amounts from Tony:

		£
31 July 19X4		900
1 October 19X4		450
7 January 19X5		450
5 June 19X5		900

(c)   Wally received the following amount from Gregory:

		£
10 April 19X5		600

Required

Write up the rent payable account and the rent receivable account in Wally's ledger for the year ended 30 June 19X5.

10   Hayward

Hayward owns many properties which he rents to various tenants, some of whom pay their rent in advance whilst others pay in arrears. He also has many different forms of borrowing from a number of banks and friends and the interest on these loans is sometimes paid in arrears and sometimes in advance.

During 19X6 the rent collected was £114,750 and the interest charged to the profit and loss account amounted to £26,250. The receivable and unearned rent revenues at two successive balance sheet dates were as follows together with the amounts of prepaid interest and interest payable at the same dates:

	31.12.X5	31.12.X6
	£	£
Rents owed by tenants	17,100	20,250
Rents prepaid by tenants	10,350	7,650
Prepaid interest	1,750	2,800
Interest payable	4,900	3,500

Required

Prepare the rent receivable and interest payable accounts for the year ended 31 December 19X6.

11 A Metro

A Metro owns a number of antique shops, and in connection with this business he runs a small fleet of motor vans. He prepares his accounts to 31 December in each year.

On 1 January 19X0 the amount prepaid for motor tax and insurance was £570.

On 1 April 19X0 he paid £420 which represented motor tax for the year ended 31 March 19X1 on six of the vans.

On 1 May 19X0 he paid £1,770 being insurance for all ten vans for the year ended 30 April 19X1.

On 1 July 19X0 he paid £280 which represented motor tax for the other four vans for the year ended 30 June 19X1.

Required

Write up the account for 'motor tax and insurance' for the year ended 31 December 19X0.

12 Maisey Hemmery

Maisey Hemmery runs a small shop and never remembers to pay her bills at the right time. Her opening trial balance at the beginning of 19X6 was as follows:

	Dr	Cr
	£	£
Capital		1,825
Cash	25	
Bank		2,500
Leasehold shop	5,000	
Provision for depreciation – leasehold shop		300
Stock	500	
Fixtures and fittings	250	
Provision for depreciation – fixtures and fittings		150
Electricity		40
Rates	100	
Bank interest		20
Trade creditors		1,095
Ground rent	115	
Assistant's wages		60
	5,990	5,990

During the year 19X6 she makes the following payments for overhead expenses.

(1)   £150 for her electricity bill for the period 1.10.X5 to 30.9.X6. (She expects her bill for the period 1.10.X6 to 30.9.X7 to be £240.)

(2)   £200 rates for the half year from 1.4.X6 and then another £200 for the half year 1.10.X6 to 31.3.X7.

(3)   £20 for the last quarter of 19X5's bank interest, then £25, £30 and £35 for the first three quarters of 19X6.

(4)   £500 for assistant's wages.

At the end of the year, her assistant is owed £30 wages and bank interest due for the final quarter is £40.

Her ground rent is £30 per annum. Maisey got rather confused between rent payments and rates payments in 19X3 and overpaid her ground rent several times.

Required

Write up the following ledger accounts for 19X6 closing off to the trading and profit and loss account (which need not be shown) at the year-end:

(a)   electricity account;
(b)   rates account;
(c)   bank interest account;
(d)   ground rent account; and
(e)   assistant's wages account.

SUMMARY

•   Carry down a balance in the expense account to reflect the fact that more or less than one year's charge has been paid.

•   If accruals are based on estimates and there is an accrual brought down from the previous period, enter the cash payments and accrual for the current period and calculate the profit and loss charge as a balancing figure.

•   Income accounts operate in the same way:

    –   for amounts received in advance, carry down a credit balance;
    –   for amounts owed to the business, carry down a debit balance.

Bad and doubtful debts

OBJECTIVES

This session looks at an example of the following performance criterion:

■   Any adjustments not dealt with in the ledger accounts are correctly entered on the extended trial balance.

INTRODUCTION

The balance sheet should contain only those debts which are expected to be recovered. Debts which will not or may not be recovered should be excluded. This can be done in two ways: the debt can be written off, or a provision can be made against it.

WRITING OFF A DEBT

This removes the debt from the books.

Dr   Bad debts expense
    Cr   Debtors

This will always be the case even if the debt had been previously provided for.

It is appropriate to write off a debt when it will not be recovered. If however there is a possibility that it will be recovered then it should be provided against.

Illustration

Lewis reviews his debtors (which total £10,000) and notices an amount due from John of £500. He knows that this will never be recovered so he wants to write it off.

	Debtors		
	£		£
Balance b/f	10,000	Bad debts expense	500
		Balance c/f	9,500
	10,000		10,000

Bad debts expense

	£		£
Debtors	500	Trading and profit and loss a/c	500

MAKING A PROVISION AGAINST A DEBT

In the event that we feel a debt might be recovered, even though it is doubtful, the debt stays in the books but a provision is created against it. The balance sheet presentation is similar to that for depreciation in that the provision is netted off the debtors figure. Unlike depreciation it is not necessary to show the provision separately.

Note: You must *never* show the provision under current liabilities.

The double entry arises from the **movement** in the provision.

		£	£
Dr	Bad debts expense	M	
	Cr Doubtful debt provision		M

M = **Movement** in the provision

Illustration

Roger has a provision for doubtful debts of £5,000. On review he considers that the provision should be increased to £7,000.

Debtors

	£		£
Balance b/f (say)	100,000		

Provision for doubtful debts

	£		£
		Balance b/f (1)	5,000
Balance c/f (2)	7,000	**Bad debt expense** (3)	2,000
	7,000		7,000
		Balance b/f	7,000

(1) to (3) is the sequence in which the entries should be made.

Bad debts expense

	£		£
Provision for doubtful debts (2)	2,000	Trading and profit and loss a/c (3)	2,000

TYPES OF PROVISION

There are two main types of provision:

- Specific – against identified debts

- General – against debtors as a whole (excluding any which have been specifically provided against)

The fact that we can divide the provision into two parts has no impact on our calculation of the **movement** on the doubtful debt provision account.

Example

Frank has a provision of £1,000 against a specific debtor and a general provision of £4,000. He decides to change this to a specific provision of £2,000 and a general provision of £5,000.

Required

Show:

- *the bad expense account; and*
- *the provision for doubtful debts account.*

Solution

See the solution to Roger. This is exactly the same problem. Frank is changing a provision of £5,000 (£1,000 + £4,000) to one of £7,000 (£2,000 + £5,000).

RECOVERY OF DEBTS WRITTEN OFF

The double entry for these amounts is:

Dr   Cash
      Cr   Bad debts expense

When the debt was written off a debit entry was made in the bad debts expense account. This entry will reverse that (albeit possibly in a different period).

RECOVERY OF DEBTS ALREADY PROVIDED AGAINST

As the debtor has remained in the books even if a provision has been made, the double entry is:

Dr   Cash
        Cr   Debtors

The necessity to remove/reduce the provision will be considered at the year-end.

COMPREHENSIVE EXAMPLE

At the end of 19X6 Bjorn had made a provision of £643 against doubtful debtors. This was made up as follows:

		£
Specific provision – A		300
– 50% × B		200
General provision		143
		643

At the end of 19X7 Bjorn's debtors total £18,450. After reviewing each debt he discovers the following, none of which have been entered in the books:

(1)   A has already paid £50 of the debt outstanding at the beginning of the year.

(2)   B has already paid his debt in full.

(3)   C went bankrupt during the year owing Bjorn £60.

(4)   D, a debtor for £485, has told Bjorn that he cannot pay.

Bjorn decides to:

- write off the remaining amounts of A and C's debts as bad;
- provide in full against D's debt; and
- maintain the general provision at 1% of the remaining debtors.

Show the ledger entries required to record the above.

Debtors' account

	£		£
Balance b/f	18,450	Cash – A	50
		Bad debts expense – A	250
		Cash – B	400
		Bad debts expense account – C	60
		Balance c/f	17,690
	18,450		18,450

Bad debts expense account

	£		£
A – Bad debt written off	250	Trading and profit and loss account	324
B – Bad debt written off	60		
Provision for doubtful debts account – increase	14		
	324		324

Provision for doubtful debts account

	£		£
		Balance b/f	643
Balance c/f	657	Bad debt expense (balancing figure)	14
	657		657
		Balance b/f (W)	657

Working

	£
Specific provision – D	485
General provision (1% × remaining debtors) = 1% (17,690 – 485) = 1% × 17,205	172
	657

QUESTIONS

1   A company's balance sheet includes a provision for doubtful debts.

(a)   Why has the provision for doubtful debts been created?

(b)   Explain how the provision for doubtful debts should be treated in the balance sheet, giving reasons for your explanation.

(AAT CA J93)

2   Give a reason why a retail shop does not have any bad debts.

(AAT CA D94)

3   If a customer, whose amount owing had been written off, subsequently paid later, how would you account for the payment?

(AAT CA J94)

4   **Mr Green**

At 31 December 19X5, Mr Green had total debtors of £12,000 and had provided against two specific debts of £150 each. The debtors concerned were X Ltd and A & Co.

In 19X6 Mr Green writes off as bad the debt from X Ltd of £150 which has already been provided for.   He also writes off as bad a debt from PQ & Co of £50 which has not been provided for.   He also decides to provide against a further debt from Mr Z of £200.

Required

Show the ledger entries required to record the above, including the individual debtors' accounts.

5   **DD Co**

DD Co makes a provision for doubtful debts of 5% of debtors.

On 1 January 19X5 the balance on the doubtful debts account was £1,680.

During the year the company incurred bad debts amounting to £1,950.   On 31 December 19X5 debtors amounted to £32,000 after writing off the bad debts of £1,950.

Required

Write up the relevant accounts for the year ended 31 December 19X5.

6   **Geoff**

Geoff has the following balances in his trial balance at 31 December 19X3:

	£
Total debtors	140,000
Bad debts written off (not previously provided for)	1,000
Provision at 1 January 19X3	10,000

The company wishes to carry forward a provision equal to 10% of total debtors.

What is the total effect of the above on the profit and loss account for the year ended 31 December 19X3?

7   Peter

Peter had the following balances in its trial balance at 3 March 19X4:

	£
Total debtors	61,000
Provision at 1 April 19X3	1,490

After the trial balance had been taken out it was decided to carry forward at 31 March 19X4 a specific provision of £800 and a general provision equal to 1% of remaining debtors. It was also decided to write off debts amounting to £1,000 which had been provided for in full at 1 April 19X3.

What is the total charge for bad and doubtful debts which should appear in the company's profit and loss account for the year ended 31 March 19X4?

8   Jason Sarmiento

Jason Sarmiento has been talking to two of his friends who run a mail order computer software company. Because of the recession, the friends are worried about bad debts and have decided to create a provision for doubtful debts. One friend suggests a provision of 5% of the total debtors' year-end balances; the other suggests a provision representing all those debtors more than four months overdue. Jason is unclear about the difference between a bad debt and a doubtful debt and what a provision is. He also wonders whether Futon Enterprises should create a provision for doubtful debts.

Write a memorandum explaining the terms *bad debt*, *doubtful debts* and *provision* and recommending whether Futon Enterprises should or should not create a provision for doubtful debts.

(AAT CA J94)

SUMMARY

Cash received from debtor (whether or not previously provided)

Debit	Cash
Credit	Debtors

Bad debts (whether or not previously provided)

Debit	Bad debts expense
Credit	Debtors

Bad debts recovered

Debit	Cash
Credit	Bad debts expense

Doubtful debts

Calculate the provision and record it as the **balance** in the provision for doubtful debts account.

The double-entry for the **movement** on the provision for doubtful debts account is the bad debts expense account.

Stock and work in progress

OBJECTIVES

This session deals with another example of the following performance criterion:

■   Any adjustments not dealt with in the ledger accounts are correctly entered on the extended trial balance.

The session also deals with a further performance criterion:

■   An agreed valuation of closing stock is correctly entered on the extended trial balance.

INTRODUCTION

The term *stock* relates to the goods in which a business deals. There are three broad categories of stock:

●   goods for resale
●   work in progress (ie. goods that are not yet complete)
●   raw materials and components

Stock can also include consumable stores used by the business but which are not sold on directly, eg. stationery.

Stock can also include services. For instance, a recruitment consultancy would include unbilled fees for work which they have already completed in work in progress.

VALUATION OF STOCK

SSAP9 *Stocks and long-term contracts* states that stock should be valued at:

'the total of the lower of cost and net realisable value of the separate items of stock or groups of similar items'.

Cost is defined as:

'that expenditure which has been incurred in the normal course of business in bringing the product or service to its present location and condition. This expenditure should include, in addition to cost of purchase, such costs of conversion as are appropriate to that location and condition'.

'The normal course of business' means that abnormal costs cannot be included.

Example

Occasionally Kidditoys has to pay a special delivery charge on deliveries of toys it urgently requires. How should this delivery charge be dealt with in the accounts?   *(AAT CA D94)*

Solution

Dr	Purchases a/c [or Carriage Inwards a/c]
Cr	Creditors a/c in Purchase Ledger

'Bringing the product to its present location' means that *normal* delivery charges can be included. The special delivery is *not* included in the cost of stock. If the delivery van carrying the toys broke down, it would not be permissible to include the additional cost associated with the breakdown in the cost of stock.

Purchase cost is defined as:

'including import duties, transport and handling costs and any other directly attributable costs, less trade discounts, rebates and subsidies'.

Costs of conversion include:

- direct production costs;
- production overheads; and
- other overheads attributable to bringing product to its present location and condition.

This means the following:

- Only production overheads – not those for marketing, selling and distribution – should be included in cost.

- Exceptional spoilage, idle capacity and other abnormal costs are not part of the cost of stocks.

- General management and non-production related administration costs should not be included in stock cost.

So far, then, we can summarise that the cost of stock is the amount it was bought for, less any discounts or other items, plus any extra costs to get it to its current location plus the cost of any work performed on it since it was bought. This means that different items of the same stock in different locations may have different costs.

However, we must also consider net realisable value (NRV). SSAP9 defines NRV as:

'the actual or estimated selling price (net of trade but before settlement discounts) less:

(a)   all further costs to completion; and
(b)   all costs to be incurred in marketing, selling and distributing'.

Let us look at an example.

Example

Steven deals in classic cars. His stock consists of:

	Cost £	NRV £
Reliant Scimitar	*2,000*	*2,500*
Morris Minor	*300*	*1,000*
Vauxhall Viva	*450*	*–*
	2,750	*3,500*

What is the value of Steven's stock?

Solution

Steven's stock should be valued at £2,300. If it were to be valued at, say, £2,750, the Vauxhall Viva would not have been valued at the lower of cost and net realisable value.

This is an application of the concept of *prudence:* the Scimitar and the Minor will hopefully sell for more than cost but we will not take credit for the profit until they are sold; the Viva has no sales value and therefore we will effectively charge the loss immediately.

NET REALISABLE VALUE

When is net realisable value likely to be less than cost? This might happen when there has been:

- an increase in costs or a fall in selling price;

- physical deterioration of stocks;

- obsolescence of products;

- a decision as part of a business's marketing strategy to manufacture and sell products at a loss;

- errors in production or purchasing.

Let us look at another example.

Example

Jenny manufactures gudgets. Details of the basic version are given below:

	Cost £	Selling price £	Selling cost £
Basic gudgets	*5*	*10*	*2*

What value should be attributed to each gudget in stock?

Solution

Stock valuation

	£
Cost	5
Net realisable value (£10 – £2)	8

Therefore stock should be valued at £5 per gudget.

It is wrong to add the selling cost of £2 to the production cost of £5 and value the stock at £7 because it is a cost that has not yet been incurred.

ESTIMATES OF COST

It may be that the business does not know how much its stock has cost. For example, a retail business may buy stocks regularly. If the price changes, it may not know which items were purchased at the old price and which at the new price.

Under such circumstances an approximate value may be used. There are three common methods for calculating such a value.

First in, first out (FIFO)

Assume that items bought first are sold first.

Last in, first out (LIFO)

Assume that sales are made from the most recent purchases.

Weighted average

Take the total cost and divide by the number of units.

Example

Rajiv made the following purchases after discovering his warehouse was empty.

- *1 April*   *20 units @*   *£5 per unit*
- *2 April*   *10 units @*   *£6 per unit*

On 3 April he sold 25 units for £20 each.

What was the value of his stock?

Solution

- **FIFO**

    Assume items bought first are sold first. The units sold will be assumed to be all those bought on 1 April and five of those bought on 2 April.

    The five units of stock are therefore assumed to have been bought on 2 April.

    Stock valuation (5 × £6) = £30

- **LIFO**

    Assume that the most recent purchases were sold first.

    The 25 units sold are assumed to be:

    10 purchased on 2 April
    15 purchased on 1 April

    The closing stock of five units is assumed to be purchased on 1 April.

    Stock valuation (5 × £5) = £25

- **Weighted average**

	£
Total cost of purchases	
20 × £5 = £100	
10 × £6 = £60	160
Number of units of purchased	30
Cost per unit	5.33
Stock valuation (5 × £5.33)	£26.65

In practice, as already stated, a business is unlikely to know exactly how much a particular item of stock originally cost. A standard policy for valuation is therefore adopted and the most common is FIFO. You should, however, make sure that you are clear about the other methods as well.

LIFO is not normally acceptable. In times of rising prices, it does not normally provide a fair approximate to purchase cost.

A FURTHER ILLUSTRATION OF NET REALISABLE VALUE

Ismail manufactures ships. In one of his dry docks he has a battleship that is half finished. It is being built for the Ruritanian government, which has agreed a price of £20m.

The costs incurred so far are £12m. Ismail expects to incur a further £12m of cost in completing the order.

What is the net realisable value of the work in progress?

	£m
Actual selling price	20
Less: Further costs of completion	(12)
Net realisable value	8

As the work in progress has cost £12m it will be shown in the balance sheet at £8m which is the lower of cost and net realisable value.

OTHER METHODS OF ESTIMATING THE COST OF STOCK

Adjusted selling price

If we know our gross profit margin and the selling price of our stock we can work out its cost.

Illustration

Gross profit margin	25%
Selling price of stock	£200

	£	%
Selling price	200	100
Cost	150	75
Profit	50	25

Cost is therefore £150.

Base stock

The idea here is that part of our stock is always the same and should therefore be valued at its historic cost. Other elements are consistently changing and should therefore be valued using an appropriate method such as FIFO.

An example of this would be oil in the bottom of a storage tank which is below the level of the outflow tap. In theory, this oil is the same oil which was in the tank when it was first filled.

This method is occasionally used in practice but it is not acceptable in most situations, since the net realisable value of the base stock is presumably nil.

Replacement cost

Stock is valued at what it would cost to buy now. This method is not likely to give a close approximation to the actual cost of the stock unless there is a very rapid turnover (or very stable prices).

GOODS ON SALE OR RETURN

If A sells goods to B on a sale or return basis, they should be included in A's stock until B sells them. They do not form part of B's stock.

THE ACCOUNTING TREATMENT OF STOCKS

In the first session, when considering the trading account, we looked at the double entry needed to deal with opening and closing stocks. The following examples will revise this.

Illustration

Let us consider a sole trader who started business on 1 January 19X5 and therefore at that date had no stocks. His trial balance at 31 December 19X5 contains a debit balance relating to purchases of £15,000 and he has no stocks remaining at that date. The sales for the year totalled £20,000.

At the end of the year we would close off the purchases account by:

			£
	Debiting	Trading and profit and loss a/c	15,000
and	Crediting	Purchase account	15,000

The purchases account would appear as follows:

Purchases account

	£		£
31.12.X5 Balance per trial balance	15,000	31.12.X5 Trading and profit and loss account	15,000

Similarly, we would close off sales to the trading and profit and loss account, and the trading and profit and loss account would be as follows:

Trading and profit and loss account

	£		£
31.12.X5 Purchases	15,000	31.12.X5 Sales	20,000
Balance (= profit)	5,000		
	20,000		20,000

Illustration

Let us consider the same illustration but at 31 December 19X5 there are £1,500 of stocks remaining.

If we merely debit the trading and profit and loss account with £15,000 of purchases then the expense 'cost of goods sold' will be overstated by £1,500. The problem is solved by crediting the trading and profit and loss account (and hence reducing the debit for cost of goods sold) with the amount of the closing stock and debiting the stock account with that same amount.

The purchases account will be unaffected but the trading and profit and loss account will appear as follows:

In T-account format:

Trading and profit and loss account

		£			£
31.12.X5	Purchases	15,000	31.12.X5	Sales	20,000
	Balance (= profit)	6,500		Stock	1,500
		21,500			21,500

As a statement:

Trading and profit and loss account (extract) for the year ended 31 December 19X5

	£	£
Sales		20,000
Purchases	15,000	
Less: Stock on hand on 31.12.X5	1,500	
Cost of sales		13,500
Gross profit		6,500

The stock account will be:

Stock account

		£		£
31.12.X5	Trading and profit and loss account	1,500	Balance c/f	1,500

Note that the effect of this entry has been to:

(a)   result in the correct profit figure in the T-accounts; and

(b)   leave a debit balance in the T-accounts for closing stock which will appear in the balance sheet as an asset.

Illustration

In the following year, 19X6, the purchases totalled £35,000, the sales were £50,000 and the closing stocks at 31 December 19X6 were £12,000.

At the end of 19X5 we left a balance of £1,500 on the stock account. This balance will remain unchanged throughout 19X6 and at the end of 19X6 it is our job to correct the position.

We must first of all remove the opening stock and then create the closing stock.

The double-entry for opening stock is to debit the trading and profit and loss account and credit the stock account with the £1,500. The double-entry for closing stock is similar to that in 19X5, ie. to debit the stock account and credit the trading and profit and loss account with the £12,000.

The stock account for 19X6 will look like this:

Stock account

		£			£
			1.1.X6	Trading and profit and loss account (opening stock)	1,500
1.1.X6	Balance b/f (opening stock for 19X6)	1,500			
		1,500			1,500
31.1.X6	Trading and profit and loss account (closing stock)	12,000			

The balance of £12,000 will appear on the balance sheet at 31 December 19X6 as a current asset.

The trading and profit and loss account is set out below:

In T-account format:

Trading and profit and loss account

		£			£
1.1.X6	Stock (opening)	1,500	31.12.X6	Sales	50,000
31.1.X6	Purchases	35,000		Stock (closing)	12,000
	Balance (= profit)	25,500			
		62,000			62,000

As a statement:

Trading and profit and loss account (extract) for the year ended 31 December 19X6

	£	£
Sales		50,000
Stock on hand on 1.1.X6	1,500	
Purchases	35,000	
	36,500	
Less: Stock on hand on 31.12.X6	12,000	
Cost of sales		(24,500)
Gross profit		25,500

QUESTIONS

1 A business manufactures and sells futons. The futons are valued at a production cost of £48 each.

Assume that two of the futons had been used as a shop window display and had faded somewhat. If it had been decided that the mattresses required replacing at a cost of £18 each to make the futons saleable at a price of £50 each, how would this have affected the closing stock valuation?

Give reasons for your answer.

(AAT CA J94)

2 A company had to pay a special delivery charge of £84 on several deliveries of urgently required games software. This amount had been debited to Office Expenses a/c.

(a) This treatment is incorrect. Which account should have been debited? (Tick the correct item)

(i) Purchases a/c
(ii) Stock a/c
(iii) Returns Inwards a/c

(b) Give the journal entry to correct the error.

(AAT CA J93)

3 A shop sold toys and games. The selling price of goods was arrived at by doubling their cost.

Assume that some of the shop's window display stock, comprising four dolls, had deteriorated. In their damaged state, the dolls could be sold for only £5 each. Their original sales price was £16 each.

(a) How would this have affected the closing stock valuation?

Give reasons for your answer.

(b) What would have been the effect on the company's profit?

(AAT CA D94)

4 Sophie is considering sending a quantity of goods to John King on a sale or return basis. How should the transaction be dealt with when the goods are first delivered to John King?

Give reasons for your answer.

(AAT CA D94)

5   Edgar

Edgar began business as a coffee importer in July 19X6. Purchases of beans were made by him as follows:

19X6	Tons	Price per ton £	£
1 July	56	20.50	1,148
12 August	42	24.00	1,008
30 September	49	26.00	1,274
15 October	35	35.20	1,232
29 November	28	37.50	1,050
10 December	24	50.00	1,200
	234		6,912

On 10 October 100 tons were sold and on 31 December 68 tons were sold. The total proceeds of the sales were £8,480.

Required

Calculate the value of closing stock under each of the following bases:

(a)   first in, first out; and
(b)   last in, first out.

6   Sally

The cost of stock shown in the balance sheet at 31 March 19X2 of Sally valued on a LIFO basis, was £8,500. Had the stock been valued on a FIFO basis it would have been £9,200. What would be the effect of adopting the FIFO valuation on the accounts for the year ended 31 March 19X2?

7   Karen

Karen sells three products: A, B and C. At the company's year-end, the stocks held are as follows:

	Cost £	Selling price £
A	1,200	1,500
B	6,200	6,100
C	920	930

At sale a 5% commission is payable by the company to its agent.

What is the total value of these stocks in the company's accounts?

8 John

John started a business on 1 January 19X6. The sales for the first year were £200,000, the purchases were £150,000 and the cost of the closing stocks at 31 December 19X6 was £20,000. The closing stocks consisted of one type of item and the net realisable value at that date was £30,000.

During 19X7, John made sales of £300,000, the purchases were £210,000 and the cost of the closing stocks at 31 December 19X7 was £42,000. The net realisable value of the stocks at that date was £38,000.

Required

Write up the stock account for 19X6 and 19X7.

SUMMARY

- Stock is valued at the lower of cost and net realisable value.

- There are methods to find the approximate cost when the actual cost is unknown:

  - FIFO;
  - LIFO; and
  - weighted average.

- The stock account is used only at the end of the year – there is no attempt within the T-accounts to keep a running stock balance.

The extended trial balance

OBJECTIVES

This section covers the performance criteria related to preparing an extended trial balance:

■   The trial balance is accurately extended and totalled.

■   Totals from the general ledger or other records are correctly entered on the extended trial balance.

■   Any errors disclosed by the trial balance are traced and corrected.

■   Any adjustments not dealt with in the ledger accounts are correctly entered on the extended trial balance.

■   An agreed valuation of closing stock is correctly entered on the extended trial balance.

INTRODUCTION

A trial balance is a list of all the balances on the ledger accounts usually *before* year-end adjustments are made. These adjustments need to be made before the preparation of the profit and loss account and balance sheet and they will include:

●   correction of errors;
●   recognition of accruals and prepayments;
●   provision of the year's depreciation charge;
●   reviewing the charge for bad and doubtful debts; and
●   inclusion of closing stock.

The extended trial balance is a worksheet which takes us from the trial balance to the profit and loss account and balance sheet.

LAYOUT OF A TYPICAL EXTENDED TRIAL BALANCE

Account	Trial balance		Adjustments		P & L account		Balance sheet	
	Dr	Cr	Dr	Cr	Dr	Cr	Dr	Cr
	£	£	£	£	£	£	£	£

The names of the ledger accounts and the corresponding amounts per the trial balance are entered into the first three columns.

The adjustments columns are used for all of the year-end adjustments mentioned above.

Example

Set out below is the trial balance of Lyttleton, a sole trader, extracted at 31 December 19X5:

	Dr £	Cr £
Capital account		7,830
Cash at bank	2,010	
Fixed assets at cost	9,420	
Provision for depreciation at 31.12.X4		3,470
Debtors	1,830	
Stock 31.12.X4	1,680	
Creditors		390
Sales		14,420
Purchases	8,180	
Rent	1,100	
Electricity	940	
Rates	950	
	26,110	26,110

On examination of the accounts, the following points are noted:

(1)   *Depreciation for the year of £942 is to be charged.*

(2)   *A provision for doubtful debts of 3% of total debts is to be set up.*

(3)   *Purchases include £1,500 of goods which were bought for the proprietor's personal use.*

(4)   *Stock at 31.12.X5 was £1,140.*

(5)   *The rent account shows the monthly payments of £100 made from 1 January to 1 November 19X5 inclusive. Due to an oversight, the payment due on 1 December 19X5 was not made.*

(6)   *The rates account shows the prepayment of £150 brought forward at the beginning of 19X5 (and representing rates from 1 January 19X5 to 31 March 19X5) together with the £800 payment made on 1 April 19X5 and relating to the period from 1 April 19X5 to 31 March 19X6.*

(7)   *The electricity charge for the last three months of 19X5 is outstanding and is estimated to be £400.*

Solution

Stage 1: The balances per the trial balance are recorded in the correct columns and the total of the debit balances is agreed to the total of the credit balances.

Stage 2: We shall now deal with the adjustments (apart from accruals and prepayments).

(a)   **Correction of errors**

The only **error** which needs to be corrected concerns the drawings of the proprietor, ie. the fact that some of the purchases were bought for his own use. To correct this we should decrease the purchases and increase the drawings, ie:

Debit   Drawings   1,500
Credit   Purchases   1,500

As there is not yet an account for drawings, we shall need to open one.

(b)   **Provision of the year's depreciation charge**

The charge for the year is £942 and we need to charge this to the **depreciation expense** account and also to increase the **provision for depreciation**, ie. the accumulated depreciation carried forward. The double-entry is:

Debit   Depreciation expense account   942
Credit   Provision for depreciation   942

Once again, we will need to set up the depreciation expense account as none exists.

(c)   **Provision for doubtful debts (3%)**

The debtors amount to £1,830 and a provision of £55 is therefore required at 31.12.X5. As no provision previously existed we will need to charge the full amount to this year's profit and loss account. The double-entry is:

Debit   Bad debts expense   55
Credit   Provision for doubtful debts   55

As neither of these accounts exist at present they will both need to be created.

(d)   **Inclusion of closing stock**

Closing stock appears in both the profit and loss account and the balance sheet.

(i)   In the profit and loss it is a reduction of cost of goods sold and hence is a *credit*.
(ii)   In the balance sheet it is an asset and hence is a *debit*.

Accordingly we set up two stock accounts: one for the balance sheet and one for the profit and loss account.

Debit   Stock (balance sheet)   1,140
Credit   Stock (profit and loss account)   1,140

If you turn to the extended trial balance on page 60 you will see that each of these pairs of double entry has been recorded in the adjustment columns. As the debit entries should always equal the credit entries it is a useful check to cast the debit and credit adjustment columns to see that the totals are equal.

Stage 3: We now have to deal with the last adjustments, ie. the accruals and prepayments.

(a)   **Rent**

The profit and loss account charge for the year should be £1,200 and there should be an accrual (creditor) of £100 at the year-end. We should therefore like to increase the profit and loss account charge by £100 (a debit entry) and to set up the accrual (a credit entry). Each accrual must be added to the relevant expense, as shown by the initial trial balance, to ascertain the profit and loss account charge and must also be added to all of the other accruals to ascertain the total 'accrual' per the balance sheet. We shall look at this again in stage 4.

(b)   **Electricity**

The profit and loss account charge for the year needs to be increased by £400 and a creditor for £400 must be established. We will deal with this in exactly the same way by recording the £400 in the adjustments column to increase the profit and loss account charge and by adding £400 to total accruals.

(c)   **Rates**

The profit and loss account charge for the year should be £150 + ($^{3}/_{4}$ × £800), ie. £750 and there should be a prepayment of £200. The adjustments column is debited with £200 to set up a prepayment and a credit of £200 is made to decrease the profit and loss account charge.

Stage 4: We have now recorded all of the adjustments and we need to prepare the trading and profit and loss account and balance sheet. This is achieved as follows:

Cross-casting each account and entering the total in the appropriate column of the profit and loss account or balance sheet. Some examples are as follows:

(a)   Fixed assets (9,420 + 0 = £9,420) are recorded in the **debit** column of the **balance sheet**.

(b)   Provision for depreciation (3,470 + 942 = £4,412) is recorded in the **credit** column of the **balance sheet**.

(c)   Purchases (8,180 – 1,500 = £6,680) is recorded in the **debit** column of the **profit and loss account**.

Note: Accruals are added to the original trial balance amount whereas prepayments are subtracted.

Adding the debit and credit sides of the profit and loss account. The differences between these two columns is a profit (if the credits exceed the debits) or a loss (if the debits exceed the credits). The difference is recorded in the correct column of the profit and loss account (so that the two sides now balance) and the double-entry is recorded in the balance sheet.

Adding the debit and credit columns of the balance sheet. These should agree unless you have made any errors.

Stage 5: The profit and loss account and balance sheet would then be prepared from the relevant columns.

You are not required to prepare these.

The completed extended trial balance follows:

Lyttleton – Extended trial balance 31 December 19X5

	Trial balance		Adjustments		P & L account		Balance sheet	
	Dr £	Cr £	Dr £	Cr £	Dr £	Cr £	Dr £	Cr £
Capital		7,830						7,830
Cash at bank	2,010						2,010	
Fixed assets	9,420						9,420	
Provision for depreciation		3,470		942				4,412
Debtors	1,830						1,830	
Stock 31.12.X4	1,680				1,680			
Creditors		390						390
Sales		14,420				14,420		
Purchases	8,180			1,500	6,680			
Rent	1,100		100		1,200			
Electricity	940		400		1,340			
Rates	950			200	750			
Stock at 31.12.X5								
– Profit and loss				1,140		1,140		
– Balance sheet			1,140				1,140	
Depreciation expense			942		942			
Provision for doubtful debts				55				55
Bad debt expense			55		55			
Drawings			1,500				1,500	
Accruals				500				500
Prepayments			200				200	
					12,647	15,560		
Profit					2,913			2,913
	26,110	26,110	4,337	4,337	15,560	15,560	16,100	16,100

Presentation of stock adjustments in the extended trial balance

The trial balance above showed three separate stock accounts on three separate lines. This presentation was adopted in order to clarify the purpose of the year-end stock adjustment and the way in which the stock figures are extended into the columns for the profit and loss account and the balance sheet.

An alternative method of presentation is used in central assessment questions and answers. All the entries for stocks are shown on one line of the extended trial balance.

Example

The extended trial balance shows the following entries for stocks:

LEDGER BALANCES		ADJUSTMENTS	
Dr	Cr	Dr	Cr
32,165		21,060	21,060

Using the figures above, complete the profit and loss a/c and balance sheet balances columns for stock. (*Example based on a question which appeared in an AAT Central Assessment*)

Solution

PROFIT AND LOSS A/C		BALANCE SHEET BALANCES	
Dr	Cr	Dr	Cr
32,165	21,060	21,060	

As before, the opening stock balance has been extended into the debit column of the trial balance and the following adjustment has been made:

Debit   Stock (balance sheet)
      Credit   Stock (profit and loss account).

with closing stock.

Presentation of accruals and prepayments in the extended trial balance

Central assessment questions and answers treat accruals and prepayments as adjustments in the extended trial balance and this approach has been followed in the Study Pack.

It is also possible to set up separate columns for accruals and prepayments. Accruals and prepayments are recorded only once alongside the relevant expense account. As before, accruals are added to the original trial balance amount, whereas prepayments are subtracted. When the trial balance is extended, the accruals and prepayments columns are added up and the totals transferred to the credit and the debit side of the balance sheet respectively. This completes the double-entry. Using **Lyttelton** as an example, the presentation would be as follows:

Account	Trial balance		Adjustments		Accruals	Prepayments	P & L account		Balance sheet	
	Dr £	Cr £	Dr £	Cr £	£	£	Dr £	Cr £	Dr £	Cr £
Rent	1,100				100		1,200			
Electricity	940				400		1,340			
Rates	950					200	750			
					500	200			500	200

TREATMENT OF GOODS TAKEN FOR OWN USE

Questions frequently ask students to adjust for goods taken from stock by the owner of a business for private use.

There are two methods of dealing with this.

Method 1

Dr   Drawings account
      Cr   Purchases account (with the *cost price* of the goods)

This is the method used in the example **Lyttleton** and in much of the material in this Study Pack.

Method 2

Dr   Drawings account (with the *selling price* of the goods, including VAT)
      Cr   Sales account
      Cr   VAT account

This is the method preferred by the AAT and many central assessment questions and answers use it.

The AAT has recently stated that *both* methods are acceptable.

As a guide, you will probably find it easier to use Method 1 (Cr Purchases) where the goods taken from stock are stated at *cost* and Method 2 (Cr Sales) where the goods taken from stock are stated at *selling price*.

THE FINAL STAGE

There is one more task to be performed, that is to return to the ledger and record the adjustments shown on the extended trial balance and then to close the books. The Study Pack for Unit 4 *Recording capital transactions* describes this process in detail.

QUESTIONS

1 Rugg

You have been asked to prepare the 19X0 accounts of Rugg, a retail merchant. Rugg has balanced the books at 31 December 19X0 and gives you the following list of balances:

	£
Capital account at 1 January 19X0	2,377
Rent	500
Stock 1 January 19X0 at cost	510
Rates	240
Insurance	120
Wages	1,634
Debtors	672
Sales	15,542
Repairs	635
Purchases	9,876
Discounts received	129
Drawings	1,200
Petty cash in hand 31 December 19X0	5
Bank balance 31 December 19X0	763
Motor vehicles, at cost	1,740
Fixtures and fittings, at cost	829
Provision for depreciation at 1 January 19X0	
Motor vehicles	435
Fixtures and fittings	166
Travel and entertaining	192
Creditors	700
Sundry expenses	433

You ascertain the following:

(1)   Closing stock, valued at cost, amounts to £647.

(2)   Rugg has drawn £10 a month and these drawings have been charged to wages.

(3)   Depreciation is to be provided at 25% on cost on motor vehicles and 20% on cost on fixtures and fittings.

(4)   Bad debts totalling £37 are to be written off.

(5)   Sundry expenses include £27 spent on electrical repairs and cash purchases of goods for resale of £72.

(6)   Rugg has taken goods from stock for his own use. When purchased by his business, these goods cost £63 and would have been sold for £91.

(7)   The annual rental of the business premises is £600 and £180 paid for rates in August 19X0 covers the year ending 30 June 19X1.

Required

Prepare an extended trial balance reflecting the above information.

2   Hick

The following is the trial balance of Hick at 31 December 19X6.

	Dr £	Cr £
Shop fittings at cost	7,300	
Depreciation provision at 1 January 19X6		2,500
Leasehold premises at cost	30,000	
Depreciation provision at 1 January 19X6		6,000
Stock in trade at 1 January 19X6	15,000	
Debtors at 31 December 19X6	10,000	
Provision for doubtful debts at 1 January 19X6		800
Cash in hand	50	
Cash in bank	1,250	
Creditors for supplies		18,000
Proprietor's capital at 1 January 19X6		19,050
Drawings to 31 December 19X6	4,750	
Purchases	80,000	
Sales		120,000
Wages	12,000	
Advertising	4,000	
Rates for 15 months	1,800	
Bank charges	200	
	166,350	166,350

The following adjustments are to be made:

(1)   Depreciation of shop fittings: £400; depreciation of leasehold: £1,000.

(2)   A debt of £500 is irrecoverable and is to be written off; the doubtful debts provision is to be 3% of the debtors.

(3)   Advertising fees of £200 have been treated incorrectly as wages.

(4)   The proprietor has withdrawn goods costing £1,200 for his personal use; these have not been recorded as drawings.

(5)   The stock in trade at 31 December 19X6 is valued at £21,000.

Required

Prepare an extended trial balance at 31 December 19X6.

3   Michael

Michael carried on business as a clothing manufacturer. The trial balance of the business as on 31 December 19X6 was as follows:

	£	£
Capital account – Michael		30,000
Freehold factory at cost (including land £4,000)	20,000	
Factory plant and machinery at cost	4,800	
Travellers' cars	2,600	
Provision for depreciation, 1 January 19X6		
Freehold factory		1,920
Factory plant and machinery		1,600
Travellers' cars		1,200
Stocks, 1 January 19X6	8,900	
Trade debtors and creditors	3,600	4,200
Provision for doubtful debts		280
Purchases	36,600	
Wages and salaries	19,800	
Rates and insurance	1,510	
Sundry expenses	1,500	
Motor expenses	400	
Sales		72,000
Balance at bank	11,490	
	111,200	111,200

You are given the following information:

(1)   Stocks on hand at 31 December were £10,800.

(2)   Wages and salaries include the following:

Michael – drawings	£2,400
Motor expenses	£600

(3)   Provision is to be made for depreciation on the freehold factory, plant and machinery and travellers' cars at 2%, 10% and 25% respectively, calculated on cost.

(4)   On 31 December 19X6 £120 was owing for sundry expenses and rates paid in advance amounted to £260.

(5)   Of the trade debtors £60, for which provision had previously been made, is to be written off.

Required

(a)   Prepare an extended trial balance at 31 December 19X6 dealing with the above information.

(b)   Prepare a trading and profit and loss account for the year ended 31 December 19X6 and a balance sheet at that date.

SUMMARY

The extended trial balance is simply a worksheet showing the adjustments made to the figures in the trial balance to lead to the profit and loss account and balance sheet.

Procedure

- Set out initial trial balance.

- Deal with adjustments.

- Deal with accruals and prepayments.

- Add the columns across into profit and loss and balance sheet.

- Add the columns down.

- Prepare profit and loss account and balance sheet from the relevant columns.

Suspense accounts

OBJECTIVES

This section looks at a method of dealing with errors in the trial balance.

It also addresses the following performance criterion:

■   Any errors disclosed by the trial balance are traced and corrected.

INTRODUCTION

A suspense account is used when the trial balance totals disagree.

If the trial balance totals disagree the difference can be posted to a suspense account. This will enable the trial balance to be extended and the accounts to be prepared. Preparation of the accounts should result in the discovery of the errors that gave rise to the suspense account in the first place. **Obviously the error(s) must be found before the accounts can be finalised.**

ERRORS AFFECTING THE TRIAL BALANCE

Errors which will cause a difference on the trial balance include the following:

•   Transposition: eg. a debit of £67 and a credit of £76 for the same transaction.

•   One-sided omission: eg. a cheque for rent £150 entered in cash book but not in the rent account.

•   Two entries on one side and none on the other: eg. discount received debited to creditors and debited to discounts received account.

•   An account entered on the wrong side of the trial balance or omitted from the trial balance.

•   Casting error: an account on the trial balance may have been added up incorrectly.

Errors which will not cause a difference on the trial balance include the following:

•   Errors of original (prime) entry: the original figure is incorrectly entered in both parts of double entry.

•   Compensating errors: where one error is compensated exactly by another in the opposite direction.

•   Errors of omission: where an entry is left out altogether.

•   Errors of commission: eg. a payment of £50 for rates is debited to the wages account.

- Errors of principle: eg. treating a fixed asset as an expense.

Only those errors which cause a difference on the trial balance need to be adjusted by means of an entry in the suspense account. For example:

- If an item has been posted to the *wrong* account, then this will not cause a difference on the trial balance although the error must be adjusted for.

- If the sales day book has been miscast then, as long as the debtors' ledger control account (and not the individual debtor's account) is the double-entry, then the miscast will not cause a difference on the trial balance as the wrong total will be posted to both the debtors' ledger control account *and* the sales account. (If, however, the individual accounts were the double-entry, then a miscast in the sales day book would cause a difference on the trial balance.)

- Failure to record a transaction will not cause a difference on the trial balance. What has happened is:

  Debit Nothing
  Credit Nothing

  The trial balance may be wrong but it is not out of balance.

- Errors in the closing stock will not cause a difference in the trial balance as closing stock does not appear in the trial balance.

COMPUTERISED ACCOUNTING SYSTEMS

The same basic principles apply to all accounting systems, whether manual or computerised. Most computer systems, however, automatically post both sides of the double-entry, meaning that the trial balance will always balance. Any differences will automatically be posted to a suspense account.

Where the accounting system is computerised, certain errors cannot occur:
- single entries (the computer will not accept them);
- two entries on one side (the computer will not accept them);
- casting errors (the computer will total accounts automatically);
- transposition errors (the computer posts the double-entry automatically);
- extraction errors (the computer posts the double-entry automatically).

Human errors can still occur:

- errors of original entry;
- compensating errors;
- errors of commission;
- omissions;
- errors of principle.

HOW TO CLEAR THE SUSPENSE ACCOUNT

- Correct the account which has the error or omission.
- The other side of the double entry should be recorded in the suspense account.

Illustration

If there has been a credit to cash but no debit to purchases, you should:

Debit Purchases
Credit Suspense

Example

On 31 December 19X0 the trial balance of John Jones, a small manufacturer, failed to agree and the difference of £967 was entered as a debit balance on the suspense account. After the final accounts had been prepared the following errors were discovered and the difference was eliminated.

(1) A purchase of goods from A Smith for £170 had been credited in error to the account of H Smith.

(2) The purchase day book was undercast by £200.

(3) Machinery purchased for £150 had been debited to the purchases account.

(4) Discounts received of £130 had been posted to the debit of the discounts received account.

(5) Rates paid by cheque £46 had been posted to the debit of the rates account as £64.

(6) Cash drawings by the owner of £45 had been entered in the cash account correctly but not posted to the drawings account.

(7) The balance on the stock account representing the opening stock of £1,200 had been omitted from the trial balance.

Required

(a) Show the journal entries necessary to correct the above errors.

(b) Show the entries in the suspense account to eliminate the differences entered in the suspense account.

Note: The control accounts are part of the double-entry.

Solution

● Journal – John Jones

		Dr £	Cr £
31 December 19X0			

1 H Smith 170

       A Smith 170

   being adjustment of incorrect entry for purchases from A Smith
   (No effect on suspense account)

2 Purchases 200

       Creditors' ledger control a/c 200

   being correction of undercast of purchases day book
   (No effect on suspense account as control account is the
   double-entry. However the error should have been found
   during the reconciliation of the control account.)

3 Machinery 150

       Purchases 150

   being adjustment for wrong entry for machinery purchased
   (No effect on suspense account)

4 Suspense account 260

       Discount received 260

   being correction of discounts received entered on wrong side
   of account

5 Suspense account 18

       Rates 18

   being correction of transposition error to rates account

6 Drawings 45

       Suspense account 45

   being completion of double-entry for drawings

7 Stock per trial balance 1,200

       Suspense account 1,200

   being inclusion of opening stock.
   There is no double-entry for this error in the ledger as
   the mistake was to omit the item from the trial balance.

Suspense account

	£		£
Difference in trial balance	967	Drawings	45
Discounts received	260	Stock per trial balance	1,200
Rates	18		
	1,245		1,245

CLOSING STOCK

Closing stock is not recorded in the trial balance since the trial balance is prepared before the year end adjustments are put through ledger accounts.

If closing stock were included in the trial balance as follows it would not cause a problem.

	£	£
	.	.
	.	.
	.	.
Cost of sales	500	.
	.	.
	.	.
Closing stock	100	.
	.	.
	.	.
	.	.

Normally the inclusion of closing stock would cause a difference on the trial balance but it does not in this case because the trial balance also includes cost of sales.

If we analyse cost of sales in more detail, our trial balance extract becomes:

		£	£
		.	
		.	
		.	
Cost of sales:	Opening stock	200	
	Purchases	400	
	Closing stock	(100) *	
		———	
		500	
Closing stock		100 *	
		.	
		.	
		.	

The two closing stock entries cancel out hence closing stock is not actually in the trial balance and it cannot cause a difference.

QUESTIONS

1   Colin

Colin returned some goods to a supplier because they were faulty. The original purchase price of these goods was £8,260.

The ledger clerk treated the return correctly in both the creditors' ledger control account and the individual creditor's account, but debited the purchases returns account with £8,620.

What is the correcting entry which needs to be made?

2   Chris

Chris extracted a trial balance but by mistake included the amount on the bank statement instead of the cash book balance. Review of the bank statement revealed the following:

(a)	Unpresented cheques	£800
(b)	Uncleared lodgements	£500
(c)	Bank charges (not yet entered in cash book)	£40
(d)	Balance per bank statement	£1,400 Dr

What is the journal entry required to clear the suspense account?

3   GA

GA extracted the following trial balance from his ledgers at 31 May 19X4:

	£	£
Petty cash	20	
Capital		1,596
Drawings	1,400	
Sales		20,607
Purchases	15,486	
Purchases returns		210
Stock (1 January 19X4)	2,107	
Fixtures and fittings	710	
Sundry debtors	1,819	
Sundry creditors		2,078
Carriage on purchase	109	
Carriage on sales	184	
Rent and rates	460	
Light and heat	75	
Postage and telephone	91	
Sundry expenses	190	
Cash at bank	1,804	
	24,455	24,491

The trial balance did not agree. On investigation, GA discovered the following errors which had occurred during the month of May.

(1)   In extracting the schedule of debtors the credit side of a debtor's account had been overcast by £10.

(2)   An amount of £4 for carriage on sales had been posted in error to the carriage on purchases account.

(3)   A credit note for £17 received from a creditor had been entered in the purchase returns book but no entry had been made in the creditor's account.

(4)   £35 charged by Builders Ltd for repairs to GA's private residence had been charged, in error, to the sundry expenses account.

(5)   A payment of a telephone bill of £21 had been entered correctly in the cash book but had been posted, in error, to the postage and telephone account as £12.

Required

State what corrections you would make in GA's ledger accounts (using journal entries) and re-write the trial balance as it should appear *after* all the above corrections have been made.

Assume that the individual debtors' accounts are the double-entry and that there are no control accounts.

4   Sylvia Smith   (AAT CA D93)

You have received the following memorandum from a colleague, Sylvia Smith:

'As you know, before I joined this company I worked for a business which operated a computerised accounting system. In such systems the suspense a/c is used by the computer to post transactions, the nominal code for which it does not recognise. On a manual system the correct nominal ledger account should always be known, therefore, what is the purpose of the suspense a/c?'

Assessment task

Write a memorandum in answer to the above query.

5   Kidditoys   (AAT CA D94)

Introduction

Kidditoys is a retail shop which specialises in the sale of unusual toys, games and other baby products. The business was started in December 1987 and is owned and run by Sophie Stewart.

About half the sales of the business are cash sales through the shop, the remainder being on mail order. Mail order customers pay cash with order.

Sophie employs one sales assistant and one packing assistant.

Her present manual system of bookkeeping comprises a purchase ledger with approximately 30 active accounts, a nominal ledger and a petty cash book. A petty cash float of £50 is maintained for sundry expenses and is replenished as required. A further cash float of £50 is maintained in the sales till. All cash receipts are banked daily.

You are an accounting technician who is helping Sophie to prepare the business's accounts up to the trial balance stage.

Fixed asset information

	Date of purchase	Cost	Expected useful economic life
		£	(Years)
Motor van	07.08.93	12,640	5
Shop fittings	10.12.87	3,240	10
Office equipment	08.04.91	4,250	5

All fixed assets are depreciated on a straight-line basis using the expected useful economic lives above and zero-estimated residual values.

Depreciation is charged a full year in the year of purchase and is not charged for in the year of sale.

Other information

Average mark-up is 100%.

The VAT rate is 17.5%.

Data

(a)   The following list of balances has been extracted from the nominal ledger at the company's year-end, 30 November 1994.

	£
Sales	392,182
Sales returns	1,214
Purchases	208,217
Purchase returns	643
Stock	32,165
Wages	50,000
Rent	27,300
Rates	8,460
Light and heat	2,425
Office expenses	3,162
Selling expenses	14,112
Motor expenses	14,728
Sundry expenses	6,560
Motor vans (cost)	12,640
Motor vans (provision for depreciation) at 1.12.93	2,528
Shop fittings (cost)	3,240
Shop fittings (provision for depreciation) at 1.12.93	1,944
Office equipment (cost)	4,250
Office equipment (provision for depreciation) at 1.12.93	2,550
Cash	100
Bank current account (debit balance)	4,420
Bank investment account	68,340
Interest received	3,280
Purchase ledger total	27,683
Capital	22,145
VAT (credit balance)	6,420
Suspense [see note (b) (ii) overleaf]	50

(b)   After extracting the balances listed in (a), the following six errors and omissions were discovered:

(i)   Credit purchases of £954 had been correctly posted to the Purchases a/c, but had been debited in the supplier's account (T Ditton).

(ii)   The shop had been entirely re-fitted during the year. The old fittings had been sold off to the local boy scouts for £50. This had been debited in the Bank a/c, but had been credited in the Suspense a/c.

The invoice for the new shop fittings, for £9,620, had been received from Kingston Displays Ltd on 15 November. This invoice had not yet been entered into the accounts. Sophie intended to pay the invoice in January after the Christmas sales period. The new shop fittings are expected to have a useful economic life of 10 years.

(iii)   Sophie paid herself a 'wage' of £2,000 per calendar month which she debited to Wages a/c.

(iv)   During the year, an invoice for £843 (for zero-rated services) had been received from a supplier (E Molesey). When payment was made, Sophie accidentally made out the cheque for £840. Sophie noticed this error and contacted E Molesey who told her to ignore such a small sum of money. No adjustment has yet been made for this discrepancy.

(v)   During the year, Sophie gave away a number of toys from the shop as presents to relatives and friends. She kept a record of these, which came to £640 at selling price, including VAT, but has not so far entered the transactions into the accounts.

(vi)   The company's current account bank statement arrived on 30 November 1994. This showed interest received for the month of November at £9. This has not yet been entered into the accounts.

(c)   The following additional matters need to be taken into account:

(i)   Depreciation for the year ended 30 November 1994 is to be provided for.

(ii)   The stock in the shop at 30 November 1994 was valued at £42,120 at selling price.

(iii)   Rent was £2,100 per month payable in advance. The rent for December 1994 had already been paid.

(iv)   Business rates are paid half yearly on 1 May and 1 November. The business rates bill for the period 1 April 1994 – 31 March 1995 amounted to £6,240.

(v)   The electricity bill for £318, covering the July, August and September quarter, had been received on 15 October. This had been entered into the purchase ledger and duly paid. Electricity usage can be considered to be relatively even throughout the year.

Assessment tasks

Task 1

Prepare journal entries for the transactions listed in (b). Narratives are required.

Task 2

Enter all the account balances, including those adjusted in Task 1 above, in the first two columns of the Extended Trial Balance. Note that some of the balances have already been filled in for you. Create additional accounts as required.

Task 3

Make appropriate entries in the adjustments columns of the Extended Trial Balance. Create additional accounts as required.

DO NOT EXTEND THE FIGURES IN THE EXTENDED TRIAL BALANCE INTO THE PROFIT AND LOSS AND BALANCE SHEET COLUMNS.

KIDDITOYS

JOURNAL ENTRIES	Dr £	Cr £

KIDDITOYS

JOURNAL ENTRIES	Dr £	Cr £

KIDDITOYS – EXTENDED TRIAL BALANCE

	Ledger Balances		Adjustments		Profit and Loss a/c		Balance Sheet Balances	
	Dr £	Cr £	Dr £	Cr £	Dr £	Cr £	Dr £	Cr £
Sales								
Sales returns								
Purchases								
Purchase returns								
Stock	32,165							
Wages	27,300							
Rent	8,460							
Rates	2,425							
Light and heat	3,162							
Office expenses	14,112							
Selling expenses	14,728							
Motor expenses	6,560							
Sundry expenses	12,650							
Motor vans (cost)								
Motor vans (provision for depreciation)								
Shop fittings (cost)								
Shop fittings (provision for depreciation)								
Office equipment (cost)	4,250							
Office equipment (provision for depreciation)								
Cash	100							
Bank current account								
Bank investment account								
Interest received								
Capital								
VAT								

SUMMARY

The suspense account is used:

(a)   when destination of posting is uncertain
(b)   when the trial balance totals disagree

Remember to correct the account with the incorrect/missing entry first; the suspense account is then the other side of the double-entry.

Accounting for partnerships and preparing manufacturing accounts

OBJECTIVES

By the end of this session, you will be familiar with the accounts produced for a partnership and will be able to prepare a manufacturing account.

INTRODUCTION TO PARTNERSHIP ACCOUNTS

A partnership exists where two or more people carry on business in common with a view to sharing the profits.

DIFFERENCE BETWEEN PARTNERSHIP ACCOUNTS AND SOLE TRADER ACCOUNTS

There is only one real difference and that is in the capital section of the balance sheet.

In the sole trader's accounts capital represents the amount owed by the business to the owner. This means there is **one** capital account.

In a partnership the business will owe money to two or more partners and hence there will be two or more capital accounts.

Illustration

Balance sheet of A and B partnership at 31 December 19X0

	£
Net assets	50,000
Capital account – Miss A	25,000
Capital account – Miss B	25,000
	50,000

CURRENT ACCOUNTS

It is common in partnerships for the capital accounts to be split into two accounts:

- the capital account – showing capital introduced by the partners
- the current account – showing the partners' shares of net profit and drawings

Obviously the balances on the two accounts added together will give the same result as a single capital account would have produced.

The reason the accounts are sometimes split in this way is that it can help to give more information about each partner's investment in the firm. For example the balance on the current account is often the amount that a partner is permitted to take from the business as drawings. Typically, he will not be allowed to withdraw his fixed capital.

Illustration 1

Suppose A and B share profits equally and profit for the year is £50,000. Their fixed capital is £15,000 each and each has a current account balance at the beginning of the year of £10,000.

Balance sheet of A and B Partnership at 31 December 19X1

		£	£
Net assets			100,000
Capital accounts			
Miss A		15,000	
Miss B		15,000	
			30,000
Current accounts			
Miss A:	b/f	10,000	
	profit share	25,000	
			35,000
Miss B:	b/f	10,000	
	profit share	25,000	
			35,000
			100,000

Drawings are treated exactly as you would expect.

Illustration 2

Miss A draws	£5,000
Miss B draws	£10,000

Balance sheet of A and B Partnership at 31 December 19X1

	£	£
Net assets		85,000
		─────
Capital accounts		30,000
Current accounts		
Miss A: b/f	10,000	
profit share	25,000	
	─────	
	35,000	
drawings	(5,000)	
	─────	
		30,000
Miss B: b/f	10,000	
profit share	25,000	
	─────	
	35,000	
drawings	(10,000)	
	─────	
		25,000
		─────
		85,000
		─────

As you can see, there is no fundamental difference between partnership accounts and sole trader accounts.

The remaining sections will consider problems that are peculiar to partnerships.

DIVISION OF PROFITS

There are many ways of dividing the profits between the partners. The most common are as follows:

- **Salaries** – to recognise the fact that some partners are more active in running the business, they may be given a 'salary'.

  For example, one partner may be given £3,000 a year.

  This should not be confused with a salary paid to an employee. It is merely one of the ways in which the profit is distributed between the partners. It does not, therefore, appear as an expense in the profit and loss account.

- **Interest on capital** – to recognise the fact that partners may have contributed different amounts of capital to the firm, they may have interest on their capital account balances.

  For example, each partner may be granted 5% of the balance on his account.

- **Profit-sharing ratio** – any profit which still has to be shared out after salaries and interest will be allocated to the partners in an agreed ratio.

Illustration

In 19X2 A and B made a profit of £60,000.

Partners are allowed interest of 10% on their capital accounts.

Miss B is allowed a salary of £5,000 for running the business.

Appropriation of profit statement

	Total £	A £	B £
Profit	60,000		
Miss B's salary	(5,000)		5,000
	55,000		
Interest	(3,000)	1,500	1,500
	52,000		
Split equally	(52,000)	26,000	26,000
		27,500	32,500

Therefore £27,500 will be credited to A's current account and £32,500 to B's current account. Of course the total of A's profit share and B's profit share must equal the amount of profit to be shared.

THE PARTNERSHIP ACT 1890

If there is no agreement as to how the profits should be split the Partnership Act 1890 states:

- no interest on capital or current accounts;

- no salaries;

- profits and losses to be shared equally; and

- 5% interest on loans made by the partners to the partnership.

Any interest on loans from partners is *not* an appropriation of profit and should, therefore, be charged in the profit and loss account.

Example

Karen and Julia are in partnership with no partnership agreement.

Karen has lent the partnership £10,000.

Trading profit for the year is £25,000.

Required

Show how the profit is shared among the partners.

Profit and loss account

	£
Trading profit	25,000
Interest	(500)
Profit available for the partners	24,500

Appropriation statement

	Total £	K £	J £
Profit	24,500		
Shared 50:50	(24,500)	12,250	12,250

INTRODUCTION TO MANUFACTURING ACCOUNTS

So far we have worked with trading accounts of the form:

	£	£
Sales		X
Opening stock	X	
Purchases	X	
	X	
Closing stock	(X)	
Cost of sales		(X)
Gross profit		X

This is perfectly satisfactory for a retail organisation that purchases and resells goods. A manufacturing company will need further details of the cost of manufacturing its products and these details can be set out in the form of a manufacturing account.

You will not be asked to prepare a full set of manufacturing accounts in the Central Assessment, but you may be asked to prepare an extended trial balance for a manufacturing company. It is therefore necessary that you understand the way in which manufacturing accounts are prepared.

Definitions

- *Direct costs* are those which can be attributed to a particular unit of production and will normally include raw materials, productive wages and other expenses capable of direct identification with production. These three are often called *direct materials, direct wages* and *direct expenses*.

- *Indirect expenses* are production expenses which cannot be attributed to a particular unit of production. They are often called *manufacturing* or *works overheads* and will include such items as factory power, plant repairs etc.

- *Prime cost* is the total of the direct expenses.

- *Factory cost or works cost* is prime cost plus a share of the factory indirect expenses.

Stocks

A trading firm has stocks in only one form (ie. goods held for resale), but a manufacturing firm will have three forms of stocks:

- *direct materials* – items of raw materials which have not yet been issued to production;
- *work in progress* – items of partly completed goods;
- *finished goods* – items which are completed but unsold.

THE PRO FORMA

Basic format

The manufacturing account summarises the costs of production in the factory:

	£
Direct materials	X
Direct labour	X
Direct expenses	X
Prime cost	X
Manufacturing overheads	X
Factory cost	X

Detailed layout of manufacturing account

Pro forma manufacturing account

	£	£
Materials consumed		
Opening stock of raw materials	X	
Purchases of raw materials	X	
	——	
	X	
Less: Closing stock of raw materials	(X)	
	——	
		X
Direct wages		X
Direct expenses		X
		——
		X
Prime cost		
Works indirect expenses		
Factory power	X	
Factory rent/rates	X	
Factory insurance	X	
Factory light and heat	X	
Plant repairs	X	
Plant depreciation	X	
	——	
		X
		——
		X
Add: Opening work in progress		X
Less: Closing work in progress		(X)
		——
Factory cost of goods produced – transfers to warehouse		X
		——

Trading and profit and loss account

The trading and profit and loss account, which takes account of selling and distribution costs and administration expenses, will be in a reasonably familiar format:

Trading and profit and loss account

	£	£
Sales		X
Less: Cost of goods sold		
Opening stock of finished goods	X	
Transfers from factory	X	
	X	
Less: Closing stock of finished goods	X	
		X
Gross profit		X
Less: Distribution costs	X	
Administrative expenses	X	
		(X)
Net profit		X

PREPARATION OF THE MANUFACTURING ACCOUNT

Illustration

The following represent details of the factory costs of J White for the year ended 31 December 19X7.

	£
Opening stock of raw materials	1,000
Raw materials purchased	12,000
Direct (manufacturing) wages	24,000
Factory rent	800
Depreciation of plant in factory	850
General indirect expenses	550
Closing stock of raw materials	1,200
Work in progress	
1 Jan 19X6	4,000
31 Dec 19X6	6,000

Given that we have a basic format, we can now use the above information to demonstrate a developed layout.

J White
Manufacturing account for the year ended 31 December 19X7

	£	£
Direct materials		
Opening stock	1,000	
Purchases	12,000	
Carriage inwards	–	
Less: Returns	–	
	13,000	
Less: Closing stock	1,200	
		11,800
Direct wages		24,000
Direct expenses		–
Prime cost		35,800
Factory overhead		
Rent	800	
Plant depreciation	850	
General expenses	550	
		2,200
		38,000
Add: Opening work in progress		4,000
		42,000
Less: Closing work in progress		(6,000)
Manufacturing cost of goods completed		36,000

Note that opening and closing stocks of raw materials and work in progress are included in the manufacturing account. Stocks of finished goods are dealt with in the trading account, as is normal.

Certain overhead costs may require apportionment amongst these functional headings. For example, rent of premises may be £1,000 per annum. How should this be split between manufacturing, administration and selling? In such a case, the likely answer is on the basis of floorspace used. Thus the apportionment might be:

	Area (m^2)	Apportionment £	
Factory	6,000	500	Manufacturing account
Administration offices	3,600	300	Profit and loss account
Sales offices	2,400	200	
	12,000	1,000	

If you are required to apportion expenses, you will be told which basis to use.

The double-entry

In the trading account the manufacturing cost of goods completed will appear in the place of purchases as shown below. Thus a credit has been made to manufacturing account and a debit to trading account.

J White
Trading account for the year ended 31 December 19X7

	£	£
Sales (say)		60,000
Less: Cost of sales		
Opening stock (say)	6,000	
Cost of manufacture	36,000	
	42,000	
Less: Closing stock (say)	5,000	
		(37,000)
Gross profit		23,000

QUESTIONS

1   Warren, Hall and Oates

Warren, Hall and Oates set up in partnership together some years ago with capital of £40,000, £38,000 and £35,000 respectively. The following are summaries of the partners' current accounts for the year ended 31 December 19X5. Study these carefully and then answer the questions which follow.

Warren – Current account

19X5		£	19X5		£
	Drawings	19,112	1 Jan	Balance b/f	55
31 Dec	Balance c/f	4,799	31 Dec	Interest on capital	5,200
			31 Dec	Salary	6,000
			31 Dec	Share of profits	12,656
		23,911			23,911

Hall – Current account

19X5		£	19X5		£
	Drawings	15,603	1 Jan	Balance c/f	120
31 Dec	Balance c/f	5,949	31 Dec	Interest on capital	4,940
			31 Dec	Salary	7,000
			31 Dec	Share of profits	9,492
		21,552			21,552

Oates – Current account

19X5		£	19X5		£
1 Jan	Balance b/f	207	31 Dec	Interest on capital	4,550
	Drawings	14,598	31 Dec	Salary	7,000
			31 Dec	Share of profits	3,164
			31 Dec	Balance c/f	91
		14,805			14,805

Required

(a) Reconstruct the appropriation scheme Warren, Hall and Oates have agreed for the division of profits and losses.

(b) Calculate the net profit of the partnership for the year ended 31 December 19X5.

(c) How would the partners have shared this profit had they made no formal agreement as to the division of profits?

(d) What would the partners' shares in profit have been had the net profit for the year ended 31 December 19X5 been:

(i) £75,000;
(ii) £30,000.

2   Alf, Ben, Connie and Dora

Alf, Ben, Connie and Dora are in partnership. The capitals they have invested in the partnership are £45,000, £30,000, £20,000 and £15,000 respectively. During the financial year ended 31 October 19X5 the partnership earned profits of £56,000.

(a) What will each partner's share in the year's profits be if:

(i) the partners share profits and losses equally;

(ii) the partners have agreed a profit-sharing ratio of 4:3:2:1 respectively;

(iii) the partners have agreed to allow interest on capitals at 10% per annum as well as sharing profits and losses in the ratio of 4:3:2:1;

(iv) the partners have agreed that interest is to be allowed on capital at 10% per annum; Connie and Dora are to receive salaries of £5,000 each; and profits are to be shared in the ratio 4:3:2:1 respectively?

(b) Show the appropriation account for the partnership for the year ended 31 October under the scheme in (a)(iv) above.

(c)   The partners had the following balances to their credit on their current accounts as at 1 November 19X4:

	£
Alf	104
Ben	270
Connie	614
Dora	317
	1,305

During the year ended 31 October 19X5 the partners withdrew the following amounts from the partnership:

	£
Alf	18,000
Ben	13,300
Connie	14,500
Dora	10,200
	56,000

From this information and the appropriation scheme in (a)(iv) above, prepare the partners' current accounts for the year ended 31 October 19X5.

3   Futon Enterprises   (AAT CA J94)

Introduction

Jason Sarmiento, trading as Futon Enterprises, is a sole trader assembling and selling futons. A futon is a Japanese-style bed, consisting of a slatted wooden frame and a mattress. Jason buys in the pre-cut timber and the mattresses and assembles the futons for sale through his retail shop in Lincoln and by mail order.

The assembly takes place in a small workshop to the rear of the shop and is carried out by a full-time assembler. The business also employs a driver, a secretary and you, the accounts clerk. Jason spends most of his time in the shop and dealing with the mail order side of the business.

The business accounts are currently operated using a manual system, though Jason is actively engaged in investigating computerised accounting systems.

A very simple sales ledger is operated and the purchase ledger contains about 20 accounts. There are few cash transactions. Any that do occur are handled through a traditional petty cash book. A £50 cash float is maintained and at weekly intervals the expenditure is posted to the nominal ledger and the float replenished.

Accounting policy

(1)   **Manufacturing**

Purchases of raw materials are posted to a Materials Account. The assembler's wages are posted to the Production Wages Account. No separate Production Overheads Account is maintained.

It has been agreed that finished goods stocks should be valued at a standard cost of production, calculated as follows per futon:

	£
Materials	36.00
Production wages	7.00
Overheads	5.00
	48.00

(2)   **Depreciation**

Rates:	Assembling machinery	10% per annum straight line
	Delivery van	30% per annum reducing balance
	Furniture and fittings	20% per annum straight line

Depreciation is charged a full year in the year of purchase and is not charged for in the year of sale.

Zero scrap values are assumed.

(3)   **Mark-up**

The company normally marks up all its products at 75% on standard production costs.

Fixed asset information

	Date of purchase	£	Cost £
Assembling machinery	1.6.90		3,650
Delivery van [see note (b) (i) on page 96]	1.8.93		12,400
Furniture and fittings:			
Shop fittings	1.6.90	7,200	
Office furniture	1.6.90	2,350	
Reception re-fit (materials only)			
[see note (b) (ii) on page 96]	1.9.93	1,240	
			10,790

Data

(a)   Listed below is the company's trial balance at 31 May 1994.

Futon Enterprises
Trial balance as at 31 May 1994

	Dr £	Cr £
Delivery vans (cost)	12,000	
Delivery vans (provision for depreciation)		7,884
Assembling machinery (cost)	3,650	
Assembling machinery (provision for depreciation)		1,095
Furniture and fittings (cost)	10,790	
Furniture and fittings (provision for depreciation)		5,730
Raw materials stock	1,320	
Finished goods stock	1,440	
Sales ledger total	1,860	
Bank		320
Cash	50	
Purchase ledger total		4,265
Sales		120,240
Materials	35,465	
Production wages	12,480	
Driver's wages	11,785	
Salaries	22,460	
Employer's National Insurance	4,365	
Motor expenses	2,160	
Rent	3,930	
Sundry expenses	3,480	
VAT		1,220
Inland Revenue		1,365
Drawings	12,400	
Capital		7,516
Suspense	10,000	
	149,635	149,635

(b)   Adjustments need to he made for the following:

(i)   A new delivery van was purchased for £12,400 on 1 August 1993. The old delivery van, originally purchased for £12,000 on 1 August 1990, was given in part-exchange; the balance of £10,000 was paid for by cheque and debited to Suspense Account.

(ii)   The reception area was re-built in the first week of September 1993. This work was carried out by the assembler as business was rather slack at that time. He spent the whole of the first week in September on this task; his pay is £12,480 per annum.

Employer's National Insurance contributions can be ignored.

(iii)   Jason gave two futons as Christmas presents in December 1993. An account was opened in the sales ledger to record these transactions.

(c)   The following additional matters need to be taken into account:

    (i)   Depreciation for the year ended 31 May 1994 is to be provided for.

    (ii)   The stocktake at 31 May 1994 has revealed the following:

       Stock of timber, mattresses and sundry materials   £1,526

       23 fully completed futons were in stock.

       There was no work in progress.

    (iii)   The electricity bill for £180 covering the- February, March, April 1994 quarter had been received on 15 May and entered into the purchase ledger. Electricity usage is relatively even throughout the year. Electricity is included within sundry expenses.

    (iv)   On 12 May, the delivery van was involved in an accident, suffering minor damage. The repairs, costing £164, have been carried out and the cost included in motor expenses. A letter has been received today from the Mercury Insurance Company agreeing to compensate for all but the first £50 of the repair costs.

    (v)   A customer, T Young, who bought two futons at the regular price in July 1993, has disappeared without paying. It has been decided to write off the amount owing.

    (vi)   The rent of £3,144 per annum is paid annually in advance on 1 September.

Assessment tasks

Task 1

Prepare journal entries for the transactions listed in (b) above. Narratives are required.

Task 2

Enter all the account balances, including those adjusted in Task 1 above, in the first two columns of the extended trial balance.

Task 3

Make appropriate entries in the adjustments columns of the extended trial balance. Create additional accounts as required.

Task 4

Extend the figures into the extended trial balance columns for profit and loss account and balance sheet. Total all columns, transferring the balance of profit or loss as appropriate.

FUTON ENTERPRISES

JOURNAL ENTRIES	Dr £	Cr £

Accounting for partnerships and preparing manufacturing accounts

FUTON ENTERPRISES – EXTENDED TRIAL BALANCE

	Ledger Balances		Adjustments		Profit and Loss a/c		Balance Sheet Balances	
	Dr £	Cr £	Dr £	Cr £	Dr £	Cr £	Dr £	Cr £
Delivery vans (cost)								
Delivery vans (depreciation provision)								
Assembling machinery (cost)								
Assembling machinery (depreciation provision)								
Furniture and fittings (cost)								
Furniture and fittings (depreciation provision)								
Raw materials (stock)								
Finished goods (stock)								
Sales ledger total								
Bank								
Cash								
Purchase ledger total								
Sales								
Materials								
Production wages								
Driver's wages								
Salaries								
Employer's NI								
Motor expenses								
Rent								
Sundry expenses								
VAT								
Inland Revenue								
Drawings								
Capital								
Depreciation delivery vans								
Depreciation assembling machinery								
Depreciation furniture and fittings								
Accruals								
Prepayments								

Financial Training

4 Punch

Punch is a sole trader engaged in the manufacture of toys. The following trial balance was extracted from the books at 31 March 19X1.

	Debit £	Credit £
Capital		39,390
Freehold land and buildings at cost	45,000	
Plant and machinery at cost	36,500	
Motor vans at cost	19,800	
Provision for depreciation – Land and buildings		2,700
– Plant and machinery		4,500
– Motor vans		3,700
Stocks at 1.4.X0 – Raw materials	12,725	
– WIP	18,000	
– Finished goods	20,500	
Purchases	82,550	
Sales		362,720
Wages – Factory	64,750	
– Administration	24,360	
– Sales	26,920	
Rent (nine months to 31.12.X0)	22,000	
Repairs to buildings	5,500	
Sales expenses	22,000	
Electricity and power	17,600	
Administration expenses	5,900	
Provision for doubtful debts		1,560
Debtors	38,970	
Creditors		42,230
Bank		6,320
Cash in hand	45	
	463,120	463,120

You are given the following information:

(1) Provision is to be made for commission due to the sales manager. The commission is 20% of his own department's net profit after charging such commission.

(2) Closing stocks on 31 March 19X1:

	£
Raw materials	9,650
WIP	21,000
Finished goods	24,500

(3) Annual depreciation is to be provided at the following rates on the straight-line basis:

Land and buildings	2%
Plant and machinery	10%
Motor vans	25%

(4)   Debtors include an amount of £700 due from Sonic Ltd. Punch does not expect to be paid and has decided to write it off.

A general provision of 5% is to be maintained on remaining debts.

(5)   Factory rent for the 12 months to 31.12.X1 is £26,500.

(6)   Expenses are to be allocated as follows:

	Factory	*Administration*
Rent	7/10	3/10
Repairs	4/5	1/5
Electricity and power	2/3	1/3
Buildings depreciation	8/10	2/10

(7)   The following amounts were outstanding at the year-end:

	£
Electricity	960
Telephone (60% Sales, 40% Admin.)	240
Accountancy fees (Admin.)	850

Required

Prepare the manufacturing, trading and profit and loss accounts for the year ended 31 March 19X1 and the balance sheet at that date.

SUMMARY

Partnership accounts

*   The amount owed by the business to each partner is reflected in the total of each partner's capital and current accounts.

*   Typically, the capital account is used for recording fixed capital.

*   Typically, the current account is used for all other items, the most important of which are profit share and drawings.

*   Profit is shared by the partners in accordance with their agreement.

*   If there is no agreement, the Partnership Act 1890 states how profit is to be shared.

Manufacturing accounts

Manufacturing accounts provide a detailed analysis of the *cost of goods produced*.

For a manufacturing business, cost of goods sold includes:

*   raw materials

*   production labour

*   production overheads (direct and indirect)

Accounting for limited companies

OBJECTIVES

This session introduces the different format required for company accounts.

INTRODUCTION

Although a sole trader's business is treated as separate from its owner they are in law regarded as one single entity.

In contrast, a company is regarded as separate from its owners (*Salomon v Salomon & Co Ltd*).

DIFFERENCES BETWEEN ACCOUNTS OF COMPANIES AND SOLE TRADERS

- The format of the company accounts, which is governed by Schedule 4 of the Companies Act 1985, as modified by the Companies Act 1989.

- The treatment of profit in the profit and loss account.

- The composition of capital in the balance sheet.

You are not required to have a detailed knowledge of the Companies Act format and disclosure requirements.

THE PROFIT AND LOSS ACCOUNT

	Sole trader £		Limited company £
Sales	X	Turnover	X
Less: Cost of sales	X	Cost of sales	X
	—		—
Gross profit	X	Gross profit	X
Other income	X	Distribution costs	X
	—		
	X	Administrative expenses	X
Less: Expenses	X	Other operating income	X
	—		—
Net profit transferred to capital account	X		X
	—	Interest payable and similar charges	X
			—
		Profit on ordinary activities before tax	X
		Corporation tax	X
			—
		Profit on ordinary activities after tax	X
		Dividends paid and proposed	X
			—
		Profit for the financial year	X
		Retained profit brought forward	X
			—
		Retained profit carried forward	X
			—

From the above proforma you can see that the main differences are:

(a)   corporation tax; and
(b)   dividends.

CORPORATION TAX

The company is a separate legal entity and is subject to tax. Tax is an appropriation of the company's profits and therefore appears in the profit and loss account.

Generally, tax will be paid nine months after the year-end so the accounting entries are:

> Debit   Profit and loss account
> Credit   Corporation tax creditor (shown as a current liability in the balance sheet)

In the next year, when the tax is likely to be paid, the entry will be:

> Debit   Corporation tax creditor
> Credit   Cash

DIVIDENDS

As far as the sole trader was concerned, when he drew money from the business the double entry was:

> Debit   Drawings account
> Credit Cash

However for a company where there may be many hundreds of shareholders, it would be far from practical for each one of them to have a drawings account. A system of dividend payments is therefore used.

The actual amount of dividend to be paid by a company will be determined by many factors, the main one being the need to retain sufficient profits to provide for the future working capital and fixed asset requirements of the company.

Some companies pay an amount on account of the total dividend before the end of the year. This is known as an *interim dividend*. The bookkeeping entry is:

> Debit   Dividend account
> Credit Cash

(The dividend account is closed off to the profit and loss account at the year-end).

It will only be at the end of the year, when the company's results for the whole accounting period are known, that the directors can declare a final dividend.

As the payment of the final dividend takes place after the year end the figure in the accounts will again represent a provision. The entries are therefore:

> Debit   Profit and loss account
> Credit Dividends proposed account (shown as current liability)

Hence we will have two debits for dividends in the profit and loss account – one paid and one proposed.

PRO FORMA BALANCE SHEET

	Cost £	Depreciation £	£
Fixed assets			
Land and buildings	X	X	X
Plant and machinery	X	X	X
Fixtures, fittings, tools and equipment	X	X	X
	X	X	X
Current assets			
Stocks		X	
Debtors		X	
Cash at bank and in hand		X	
		X	
Creditors: Amounts falling due within one year			
Trade creditors		X	
Accruals		X	
		X	
Net current assets			X
Total assets less current liabilities			X
Creditors: Amounts falling due after more than one year			
12% debentures			X
			X
Capital and reserves			
Share capital			X
Share premium account			X
Other reserves			X
Profit and loss account			X
Shareholders' funds			X

SHARE CAPITAL

When a company is formed it usually raises its initial capital by issuing a number of **shares**.

The people who buy the shares are the owners of the company are known as its **members** or **shareholders**.

Shareholders

The proportion of the company which each member owns can thus be calculated by reference to the number of shares he holds. For example, if a member holds 750 shares in a company which has 1,000 shares in issue, he has a 75% stake in the company.

The advantage of the share system is that members can easily transfer their interest in the company by selling their shares, and the company can raise new capital by issuing more shares.

Shares have a face value which is also called the nominal value or the par value.

Suppose a company issues 100 shares with a nominal value of £1 for £100 in total.

>   Mrs X 25 shares
>   Mrs Y 75 shares

The double entry is:

>   Debit   Cash   100
>   Credit   Share capital   100

If Mrs Y sells her shares to Mrs Z this has no effect on the amount of share capital received by the company, so no entry is made in the share capital account.

If the stock market decides that the shares are worth only 80p each no entry is made in the share capital account because, again, this has no effect on the capital received by the company.

Types of share capital

A company may issue different types (classes) of shares, by far the most important of which are:

- **Ordinary shares**

   The majority of companies will have only this type of share, whose holders usually have a right to vote at meetings and are therefore effectively the owners of the company.

- **Preference shares**

   'Preference' in this context means that the owners of these shares will have priority over the ordinary shareholders in the payment of their dividend, which is usually of a fixed amount.

   In addition, if the company winds up (ceases to exist) the preference shareholders will normally be repaid their capital before the ordinary shareholders.

The difference between these two classes of shares is in essence the difference between the risk-takers (the ordinary shareholders), whose reward will be geared to how well the company performs, and the non-risk-takers (the preference shareholders) whose entitlement is fixed.

RESERVES

Reserves are the cumulative total of the company's retained profits.

A company may if it wishes, set aside some of its profits for a specific purpose, eg:

	£
Called-up share capital	1,000
Profit and loss account	1,000
	2,000

The company wishes to set aside £500 for replacement of fixed assets.

	£
Called-up share capital	1,000
Fixed asset replacement reserve	500
Profit and loss account	500
	2,000

This does not affect its total reserves, which remain at £1,000.

SHARE PREMIUM ACCOUNT

This arises when a company issues shares for more than their nominal value.

Example

Enterprise Ltd makes an issue of 10,000 £1 ordinary shares for £1.60 each. The entries are:

    Debit   Cash account £16,000

    Credit   Share capital account £10,000
             Share premium account £6,000

Note that a share premium account does not arise if the market value subsequently increases to more than the nominal value.

DEBENTURES

Debentures are a long-term loan. They are named after the legal agreement detailing the loan.

It is likely that there will be a number of debenture holders in the same way that there are a number of shareholders. In other words, the company may well be borrowing from a number of people or organisations rather than just one.

TYPES OF COMPANY

There are two types of limited company, public and private. A public company must include in its name the letters 'plc' standing for *public limited company*. Private companies must include *Limited* (*Ltd*) in their name.

The main difference is that a private company may not offer its shares or debentures to the public and so all companies listed on the Stock Exchange are public companies.

QUESTIONS

1   Transit Ltd

Believe it or not, you are now ready to tackle your first set of company accounts! Just before you launch yourself into the question that follows remember that *everything you have learnt about double-entry bookkeeping and the presentation of year-end accounts is valid in the context of companies*, subject only to the points we have added in this session.

The following is the trial balance of Transit Ltd at 31 March 19X8:

	£	£
Issued share capital (ordinary shares of £1 each)		42,000
Leasehold properties, at cost	75,000	
Motor vans, at cost (used for distribution)	2,500	
Provision for depreciation on motor vans to 31 March 19X7		1,000
Administration expenses	7,650	
Distribution expenses	10,000	
Stock, 31 March 19X7	12,000	
Purchases	138,750	
Sales		206,500
Directors' remuneration (administrative)	25,000	
Rents receivable		3,600
Investments at cost	6,750	
Investment income		340
7% Debentures		15,000
Debenture interest	1,050	
Bank interest	162	
Bank overdraft		730
Debtors and creditors	31,000	24,100
Interim dividend paid	1,260	
Profit and loss account, 31 March 19X7		17,852
	311,122	311,122

You ascertain the following:

(1)   All the motor vans were purchased on 1 April 19X5. Depreciation has been, and is to be, provided at the rate of 20% per annum on cost from the date of purchase to the date of sale. On 31 March 19X8 one van, which had cost £900, was sold for £550, as part settlement of the price of £800 of a new van, with the balance on credit. No entries with regard to these transactions were made in the books.

(2)   The estimated corporation tax liability for the year to 31 March 19X8 is £12,700.

(3)   It is proposed to pay a final dividend of 10% for the year to 31 March 19X8.

(4)   Stock at the lower of cost or net realisable value on 31 March 19X8 is £16,700.

(5)   The investments were sold shortly after the year-end.

Required

Prepare, without taking into account the relevant statutory provisions:

(a)   a profit and loss account for the year ended 31 March 19X8;

(b)   a balance sheet at that date.

2   Pirbright Precision Ltd

The bookkeeper of Pirbright Precision Ltd has extracted the following trial balance at 31 March 19X4.

	£	£
Administrative expenses	8,474	
Bank balance per cash book	715	
Creditors and accruals		7,855
Debentures		4,000
Debtors and prepayments	12,390	
Fixtures and fittings	2,280	
Motor vehicles	17,284	
Plant and machinery	16,327	
Premises	12,000	
Profit and loss account – balance at 1 April 19X3		7,613
Provision for depreciation		
Fixtures and fittings		1,250
Motor vehicles		7,212
Plant and machinery		9,557
Premises		1,200
Purchases	66,751	
Sales		102,142
Selling and distribution expenses	2,610	
Share capital		20,000
Share premium account		5,000
Stock	9,880	
Taxation due at 1 April 19X3		1,400
Wages and salaries (all administrative)	18,518	
	167,229	167,229

The directors of the company suspect that some of the figures are incorrect, and further enquiry reveals the following.

(1)   The bookkeeper has admitted that, originally, the trial balance did not agree and, to make it balance, the difference has been entered in the administrative expenses account.

(2)   Fixtures and fittings, which were purchased on 1 April 19X2 for £1,000, were sold for £400 on 12 January 19X4. The sale proceeds were credited to the fixtures and fittings account, and the only other entry made in the books in respect of this disposal was to debit cash.

(3)   No depreciation has been charged for the year ended 31 March 19X4. The company's depreciation policy is to take a full year's depreciation in the year of acquisition and none in the year of disposal at the following rates:

Fixtures and fittings	20% pa on cost
Motor vehicles	25% pa on reducing balance
Plant and machinery	10% pa on cost
Premises	2% pa on cost

Of the plant and machinery, items costing £4,000 in total had been acquired more than 10 years before 31 March 19X4.

(4)   Payments of sales commission of £1,385 had been entered in the cash book, but not posted to the expense account. At 31 March 19X4, commission due but unpaid amounted to £230.

(5)   The taxation liability for the year ended 31 March 19X3 was eventually agreed at £1,560. This amount was paid on 1 January 19X4 and debited to administrative expenses. The directors estimate the current year's liability to be £10,400.

(6)   No account has been taken of bank charges debited to the company's bank statement on 31 December 19X3 of £187.

(7)   The stock figure of £9,880 shown on the trial balance represented stock at cost at 31 March 19X4. This figure included £500 which had been taken by the company on sale or return and treated as a credit purchase. Stock at 1 April 19X3 was valued at £8,220.

After these adjustments had been made, the trial balance agreed.

Required

(a)   Show by means of a suspense account how the original trial balance difference was made up.

(b)   Prepare a profit and loss account for the year ended 31 March 19X4, together with a balance sheet at that date.

3   Bassingham Ltd   (AAT CA J93)

Introduction

Bassingham Ltd are wholesalers of computer software, based in Lincolnshire. The company was started eight years ago by Mary Bassingham and her husband. Your role is that of accounting technician. In that role, you are responsible for the preparation of the company's accounts to trial balance.

At present, the company operates a manual system of bookkeeping with sales ledger, purchase ledger, nominal ledger and cash book.

Notes

(1)   The company sells all its computer software at cost plus a mark-up of 50%.
(2)   The company does not maintain control accounts.

Data

(a)   You have extracted the following list of balances from the nominal ledger at the company's year-end, 31 March 1993.

	£
Purchases	157,712
Sales	326,845
Salaries	59,200
Rent and rates	32,800
Motor expenses	3,840
Light and heat	972
Office expenses	22,485
Interest on loan	1,800
Stock (1 April 1992)	27,200
Provision for doubtful debts	2,240
Fittings and equipment (cost)	31,400
Fittings and equipment (accumulated depreciation)	12,350
Motor vehicles (cost)	24,200
Motor vehicles (accumulated depreciation)	12,100
Share capital	2,000
Loan from T Harby	20,000
Profit and loss (credit balance)	34,402

Total of balances in the sales ledger: £76,040

Total of balances in the purchase ledger: £28,032

The cash book revealed balances of:

Bank A/c	£230 (Dr)
Cash A/c	£180

(b)   After obtaining the account balances above, four errors were discovered:

(i)   Credit purchases of £1,762 had been correctly debited to Purchases a/c, but had been credited to the supplier's account (R Swinderby) at £1,672.

(ii)   Computer software has been sent to T Brough, a customer, on a sale-or-return basis (selling price: £360). This transaction has been entered in the books as a credit sale to T Brough.

(iii)   During the year, a new word-processor had been bought at a cost of £3,860. This had been debited to Office Expenses a/c.

(iv)   The company had owned two motor vehicles. Earlier in the year, as a cost-saving measure, one of these had been sold for £4,250. The only entries made for this had been:

Dr	Bank A/c	£4,250
Cr	Sales A/c	£4,250

You have now discovered that the motor vehicle had originally cost £12,100 and had been depreciated at 25% per annum straight line over the two years to 31 March 1992.

(c)   The following additional matters need to be taken into account:

(i)   The company's depreciation policy is as follows:

Fittings and equipment   20% per annum straight line
Motor vehicles   25% per annum straight line

(ii)   The company's bank statement arrived on 2 April 1993, containing the following entries which had not been entered in the accounts:

1993	Payment	£
28 March	Bank charges	83
29 March	Cheque dishonoured	173

It was subsequently discovered that the dishonoured cheque had been received earlier in March from N Scarle, a trade debtor.

(iii)   Bad debts of £303 for a debt owed by N Disney, who had now been declared bankrupt, have not yet been written off.

(iv)   The provision for doubtful debts is to be 2% of the debtors figure.

(v)   The stock on 31 March 1993 had been valued at £38,120. This did not include the sale-or-return items referred to in (b)(ii) above.

(vi)   Interest on the loan, fixed at a rate of 12% per annum, is paid quarterly. Payment for the quarter 1 January to 31 March 1993 is due for payment on 10 April.

Assessment tasks

Task 1

Draft a trial balance from the data given in part (a) above. Enter any imbalance in a Suspense a/c.

Task 2

Prepare journal entries to correct the errors detailed in part (b) above. Include narratives.

Task 3

Enter all the account balances, after incorporating the corrections from Task 2 above, in the first two columns of the extended trial balance.

Task 4

Make appropriate entries in the adjustment columns of the extended trial balance for the matters referred to in part (c) above, adding any additional accounts that may be required.

Total these columns.

Task 5

Extend the figures into the extended trial balance columns for profit and loss account and balance sheet. Total all of these columns, transferring the balance of profit or loss as appropriate.

BASSINGHAM LTD

TRIAL BALANCE AS AT 31 MARCH 1993

	£	£
	Dr	Cr
Purchases a/c		
Sales a/c		
Salaries a/c		
Rent & Rates a/c		
Motor expenses a/c		
Light & Heat a/c		
Office expenses a/c		
Interest on loan a/c		
Stock a/c		
Provision for doubtful debts a/c		
Fittings & Equipment (cost) a/c		
Fittings & Equipment (acc. dep'n.) a/c		
Motor vehicles (cost) a/c		
Motor vehicles (acc. dep'n.) a/c		
Share capital a/c		
Loan a/c		
Profit & Loss a/c		
Debtors		
Creditors		
Bank a/c		
Cash a/c		

JOURNAL ENTRIES	Dr £	Cr £

EXTENDED TRIAL BALANCE 31 MARCH 1993

	Ledger		Adjustments		Profit and loss a/c		Balance sheet balances	
	Dr	Cr	Dr	Cr	Dr	Cr	Dr	Cr
	£	£	£	£	£	£	£	£
Purchases a/c								
Sales a/c								
Salaries a/c								
Rent & Rates a/c								
Motor expenses a/c								
Light & Heat a/c								
Office expenses a/c								
Interest on loan a/c								
Stock a/c								
Provision for doubtful debts a/c								
Fittings & Equipment (cost) a/c								
Fittings & Equipment (acc. dep'n.) a/c								
Motor vehicles (cost) a/c								
Motor vehicles (acc. dep'n.) a/c								
Share capital a/c								
Loan a/c								
Profit & Loss a/c								
Sales ledger balances								
Purchase ledger balances								
Bank a/c								
Cash a/c								

4   Country Crafts Ltd   (AAT CA D93)

Introduction

Country Crafts Ltd is a small business started in 1988. It buys in craft items – for example, pottery, hand-made clothes and wooden toys – from a large number of small craft producers and then sells them to craft shops throughout the country.

The rented premises consist of a warehouse containing racks and bins to hold the craft products along with an adjoining office and garage. The company owns two delivery vans, used for both collections and deliveries, and two company cars.

The company was started by two friends, Sandip Patel and Abdul Mohim, who met on a small business training course in Leicester. Sandip has responsibility for buying and selling and has built up a network of small craftworkers who make stock for him. Abdul is responsible for the running of the warehouse and the office and the administration of the business.

In addition to the two owners, the business employs two drivers, a warehouseman, two accounts clerks and a secretary.

You are the senior of the two accounts clerks and you are responsible for the nominal ledger.

The company's accounts are currently operated using a manual system, but computerisation of the accounts should take place in the near future and some equipment has recently been purchased.

The sales ledger holds at present about 100 accounts; the company has no cash customers.

All purchases of craft products are on credit and the purchase ledger contains about 80 accounts.

There are very few cash transactions. Any that do occur – for example, window cleaning, office sundries and travel expenses – are dealt with by a simple petty cash system. A £50 float is maintained, expenditure is recorded in a simple petty cash book and at irregular intervals the expenditure is posted to the nominal ledger.

Depreciation policy

Rates:	Motor vehicles	25%	straight line
	Office furniture	10%	straight line
	Computer equipment	$33^1/_3\%$	straight line

Depreciation is charged a full year in the year of purchase and is not charged for in the year of sale.

Zero scrap values are assumed.

Fixed asset information

Motor vehicles

Delivery vans	H247AFE	K174RFU
Date of purchase	09.08.90	12.08.92
Cost	£16,200	£19,800

Company cars	J168TFE	J169TFE
Date of purchase	11.09.91	11.09.91
Cost	£9,200	£9,200

Office furniture

All office furniture was purchased upon incorporation of the business on 1 September 1989.

Cost: £4,850

Computer equipment

Date of purchase	1 June 1993
Cost	£16,830

Mark-up policy

The company marks up all its products by 100% on cost.

Data

(a)   Listed below is the company's trial balance at 31 December 1993.

Country Crafts Ltd
Trial Balance as at 31 December 1993

	Dr	*Cr*
Motor vans (cost) a/c	36,000	
Motor cars (cost) a/c	18,400	
Office furniture (cost) a/c	4,850	
Computer equipment (cost) a/c	16,830	
Motor vans (provision for dep'n) a/c		17,100
Motor cars (provision for dep'n) a/c		9,200
Office furniture (provision for dep'n) a/c		1,940
Computer equipment (provision for dep'n) a/c		
Stock a/c	24,730	
Debtors control a/c	144,280	
Bank a/c		610
Cash a/c	50	
Creditors control a/c		113,660
Sales a/c		282,490
Purchases a/c	152,140	
Rent a/c	12,480	
Heat and light a/c	1,840	
Wages and salaries	75,400	
Office expenses a/c	7,900	
Motor expenses a/c	14,890	
Depreciation (motor vans) a/c		
Depreciation (motor cars) a/c		
Depreciation (office furniture) a/c		
Depreciation (computer equipment) a/c		
Share capital a/c		50,000
Profit and loss a/c		35,850
VAT a/c		12,640
Suspense a/c	13,700	
	523,490	523,490

(b)   Adjustments need to be made for the following:

(i)   On 2 December 1993 a new delivery van, L673NFU, was purchased for £22,600. Van H247AFE was given in part-exchange, the balance of £17,600 being paid for by cheque and debited to the Suspense a/c.

(ii)   On 4 December 1993, as a cost-saving measure, company car J168TFE was sold for £3,900 and the receipt credited to the Suspense a/c.

(iii)   On 20 December 1993 the company had allowed a local organisation to use its car park and adjacent field for a car boot sale. For this service, the company was paid £250. This amount had been credited to Sales a/c.

(c) The following additional matters need to be taken into account:

(i)   Depreciation for the year ended 31 December 1993 is to be provided for.

(ii)   On 15 December 1993 a rack full of china craft products fell in the warehouse. These products, valued at £2,300 at selling price, were so badly damaged that they had to be thrown away. The Raven Moon Insurance Company have agreed to compensate for the damage except for the first £200. A claim has been submitted, but so far no payment has been received.

(iii)   The stocktake on 30 December 1993 revealed stock at cost price of £31,640.

Two batches of stock, however, were of particular note:

–   A batch of Baby Beatrice mugs, value at selling price £320, were judged to be saleable for only £120.

–   A batch of Windsor Fire Damage plates, value at selling price £620, were judged to be saleable for only £350.

(iv)   Several small customers had been going out of business recently, probably because of the recession. The company's accountant had therefore judged it prudent to create a provision for doubtful debts representing 5% of the trade debtors figure at the year-end.

(v)   Petty cash transactions for December were as follows:

December 3	Window cleaning	£10.00
December 8	Tea and coffee	£4.40
December 12	Xmas decorations	£28.60
December 30	Petty cash float replenished to	£50.00

These transactions, including the withdrawal from the bank, have not yet been entered into the company's books.

(vi)   The electricity bill for the September, October, November quarter for £315 had been received on 16 December and entered into the purchase ledger. It is normal for the electricity bill for the December, January, February quarter to be double that for the previous quarter.

(vii)   The rent of £7,488 per annum is paid annually in advance on 1 September.

Assessment tasks

Task 1

Prepare journal entries for the transactions listed in (a) above. Narratives are required.

Task 2

Enter all the account balances, including those adjusted in Task 1, in the first two columns of the extended trial balance.

Task 3

Make appropriate entries in the adjustment columns of the extended trial balance.

Task 4

Extend the figures into the extended trial balance columns for the profit and loss account and balance sheet. Total all columns, transferring the balance of profit or loss as appropriate.

JOURNAL ENTRIES	Dr £	Cr £

COUNTRY CRAFTS LTD – EXTENDED TRIAL BALANCE

	Ledger balances		Adjustments		Profit and loss		Balance sheet balances	
	Dr	Cr	Dr	Cr	Dr	Cr	Dr	Cr
	£	£	£	£	£	£	£	£
Motor vans (cost)								
Motor cars (cost)								
Office furniture (cost)								
Computer equipment (cost)								
Motor vans (PD)								
Motor cars (PD)								
Office furniture (PD)								
Computer equipment (PD)								
Stock								
Debtors control								
Bank								
Cash								
Creditors control								
Sales								
Purchases								
Rent								
Heat and light								
Wages and salaries								
Office expenses								
Motor expenses								
Dep'n (motor vans)								
Dep'n (motor cars)								
Dep'n (office furniture)								
Dep'n (computer equipment)								
Share capital								
Profit and loss								
VAT								

	Ledger balances		Adjustments		Profit and loss		Balance sheet balances	
	Dr	Cr	Dr	Cr	Dr	Cr	Dr	Cr
	£	£	£	£	£	£	£	£

SUMMARY

- Differences between sole traders' and companies' accounts:

    - treatment of profit;

    - composition of capital in the balance sheet; and

    - requirements of the Companies Acts 1985 and 1989 (note a company is a separate legal entity).

- Corporation tax:

    - a tax based on profits for a year; and
    - amount due shown as a current liability.

- Dividends:

    - amounts paid by the company to its shareholders, corresponding to drawings by a sole trader.

- Shares:

    Ordinary

    - give control of the company; and
    - dividend dependent upon profitability.

    Preference

    - do not give control; and
    - priority over ordinary shares in payment of dividend and (normally) on winding up.

- Reserves:

  - cumulative total of a company's retained profits. There may be several different reserves intended for specific purposes.

- Share premium account:

  - amount paid for shares over and above their nominal value.

- Debenture:

  - an acknowledgement by a company of a long-term loan made to it.

- Public company:

  - name has suffix 'plc'; and
  - may issue shares to the public.

- Private company

  - name has suffix 'Ltd'; and
  - may not issue shares to the public.

Review of Module One

You have now completed the first module of the Study Pack. You have developed the knowledge and understanding required for Unit 4 *Recording capital transactions* by covering the following:

- accruals and prepayments
- bad and doubtful debts
- stocks

You have also covered the preparation of an extended trial balance and the correction of errors using a suspense account.

So far we have mainly considered the accounts of sole traders, but the principles of recording and processing transactions are the same for all types of bookkeeping. Do not be discouraged if you initially have difficulty in mastering double-entry. It will become easier with practice until eventually it becomes second nature.

You must become familiar with the way in which information is presented so that you can record and process transactions quickly and accurately. It is vital that you attempt as many practice questions as possible.

Finally, we have looked at the form and preparation of:

- partnership accounts
- manufacturing accounts
- limited company accounts

You will not be required to prepare final accounts for Unit 5 (although you may be asked to prepare an extended trial balance for a manufacturing business or for a limited company). However, it is important that you understand the way in which accounts are prepared for the different types of trading entity. You will study the preparation of final accounts at Technician level.

You should now possess much of the knowledge and understanding necessary to complete Element 5.1 *Record income and expenditure* and Element 5.3 *Prepare an extended trial balance*.

Module Two will look at accounting principles and the preparation of accounts from incomplete records. Finally, the Study Pack will cover Unit 8 *Prepare VAT returns*.

Accounting principles

OBJECTIVES

The purpose of this session is to remind you of the main accounting principles and concepts including those contained in the accounting standards that you have already studied:

- SSAP2 *Disclosure of accounting policies*
- SSAP9 *Stocks and long-term contracts*
- SSAP12 *Accounting for depreciation*
- SSAP5 *Accounting for value added tax*

The session will also introduce SSAP13 *Accounting for research and development* and SSAP21 *Accounting for leases and hire purchase contracts*.

INTRODUCTION

As an accounting technician, you will often be required to explain the correct accounting treatment of particular items. This is normally determined by the requirements of accounting standards or by applying accounting concepts or principles.

ACCOUNTING STANDARDS

The standard-setting process

Statements of Standard Accounting Practice (SSAPs) and Financial Reporting Standards (FRSs) are documents whose basic objective is to ensure that acceptable standards are achieved in the preparation of accounts.

SSAPs were issued by the Accounting Standards Committee (ASC) over a period of many years. Not all of the original SSAPs are still in force. Inevitably SSAPs have been withdrawn over the years because they have not achieved their objective or because circumstances have changed.

As part of the process of preparing a SSAP, the ASC produced an **Exposure Draft** (ED). This was a draft of the proposed SSAP for comment and feedback from interested parties prior to issuing the final version of the SSAP. Not all EDs became SSAPs. Although EDs were not compulsory, they were usually treated by accountants as examples of best practice.

In August 1991 the Accounting Standards Board (ASB) replaced the ASC as the main authority on accounting practice. At that point, there were a large number of SSAPs still in force and a number of EDs.

The ASB adopted all the existing SSAPs (but not the EDs) although they remain under review. The ASB also decided to issue its own standards or **FRSs**. The ASB also has its own process of consultation and drafting and issues **Financial Reporting Exposure Drafts** (FREDs).

Applying accounting standards

The aim of the ASB is to establish and improve standards of financial accounting and reporting, for the benefit of users, preparers and auditors of financial information.

Accounting standards:

- are authoritative statements of how particular types of transaction and other events should be reflected in financial statements

- are applicable to all financial statements that are intended to give **a true and fair view**

- need not be applied to immaterial items

Compliance with accounting standards will normally be necessary for financial statements to give a true and fair view. Only in exceptional circumstances will departure from the requirements of an accounting standard be necessary in order for financial statements to give a true and fair view.

Accounting standards should achieve **consistency** of accounting treatment for similar items in the accounts of different enterprises and also for similar items within the accounts of the same enterprise. The standards also specify information which must be **disclosed** within the accounts of an enterprise.

This does not mean that all enterprises must adopt identical accounting treatments. In practice, most accounting standards allow a degree of choice between different methods and an enterprise should select the method which is most appropriate to its circumstances.

Members of professional bodies are expected to observe accounting standards, whether they are acting as directors or officers of a company, or as auditors or reporting accountants. They should use their best endeavours to ensure that accounting standards are observed by others and that significant departures found to be necessary are adequately disclosed and explained in the financial statements.

Truth and fairness

Financial accounts prepared for publication must show a **true and fair view** of the results and state of affairs of an organisation.

The term *true and fair view* does not have a strict definition. In relation to limited company accounts, it is a legal concept the meaning of which may ultimately be decided in the courts.

Truth implies that the figures are mathematically accurate and factually correct.

Fairness implies that the information is presented in a manner which is free from bias.

ACCOUNTING CONCEPTS, BASES AND POLICIES (SSAP2)

Introduction

SSAP2, *Disclosure of accounting policies* states in its introduction that 'it is fundamental to the understanding and interpretation of financial accounts that those who use them should be aware of the main assumptions on which they are based'.

Definition of concepts, bases and policies

Fundamental accounting concepts

These are the broad basic assumptions which underlie the periodic financial accounts of business enterprises. SSAP2 recognises the four fundamental concepts. The relative importance of each will vary according to the circumstances of the particular case.

The four fundamental accounting concepts are:

- going concern
- accruals
- consistency
- prudence

Accounting bases

These are the methods developed for applying fundamental accounting concepts to financial transactions and items, for the purpose of financial accounts. In order to decide in which periods revenue and expenditure will be brought into the profit and loss account and the amounts at which material items should be shown in the balance sheet, business enterprises will select specific accounting bases most appropriate to their circumstances and adopt them.

Depreciation is a method developed to apply the accruals (matching) concept to the cost of a fixed asset.

Accounting policies

These are the specific accounting bases judged by the business enterprises to be most appropriate to their circumstances and adopted by them for the purpose of preparing their financial accounts.

Most companies have a policy of depreciating fixed assets.

Standard accounting practice

Disclosure of adoption of concepts which differ from those generally accepted

If accounts are prepared on the basis of assumptions which differ in material respects from any of the generally accepted fundamental concepts, the facts should be explained. In the absence of a clear statement to the contrary, there is a presumption that the four fundamental concepts have been observed.

Disclosure of accounting policies

The accounting policies followed for dealing with items which are judged material or critical in determining profit and loss for the year and in stating the financial position should be disclosed by way of notes to the accounts. The explanation should be clear, fair and as brief as possible.

The disclosure of accounting policies enables users of accounts to *compare* the accounts of different enterprises even if they have adopted different accounting policies.

FUNDAMENTAL ACCOUNTING CONCEPTS

Going concern

The enterprise will continue in operation for the foreseeable future. This means in particular that the profit and loss account and balance sheet assume no intention or necessity to liquidate or curtail significantly the scale of operation.

Example

- Assets are carried at net book value. This implies that the business is not about to be sold or liquidated because the assets would then have to be included at their net realisable value (expected sales proceeds less any selling costs).

Accruals

Revenue and costs are accrued (that is, recognised as they are earned or incurred, not as money is received or paid), matched with one another so far as their relationship can be established or justifiably assumed, and dealt with in the profit and loss account of the period to which they relate.

Examples

- The cost of fixed assets is spread over the accounting periods expected to benefit from their use (depreciation).

- The profit and loss account includes expenses relating to a period rather than simply amounts paid during the period.

- Cost of sales is purchases plus opening stocks less closing stocks.

- The profit and loss account includes all sales made during the period, rather than total cash received from sales during the period. Sales in respect of which cash has not yet been received are included in the balance sheet as debtors.

- Monies received from customers where goods have not yet been despatched is not included in sales but taken to the balance sheet as a creditor. (This might occur in a mail order business or where customers are required to pay a deposit.)

- Development expenditure may be deferred (ie. not immediately included in the profit and loss account) and matched with the income which it is expected to generate in future accounting periods (SSAP13, discussed later in this session).

Consistency

There is consistency of accounting treatment of like items within each accounting period and from one period to the next.

Examples

- All motor vehicles are depreciated using the same rate and method of depreciation.

- The same methods of calculating the cost of stock (eg. FIFO, LIFO, average cost) are used from one period to the next.

Prudence

Revenues and profits are not anticipated but are recognised by inclusion in the profit and loss account only when realised in the form of cash or by other assets, the ultimate cash realisation of which can be assessed with reasonable certainty (eg. debtors). Provision is made for all known liabilities (expenses and losses) whether the amount of these is known with certainty or is a best estimate in the light of the information available.

Examples

- Provision is made against all potential losses from bad or doubtful debts.

- Stocks are included in the balance sheet at the lower of cost or net realisable value.

- Development costs cannot be deferred unless the development of the new product or service is reasonably certain to generate profits (SSAP13).

When the accruals concept is inconsistent with the prudence concept, the latter prevails.

RECOGNISING SALES

A business may make both cash and credit sales. There are several stages in a sales transaction, for example:

Stage 1	The customer places the order.
Stage 2	Goods are delivered to the customer.
Stage 3	The customer is invoiced.
Stage 4	The customer pays for the goods.

At what point is the sale treated as having taken place?

Sales revenue may be regarded as arising when:

- the transaction can be measured objectively in monetary terms (ie. when quantity and price are known); and

- the transaction is complete or certain to be completed; and

- the critical event in the transaction cycle is complete (eg. securing the order or obtaining payment).

Generally, a sale is recognised when goods or services have been exchanged for cash or a legally enforceable promise to pay.

It is not appropriate to recognise the sale at Stage 1, because the transaction is not yet certain and the exchange has not yet occurred. Recognition at this stage would be a contravention of the prudence concept (revenue cannot be anticipated until its realisation is reasonably certain).

If the sale is a cash sale it may be appropriate to recognise it at Stage 2, as payment will take place immediately, without invoicing.

Stage 3, invoicing, is almost always the critical event if the sale is a credit sale. At this stage, there is a legal contract between buyer and seller and most of the uncertainties surrounding the transaction are removed. In terms of the prudence concept, the business has an asset (a debtor) which is reasonably certain to be realised in the form of cash.

Stage 4, payment, is the critical event in a cash sale and normally occurs at the same time as Stage 2. If the sale is a credit sale, it is usually inappropriate to defer recognition to this stage. The critical event is normally invoicing; to fail to recognise the sale beyond that point would be to contravene the accruals concept.

Where there is a conflict between accruals and prudence, prudence prevails. This may occur if the customer is felt to be a bad risk (although, strictly speaking, the correct accounting treatment in this case would be to recognise the sale and to provide for the doubtful debt as an expense). Prudence may also be necessary if the customer has the right to return the goods within a certain period after delivery.

OTHER ACCOUNTING PRINCIPLES

Materiality

An item is **material** if its omission or misstatement will influence the economic decisions of users taken on the basis of the accounts.

The misstatement or omission of an immaterial item will not prevent the accounts from giving a true and fair view. Accounting standards do not apply to immaterial items.

Example

- A business buys some computer software. Strictly speaking, this is capital expenditure because it will be used on a continuing basis. The effect of capitalising and depreciating individual small items is unlikely to be material in the context of the accounts as a whole. Therefore, the software is treated as revenue expenditure and written off to the profit and loss account in the period in which the expenditure was incurred.

Judgement is needed in order to decide whether or not an item is material. The materiality of an item should always be judged in the context of its effect upon the financial statements as a whole.

Economic (or commercial) substance over legal form

Accounts must reflect the commercial effect (substance) of transactions rather than their strict legal form.

Most transactions are reasonably straightforward and their commercial effect is the same as their strict legal form. However, in some instances this is not the case.

Example

- A sells goods to B. A undertakes to repurchase the goods from B in twelve months time.

  The strict legal form of the transaction is that A has sold goods to B.

  The commercial effect of the transaction is that B has made a loan to A.

In theory, A could record the transaction as a sale. To do so would be likely to enhance the appearance of A's financial statements. In particular, the company would appear to be a safer investment than if A had recorded the transaction as a loan. This would, however, be very misleading.

Historic cost

Historical cost accounting means expressing items in accounts at the **actual value of a transaction at the time that it was incurred** (remember that balances in the balance sheet are the result of original transactions).

Examples:

- Fixed assets are recorded at purchase price or production cost.

- Assets with a finite life must be depreciated over their useful economic life.

- Current assets (eg. stock) must be shown at the lower of cost and NRV.

SSAP9: STOCKS AND LONG-TERM CONTRACTS

SSAP9 applies the concepts of accruals and prudence.

- Stock has been purchased in the current accounting period and will be sold in the next. Consequently an asset has been bought, the cost of which should be matched with the revenue generated from it. By crediting the closing stock value to cost of sales and temporarily suspending it on the balance sheet, the cost is transferred from one accounting period to the next.

- If at the balance sheet date the amount to be recovered on selling the stock is less than the purchase price, then it is prudent to write the stock down to this value. The diminution in value occurred in the period up to the balance sheet date, as it was discovered at this date. By including stock at this reduced valuation, the period in which the loss arose is being charged with the loss in value.

Choosing a valuation method

SSAP9 does not discuss different methods of stock valuation. It merely says that the method used must be selected with a view to providing the fairest possible approximation to the expenditure actually incurred in bringing the product to its present location and condition. The business must select the most appropriate method and apply it consistently.

In most cases the most appropriate method used will be first in, first out (FIFO), as it is likely that most businesses will use the oldest stock first, especially where stocks deteriorate over time. Weighted average cost may be appropriate where stock units are identical or near identical, or where stock turnover is relatively quick.

Last in, first out (LIFO) is not normally appropriate as it may result in stocks being stated in the balance sheet at amounts which bear little relationship to current cost. However, very rarely there may be circumstances in which LIFO would give the fairest approximation to actual unit cost, for example, if stocks were stored in such a way that the most recently purchased items had to be used first.

ACCOUNTING FOR FIXED ASSETS

Recording the purchase of fixed assets

An organisation may purchase tangible fixed assets from a third party or construct them itself. Most fixed assets are purchased and should be recorded initially at purchase cost. The asset is initially recorded as follows:

Dr   Fixed assets
Cr   Cash at bank

for the purchase of an asset by cash or cheque.

Or alternatively as follows, if it is purchased on credit:

Dr   Fixed assets
Cr   Creditors

Only the purchase cost of the asset itself should be capitalised. Particular care needs to be taken when recording the cost of motor vehicles as the invoice normally includes items such as petrol, road fund licences and warranties. These are revenue expenditure and should be written off to the profit and loss account.

Recording the production cost of fixed assets

If a business constructs a fixed asset, the asset should be recorded at production cost.

Fixed assets and VAT

Standard-rated VAT can be reclaimed on capital expenditure, as long as the business holds the correct documentation.

This means that the cost of assets which appears in the balance sheet is stated **net** of VAT. Remember, however, that motor cars are the exception to the rule; businesses are not allowed to reclaim VAT paid on new car purchases.

SSAP12: ACCOUNTING FOR DEPRECIATION

Introduction

Fixed assets do not have an infinite life within a business. They have finite useful economic lives. The length of that life will depend upon a number of factors.

It may be:

- **predetermined**, eg. a lease on property;

or it may be affected by:

- **depletion**, eg. coal mines, sand and gravel quarries;

- **physical deterioration**, eg. machinery which rusts;

- **time**, eg. patents and copyrights;

- **economic obsolescence**, eg. computer equipment.

If assets are originally recorded in the accounting records at cost, then the reduction in the asset's value over time must be recorded. Each year a charge will be made to the profit and loss account. This charge is known as **depreciation**.

SSAP12 *Accounting for depreciation* states that all fixed assets having a finite useful economic life should be **depreciated**. SSAP12 defines **depreciation** as:

- 'the measure of the wearing out, consumption or other reduction in the useful economic life of a fixed asset whether arising from use, effluxion of time or obsolescence through technology or market changes'.

The aim of depreciation is to spread the cost of a fixed asset over its useful economic life. This is an application of the accruals concept. The cost of a fixed asset must be allocated to (matched with) the accounting periods expected to benefit from their use.

Although assets may have finite lives, because they lose value, depreciation is not an attempt to show the loss of value. The depreciation charge reduces the profits of the business, but it does not make cash available to replace assets.

Some fixed assets, such as buildings, may increase in value over time, but they must still be depreciated.

Estimating depreciation

There are three factors to consider when estimating the depreciation expense for any one year. These are:

- the carrying value of the asset;

- the length of the asset's expected useful life to the business;

- the estimated residual value of the asset at the end of its useful life in the business of the enterprise.

Recording depreciation

Depreciation is an expense in the profit and loss account and it also reduces the value of the asset in the balance sheet.

The double-entry necessary to record the depreciation charge each year in the ledgers is as follows:

Debit   Depreciation account
Credit   Provision for depreciation account

Methods of depreciation

The straight-line method

This method requires an equal depreciation charge in each period of the asset's life.

$$\text{Annual charge} = \frac{\text{Cost} - \text{Residual value (if any)}}{\text{Useful economic life}}$$

The reducing balance method

This method applies a fixed percentage to the net book value.

Choosing a method of depreciation

SSAP12 does not specify which method of depreciation should be used, nor does it discuss the various methods and their merits. It states that the enterprise should adopt the most appropriate method and apply it consistently from year to year. The method chosen for each category of fixed asset should also be applied consistently to all assets in that category.

The purpose of depreciation is to allocate the cost of a fixed asset to the periods expected to benefit from its use. Therefore the method chosen should be the method which provides the fairest allocation. In practice, this will normally be the straight-line method. This is the method which is also the easiest to apply and the one in which it is easiest to make revisions to estimates.

The reducing balance method may be appropriate in the following situations:

- where an asset is likely to provide greater benefits to the organisation or to have more use in its earlier years;

- where an asset is likely to require significant maintenance; this means that the low depreciation charge corresponds to the higher maintenance charges in the final years of the asset's useful economic life;

- where in practice an asset will have an almost indefinite useful economic life; some small businesses treat basic office furniture in this way.

SSAP5: ACCOUNTING FOR VAT

SSAP5 gives guidance on how to account for VAT in line with VAT legislation.

The sales accounts in the nominal ledger should exclude VAT on taxable outputs.

Assets and liabilities should be recorded net of recoverable VAT.

The amount due to or from HM Customs and Excise should be included as part of creditors or debtors.

SSAP13: ACCOUNTING FOR RESEARCH AND DEVELOPMENT

SSAP13 *Accounting for research and development* applies the general principles of SSAP2 to the specific case of research and development expenditure.

Definitions

- **Pure research** – experimental or theoretical work undertaken primarily to acquire new scientific or technical knowledge, but not directed towards any specific aim or application.

- **Applied research** – original or critical investigation to gain new scientific or technical knowledge and directed towards a specific practical aim or objective.

In practice, the distinction between pure and applied research is not important as the accounting treatment is the same.

- **Development** – use of scientific or technical knowledge:

    - to produce new or substantially improved materials, devices, products or services; or

    - to install new or substantially improved processes or systems prior to the start of commercial production or commercial applications.

Accounting treatment

Normally **research and development expenditure** must be charged to the profit and loss account as an expense in the year in which it is incurred. This is because it is not prudent to anticipate any future benefits with which to match the cost.

Development expenditure may be deferred to future periods (included in the balance sheet as an intangible fixed asset) if **all** the following criteria are met:

- The project to which the expenditure relates is separate from other activities.

- The expenditure can be identified separately.

- The outcome of the project has been considered and it is reasonably certain that it is:

    (i)   technically feasible;
    (ii)   commercially viable (bearing in mind market conditions, the law and other factors).

- The deferred development costs, plus any further costs needed to complete the project and sell the produce, must be less than the sales which will be generated by the project.

- The organisation has adequate financial and other resources to complete the project.

Note that although the Standard permits a choice of treatment, whichever treatment is adopted must be applied **consistently**.

Amortisation

If development expenditure is deferred to future periods, it must be **amortised** starting from the time that the product goes into commercial production. The costs are allocated to the accounting periods in which the product is expected to be sold or used (following the accruals concept).

The standard does not specify a particular method of allocating amortisation. If the expected total sales quantity is known, this can be used as a basis for amortisation. In the absence of this, we can use the straight-line method over the expected period of production.

Note that amortisation commences with commercial production, whereas development costs occur prior to the start of commercial production.

Illustration

A company has incurred development expenditure of £250,000 in relation to Product X. This development expenditure meets all the criteria for deferral laid down in SSAP13.

Production of Product X has now commenced and sales are expected to take place as follows:

	Number of units
19X1	75,000
19X2	150,000
19X3	75,000

After 19X3 sales are expected to decline dramatically.

The deferred development expenditure will be amortised as follows:

	Charge £
19X1 (75/300 × £250,000)	62,500
19X2 (150/300 × £250,000)	125,000
19X3 (75/300 × £250,000)	62,500

The note to the balance sheet will appear as follows:

Intangible fixed assets – development costs

	19X1 £	19X2 £	19X3 £
Cost at beginning and end of year	250,000	250,000	250,000

	19X1 £	19X2 £	19X3 £
Amortisation			
At beginning of year	–	62,500	187,500
Charge for year	62,500	125,000	62,500
At end of year	62,500	187,500	250,000
Net book value at end of year	187,500	62,500	–
Net book value at beginning of year	250,000	187,500	62,500

Other points

Deferred development expenditure must be reviewed at each year-end in order to assess whether the criteria for deferral are still met. Development costs must be written off through the profit and loss account if they are considered irrecoverable. (This is an application of the prudence concept.)

Fixed assets used for research and development should be capitalised and written off over their useful economic lives through the profit and loss account (the normal treatment for fixed assets).

SSAP21: ACCOUNTING FOR LEASES AND HIRE PURCHASE CONTRACTS

Introduction

A business may acquire fixed assets in several ways:

- for **cash**

- on **credit** terms – a trade creditor is recorded in current or long-term liabilities

- subject to a **hire purchase** (HP) agreement or a **lease**

Nature of hire purchase and lease agreements

Under a hire purchase agreement or a lease, the lessee acquires the right to use an asset in return for the payment of a sum of money in equal instalments over a certain period.

There are two important things to note:

- The total amount paid will tend to be higher than the price for which the asset could have been purchased outright. The difference represents the **interest** for the credit given.

- Under a **hire purchase agreement**, the ownership of the asset does not **legally** pass from the vendor to the purchaser until the purchaser has paid the last instalment. Under a **lease**, title *never* passes to the lessee.

The problem

We could account for these assets based on the strict **legal form** of the transaction. This would mean that the instalments paid would be charged to the profit and loss account as rentals. The asset would not be included in the balance sheet.

However, the **commercial effect** of most hire purchase agreements is that the business effectively owns the asset. The **risks and rewards of ownership** have been transferred to the purchaser. The asset is used by the business to generate income. If we did not include this asset in the balance sheet as soon as it started generating income, then we would not be showing a true picture.

The commercial effect of many **lease agreements** is similar. The business has the risks and rewards of ownership, regardless of the fact that it will never legally own the asset.

The solution

SSAP21 *Accounting for leases and hire purchase contracts* requires businesses to account for the **economic substance** of leases rather than their strict **legal form**.

SSAP21 identifies two types of lease agreement: a **finance lease** and an **operating lease**. Hire purchase agreements are normally accounted for in the same way as finance leases.

Finance lease

A finance lease is a lease which *transfers substantially all the risks and rewards of ownership of an asset to the lessee*.

The lessee has substantially all the risks and rewards of ownership where he bears the risk of obsolescence, pays for maintenance and has unencumbered use of the asset for all or most of its life.

SSAP21 states that we should presume that a lease is a finance lease where the present value of the minimum lease payments amounts to 90% or more of the fair value of the asset at the start of the lease. However, we should only need to refer to this aspect of the definition if we are unsure about whether substantially all the risks and rewards are transferred. You will almost certainly be told whether a lease is a finance lease or an operating lease.

Operating lease

An operating lease is a lease other than a finance lease.

Commercial substance of finance and operating leases

A **finance lease** is similar in substance to the ownership of an asset, financed by a loan repayable by instalments over the period of the lease. The lessee would normally have sole use of the asset and would be responsible for its maintenance, repair and insurance even though legal title to the asset remains with the lessor. An **operating lease**, on the other hand, is the 'short-term' hire of an asset.

Accounting for finance leases

SSAP21 requires that finance leases be included in the lessee's balance sheet in order to reflect the 'ownership' of the asset. This is financed by the lease commitments (future instalments), which are included in creditors. The profit and loss account is charged with depreciation on the asset and an amount representing the finance charges (interest) inherent in the lease payments.

The double-entry

To deal with a finance lease, we need to make the following entries:

1. When the asset is first acquired:

		£	£
Dr	Fixed assets cost	X	
Cr	Lease creditor		X

with the fair value of the asset (normally the price for which the asset could have been purchased for cash)

2. As each instalment is paid:

		£	£
Dr	Lease creditor	X	
Cr	Cash		X

3. Depreciation for each year:

		£	£
Dr	P&L depreciation expense	X	
Cr	Accumulated depreciation		X

4. Finance charge for each year:

		£	£
Dr	P&L Interest	X	
Cr	Lease creditor		X

Note that interest accrues over the period for which the loan is outstanding. We always assume that we pay interest in arrears, so that if there is a payment at the start of the lease, it will not contain interest, as the loan will not have been outstanding for any period of time over which interest can have accrued. Also, no interest accrues once we have made the final payment as this is when the last of the loan is paid off.

Example

On 1 January 19X1 a lessee enters into a lease for an item of plant. The following details are relevant:

Fair value of asset: £10,000

Residual value: Nil after 5 years

Lease terms: £2,500 pa in advance for 5 years, the first rental payable on 1.1.X1

The finance charge of £2,500 (£12,500 – £10,000) is to be apportioned as follows:

Year	£
1	1,000
2	750
3	500
4	250
	2,500

Show how this transaction would be recorded in the ledger accounts of the lessee for the first two years, and show also how the transaction would be reflected in the profit and loss account and balance sheet over the five years.

Solution

The ledger entry at the beginning of the lease will be:

		£	£
Dr	Leased assets	10,000	
	Cr Obligations under finance leases		10,000

being the recording of the 'purchase' of an asset under a finance lease at its fair value and the assumption of a liability.

The annual depreciation charge will be:

$$\frac{£10,000}{5} = £2,000 \text{ pa}$$

The leased asset will be depreciated in exactly the same way as any other fixed asset:

		£	£
Dr	Depreciation charge	2,000	
	Cr Fixed assets (acculumated depreciation)		2,000

being the annual depreciation charge.

The entries in the leasing obligation (creditor) account will be as follows:

		£			£
1.1.X1	Cash	2,500	1.1.X1	Leased asset a/c	10,000
31.12.X1	Balance c/f	8,500	31.12.X1	Interest expense	1,000
		11,000			11,000
1.1.X2	Cash	2,500	1.1.X2	Balance b/f	8,500
31.12.X2	Balance c/f	6,750	31.12.X2	Interest expense	750
		9,250			9,250
			1.1.X3	Balance b/f	6,750

Note: The balance sheets would reflect the net book value of the asset in fixed assets and the outstanding principal of the loan together with the accrued interest for the year, which will be paid on the first day of the next period.

The balance sheet over the five years would appear as follows:

Balance sheets

Year	1	2	3	4	5
	£	£	£	£	£
Fixed assets					
Leased plant:					
Cost	10,000	10,000	10,000	10,000	10,000
Accumulated depreciation	2,000	4,000	6,000	8,000	10,000
Net book value	8,000	6,000	4,000	2,000	–
Finance lease creditors	8,500	6,750	4,750	2,500	–

The profit and loss account would include the following charges in respect of the leased asset:

Year	1	2	3	4	5
	£	£	£	£	£
Depreciation	2,000	2,000	2,000	2,000	2,000
Finance charges	1,000	750	500	250	–

Accounting for operating leases

An operating lease is a lease other than a finance lease. Perhaps the easiest way to visualise an operating lease is in terms of the short-term hire of an asset such as a car or video recorder. There is no suggestion that the risks and rewards of ownership are transferred from the lessor to the lessee. Thus the asset is treated as a fixed asset in the books of the lessor and the rental is treated as income for the lessor and as an expense for the lessee. The rental under an operating lease should be charged on a straight-line basis over the lease term.

QUESTIONS

1   Mary Bassingham   (AAT CA J93)

Write memoranda in reply to the following comments from Mary Bassingham.

(a)   Depreciation policy:

We depreciate our fittings and equipment at 20% per annum straight line. This means that these fittings and equipment will have no value after five years. At the present rate of technical innovation, the word-processor will probably have little value after four years, whilst much of the office equipment such as filing cabinets and office furniture will clearly last much longer.

Should we not review our depreciation policy?

(b)   Accounting standards:

From what I knew of accounting standards, I thought they were to ensure that all companies' accounts were prepared on the same basis. However, the large company my brother works for depreciates its equipment using a different method from our's (reducing balance I think it's called) and they revalue their premises upwards.

Who is right and why? If we are both right, what is the purpose of standards?

2   James McBride   (AAT CA D93)

You have received the following memorandum from one of the two junior accounts clerks, James McBride:

As you know, I am studying for my AAT qualifications at Uppingham College. Most of the work so far has been straightforward, but there are two areas where I am a little uncertain. I understand that accounting concepts are basic principles laid down in SSAP2 and the Companies Act 1985 governing the preparation of company accounts; however, we don't always appear to adhere to these concepts. For example, I always understood that we should be objective and give the most accurate value possible to our stocks, but we know that the value of some of our stocks has risen – recent purchases of some items cost more than earlier purchases – but we must still value the stock we purchased earlier at the original cost price. On the other hand, if the value of any item falls to less than we could sell it for, as with some of our recent Royal Family souvenirs, we have to write off the loss in value of the stock even before it is sold. This seems also to go against the concept of consistency. Can you explain please?

Assessment task

Write a memorandum in reply to this query.

3   Cash accounting   (AAT CA J94)

Jason believes that the complication of the accounting system to incorporate additional profit analysis will result in more work for you, the accounts clerk. To help you take on this additional workload, he has suggested that the accounting system be changed to a cash accounting basis. This would entail recording sales only when the customer pays and recording purchases and expenses only when payments are made. Jason also believes that depreciation can be eliminated with the cost of the asset being charged in full upon purchase.

Assessment task

Write a memorandum in reply to Jason's suggestions.

4   Sophie Stewart   (AAT CA D94)

As you are a friend who is also an accounting technician, Sophie has consulted you about two aspects of her accounting system.

Task 1

Mail order customers send cash with order and so far Sophie has always been able to fulfil the order immediately. However, she is considering branching out into some new product lines which will involve purchasing her stock from a number of different suppliers. She is a little worried, therefore, about always being able to guarantee a supply of stock for her mail order customers. She is particularly concerned about how to deal with the following two possible scenarios:

(i)   Stock will not be available for a month.

(ii)   Goods ordered by a customer are no longer available.

Write a note, not a memorandum, to Sophie explaining how to deal with these two situations.

Task 2

Sophie would like to value her stock at selling price in her annual accounts to give her a better idea of the profit it is likely to generate. For example:

(i)   When the sales value of stock rises, for example, when a particular product becomes popular or when the manufacturer increases the price, Sophie would like to value the stock (both that already in stock and that which she purchases in the future) at the new selling price.

(ii)   When the sales value of stock falls because it is out of date or slightly shop-soiled, Sophie would like to reduce the value of her stock.

Explain in a note how Sophie should deal with the valuation of her stock. Your note should refer to relevant accounting standards and concepts.

SUMMARY

- Fundamental accounting concepts: the broad basic assumptions which underlie the accounts of businesses:

  - going concern;
  - accruals;
  - consistency;
  - prudence.

- Accounting bases: methods developed for applying the fundamental concepts to financial transactions and items.

- Accounting policies: specific accounting bases adopted for the purpose of preparing financial accounts.

- A sale is normally recognised when goods or services have been exchanged for cash or a legally enforceable promise to pay.

- SSAP9 *Accounting for stocks* applies the concepts of accruals and prudence in valuing stock at the lower of cost and net realisable value, together with methods to find the approximate cost when the actual cost is unknown.

- SSAP12 *Accounting for depreciation* uses the concept of accruals to allocate the cost less the residual value of fixed asset over its useful economic life.

- SSAP13 *Accounting for research and development* discusses the treatment of an item when accruals and prudence are in conflict.

- SSAP21 *Accounting for leases and hire purchase contracts* requires businesses to account for commercial substance of lease agreements.

Incomplete records (1) – net assets approach, margins and mark-ups

OBJECTIVES

This session is the first of three which cover the performance criteria for preparing accounts from incomplete records.

It addresses the following performance criteria:

- Existing primary information is accurately summarised.

- Other relevant information is correctly identified and recorded.

- Investigations into the client's business transactions are conducted with tact and courtesy.

INTRODUCTION

Preparing accounts from incomplete records means preparing accounts where less than a complete ledger system has been maintained.

There are many reasons why businesses may not keep proper records. The owner of the business may not understand accounts, or may not have the time or the inclination to maintain a proper system. Occasionally accounting records may be lost, due to a fire or computer breakdown or other disaster. In some cases, the records may be so incomplete that you have to do some detective work to calculate some of the figures.

There are a number of techniques which can be used in various different situations. Normally you will have to use a combination of these.

If you are required to prepare accounts from incomplete records, you are likely to be working in a professional practice and acting for a client. You will almost certainly have to request information and explanations, either verbally or in writing.

Depending on the circumstances you may need information on:

- the client's general business practices (eg. mark-ups on cost, gross profit margins, whether all cash takings are banked, level of drawings, whether any business expenses are paid from the client's private bank account);

- specific transactions (eg. because cash payments or receipts are not supported by documentation or because there are discrepancies between the bank statement and the invoices).

It is easy to see that some of these areas are potentially sensitive. Questions about private expenses paid from the business bank account could be seen as an intrusion of privacy if they were worded in the wrong way. Similarly, a client could interpret aggressively worded enquiries about discrepancies in cash takings as an accusation of fraud!

Therefore it is important that questions are asked in a tactful and courteous manner.

THE NET ASSETS APPROACH

The net assets approach is used for a particular type of incomplete records situation: where the opening and closing net assets of a business are known, or can be easily ascertained, but where there is no detail concerning the transactions for the year.

Thus a detailed profit and loss account cannot be constructed, but the total profit (or loss) for the period can be ascertained from the accounting equation, ie.

	£
Net assets at the year-end	X
Net assets at the start of the year	(X)
	A
Profit for the year	X
Capital introduced in the year	X
Drawings in the year	(X)
	A

You have already attempted some simple examples of the use of the accounting equation. An example should be sufficient to remind you.

Example

Archibald started a business on 1 January 19X1 with £2,000. On 31 December 19X1 the position of the business was as follows:

	£
It owned:	
Freehold lock-up shop cost	4,000
Shop fixtures and equipment, cost	500
Stock of goods bought for resale, cost	10,300
Debts owing by customers	500
Cash in till	10
Cash at bank	150
It owed:	
Mortgage on shop premises	3,000
Creditors for goods	7,000
Accrued mortgage interest	100

Archibald had drawn £500 for personal living expenses.

The shop fittings are to be depreciated by £50 and certain goods in stock which had cost £300 can be sold for only £50.

No records had been maintained throughout the year.

You are required to calculate the profit earned by Archibald's business in the year ended 31 December 19X1.

Solution

This sort of question is answered by calculating the net assets at the year-end as follows:

Net assets at 31 December 19X1

	Cost £	Dep'n £	£
Fixed assets			
Freehold shop	4,000	–	4,000
Fixtures etc.	500	50	450
	4,500	50	4,450
Current assets			
Stock at lower of cost and			
net realisable value			
(10,300 – 300 + 50)		10,050	
Debtors		500	
Cash and bank balances		160	
		10,710	
Current liabilities			
Trade creditors	7,000		
Mortgage interest	100		
		(7,100)	
			3,610
			8,060
Mortgage			(3,000)
Net assets			5,060

The profit is now calculated from the accounting equation.

Change in net assets during the year = Profit plus capital introduced less drawings

£5,060 – 2,000 = Profit + Nil – 500

Therefore, profit = £3,560

Archibald's balance sheet is made up of the above together with the bottom half which can be established after calculating the profit, ie.

	£
Capital	2,000
Profit (balancing figure)	**3,560**
	5,560
Drawings	(500)
	5,060

As you can see, the 'incomplete records' part of the question is concerned with just one figure. The question is really about the preparation of the balance sheet.

MARGINS AND MARK-UPS

This is a technique which you might use in preparing the accounts of a retailer.

If I buy an item for £100 and sell it for £150, my profit is £50. In percentage terms this could be stated as either (a) $33^1/3$% on selling price or (b) 50% on cost price.

Make sure that you do not get confused with terminology as sometimes you may be working with a percentage based on cost and sometimes the percentage may be based on selling price.

- If the percentage is based on sales, it is called 'gross profit on sales', 'gross profit', or 'gross profit margin'.

- If the percentage is based on cost of sales, the term is 'mark-up' or 'gross profit on cost of sales'.

The best way of ensuring that you achieve the right answer is to say that whatever the gross profit percentage is 'on' is 100%, from which the relative percentage of the other figure – the cost or selling price – can be easily deduced.

Illustration 1

Deduce the cost of goods which have been sold for £1,200 on which a gross profit of 25% has been achieved.

Always approach this situation in the same way.

- First, work out the 'cost structure'.

  The phrase 'gross profit' means 'gross profit on sales'. Following the rule above we therefore make sales equal to 100%. We know the gross profit is 25%, therefore the cost of sales must be 75%.

	%
Sales	100
Less: Gross profit	25
Therefore cost of sales	75

- Work out the missing figure, in this case 'cost of sales'.

Cost of goods sold   =   75% of sales

$$= \frac{75}{100} \times 1,200 \ = \ £900$$

Illustration 2

Calculate the cost of goods which have been sold for £1,200 on which a mark-up on cost of sales of 25% has been achieved.

- **The cost structure**

  The fact that the gross profit here is on cost of sales rather than sales as above makes all the difference. When we construct the 'cost structure', cost of sales will be 100%, gross profit will be 25%, so that sales must be 125%.

  In other words:

	%
Sales	125
Less: Mark-up	25
Therefore cost of sales	100

- **Calculate the missing figure, again the cost of sales**

$$= \frac{100}{125} \ \text{of sales}$$

$$= \frac{100}{125} \times 1,200 = £960$$

EXAMPLES

The following simple examples will establish whether this technique is understood.

		£
(a)	Mark-up on cost of sales = 10% Sales were £6,160 Cost of sales	?
(b)	Gross profit on sales = 20% Cost of sales was £20,000 Sales	?
(c)	Mark-up on cost of sales = 33$\frac{1}{3}$% Cost of sales was £15,000 Sales	?
(d)	Gross profit on sales = 25% Cost of sales was £13,200 Sales	?
(e)	Sales were £20,000 Cost of sales was £16,000 Gross profit on sales and on cost of sales	? ?

Solutions

(a)

	%	£
Cost of sales	100	
Add: Mark-up	10	
Therefore sales	110	
Therefore cost of sales	$\frac{100}{110}$ × £6,160	**5,600**

(b)

	%	£
Sales	100	
Less: Gross profit	20	
Therefore cost of sales	80	
Therefore sales	$\frac{100}{80}$ × £20,000	**25,000**

(c)

		£
Cost of sales	100	
Add: Mark-up	33¹/₃	
Therefore sales	133¹/₃	

Therefore sales $\dfrac{133\frac{1}{3}}{100} \times £15,000$ **20,000**

(d)

Sales	100	
Less: Gross profit	25	
Therefore cost of sales	75	

Therefore sales $\dfrac{100}{75} \times £13,200$ **17,600**

(e)

Sales	20,000
Less: Cost of sales	16,000
Therefore gross profit	4,000

Gross profit on sales $\dfrac{4,000}{20,000} \times \dfrac{100}{1} = \mathbf{20\%}$

Gross profit on cost of sales $\dfrac{4,000}{16,000} \times \dfrac{100}{1} = \mathbf{25\%}$

QUESTIONS

1 Clarence

You are given the following information relating to Clarence's business for the year ended 31 December 19X3.

Cash paid to trade creditors £9,000

	1 January £	31 December £
Creditors	2,100	2,600
Stock	1,800	1,600

Mark-up on cost of sales 20%

Required

Compute the sales for the year.

2   Alistair

Alistair's business made purchases of £18,000 during the month of January 19X6. His stock was £2,000 on 1 January and £4,000 on 31 January. His gross profit margin is 25% of sales.

What were his sales for the month?

3   Anita Ltd

The accountant of Anita Ltd gives you the following information for the year ended 31 December 19X7:

Stock at 1 January	£3,025
Stock at 31 December	£1,500
Purchases	£12,108
Gross profit margin	30%

What was the company's gross profit for the year?

SUMMARY

- Establish the cost structure.

- Use this relationship together with known information to find the unknown.

Incomplete records (2) – working control accounts

OBJECTIVES

This section covers the following performance criteria:

■　　Existing primary information is accurately summarised.

■　　Essential accounts and reconciliations are correctly prepared.

■　　Other relevant information is correctly identified and recorded.

INTRODUCTION

This is also a technique in which known information is used to calculate the unknown. This time the working is in the form of a ledger account rather than a trading account.

EXAMPLES OF WORKING CONTROL ACCOUNTS

Example

Benedict has made the following credit sales in the year ended 31 December 19X2:

	£
Richard	*100*
Andrew	*75*
Gill	*150*
Sadie	*25*

He also sold goods to Mervyn, but has lost all record of the transaction. He has received £330 from debtors in the year including £30 from Mervyn. At the end of last year, £80 was owed by customers. The balance outstanding is now £160. What is the amount of the sales to Mervyn?

Required

Prepare a working debtors' ledger control account.

Solution

Working debtors' ledger control account

	£		£
Balance owed b/f	80	Cash received	330
Sales in year per question		Balance owed c/f	160
omitting Mervyn	350		
	430		
Sales to Mervyn	?		
	490		490
Balance b/f	160		

Since the debit side is too small, sales to Mervyn must be the difference between £490 and £430, ie. £60.

Think this through carefully to ensure that you understand it. Note also that this approach using a balancing figure will frequently be used in incomplete records: You will often need to fill in all the information that you have at your disposal and then calculate the balancing figure and determine what 'caused' the balancing figure. In the above example, the balancing figure is £60, and the only possible cause is that Benedict made sales of £60 to Mervyn.

Now try to do the following example without reference to the answer.

Example

Dominic paid his creditors £5,000. At the beginning of the period he owed £1,500 and at the end he owed £750.

What were his purchases?

Solution

Working creditors' control account

	£		£
Cash	5,000	b/f	1,500
c/f	750	**Purchases**	**4,250**
	5,750		5,750
		b/f	750

So far the working control accounts appear to be little different from the actual control accounts that would exist in the nominal ledger. However, consider the following.

Example

William received £50,000 cash from his customers. Unfortunately he does not know how much was paid by debtors and how much by cash customers.

He does know that:

      Opening debtors =   £10,000
      Closing debtors   =   £15,000

What were his sales?

Solution

Working debtors' control account

	£		£
b/f	10,000	Cash	50,000
Sales	55,000	c/f	15,000
	65,000		65,000
b/f	15,000		

Here we have included in the control account all the cash received even though some of it was not from debtors. This, of course, does not happen in the nominal ledger.

We can show that this gives us the right answer by reworking the problem using known figures. Suppose that the £50,000 cash received was entirely from cash sales.

Total sales:

	£
Cash sales	50,000
Credit sales (see below)	5,000
	55,000

Working debtors' control account

	£		£
b/f	10,000	Cash	Nil
Sales on credit	**5,000**	c/f	15,000
	15,000		15,000

Suppose now that the cash sales were only £25,000.

Total sales:

	£
Cash sales	25,000
Credit sales (see below)	30,000
	55,000

Working debtors' control account

	£		£
b/f	10,000	Cash (50,000 – 25,000)	25,000
Sales on credit	**30,000**	c/f	15,000
	40,000		40,000

The sales figure given by the working debtors' control account is directly related to the amount of cash that is posted to this account. Therefore if the cash figure includes both credit sales and cash sales, the sales figure will also contain both these elements, and it is not necessary to know the split between cash and credit.

For every £1 of cash sales that go into the working control account it can be said that:

- credit sales will be artificially inflated by £1; and
- cash sales will be artificially deflated by £1.

Overall the sales figure remains correct.

Therefore, including all cash receipts in the working debtors' control account will result in a correct overall sales figure.

QUESTIONS

1 Andrew

Andrew started a business on 1 October 19X7. The following information is available for the year ended 30 September 19X8:

Cash received from customers	£20,150
Cash paid to suppliers	£21,120
Trade debtors at 30 September 19X8	£5,960
Trade creditors at 30 September 19X8	£2,340
Mark-up on cost	40%

What is the cost of stock at 30 September 19X7?

2   Desdemona

The following information relates to Desdemona's business for the year ended 31 December 19X4:

		£
Opening stock		1,200
Closing stock		900
Due to suppliers 1.1.X4		850
Due to suppliers 31.12.X4		760
Cash paid to suppliers for year		4,600
Due from debtors 1.1.X4		310
Cash received from debtors		7,420

There were no debtors at the year-end.

Required

Compute the sales, purchases and gross profit which should be expressed as a percentage on sales and on cost.

SUMMARY

- Draw up a working control account.

- Fill in the known items.

- The unknown item is the balancing figure.

Incomplete records (3) – working cash and bank accounts

OBJECTIVES

This session addresses the following performance criteria:

- Essential accounts and reconciliations are correctly prepared.

- Existing primary information is accurately summarised.

- Other relevant information is correctly identified and recorded.

INTRODUCTION

The working cash account works on the same principle as the working control account, namely information known is used to calculate unknown information.

Typically a working cash account is used where the cash received is unknown but there is full knowledge of what has been done with the cash.

EXAMPLES

Example 1

Henry's sales are all for cash. During the year he:

- *banked £50,000;*
- *paid wages of £5,000 out of the till; and*
- *paid expenses in cash of £10,000.*

What were Henry's sales?

Solution

Working cash account

	£		£
Cash sales	65,000	Bankings	50,000
		Wages	5,000
		Expenses	10,000
	65,000		65,000

The rationale is that if £65,000 of cash was taken out of the till for various purposes then £65,000 must have come in.

Now try the following example without looking at the solution.

Example 2

Henrietta runs a milliner's shop making all her sales for cash. You ascertain the following information:

	£
Cash in the till at the beginning of the year	*50*
Cash in the till at the end of the year	*75*
Bingo winnings put into the till	*500*
Bankings	*15,000*
Cash wages	*1,000*
Cash expenses	*5,000*

What were Henrietta's sales?

Solution

Working cash account

	£		£
Balance b/f	50	Bankings	15,000
Capital	500	Wages	1,000
Cash sales	**20,525**	Expenses	5,000
		Balance c/f	75
	21,075		21,075

The rationale is that £21,075 has been 'used' for bankings, expenses and providing a float to start the next period therefore £21,075 must have been received.

Of this 'receipt':

- is from last period; and
- is an injection of capital.

Therefore £20,525 must have been sales.

THE WORKING BANK ACCOUNT

The working bank account works in exactly the same manner except that it considers activity in the bank account.

Using the principles you have learned in working cash accounts, attempt the following question without reference to the answer.

Illustration

Henry writes cheques only for his own use.

He knows that his bankings were £50,000.

The opening and closing bank balances were £10,000 and £40,000 respectively. What were his drawings?

Working bank account

	£		£
Balance b/f	10,000	**Drawings**	**20,000**
Bankings	50,000	Balance c/f	40,000
	60,000		60,000
Balance b/f	40,000		

Combined cash and bank account

If there are two missing items it is convenient and acceptable to combine the working cash account and the working bank account.

Illustration

In the case of Henry this would be written as:

Working cash and bank account

	Cash £	Bank £		Cash £	Bank £
			Drawings		**20,000**
			Bankings	50,000	
Balance b/f		10,000	Wages	5,000	
Bankings		50,000	Expenses	10,000	
Cash sales	**65,000**		Balance c/f		40,000
	65,000	60,000		60,000	60,000

COMPREHENSIVE EXAMPLE

Simone runs a television and video shop. All purchases are made on credit. Sales are a mixture of cash and credit. For the year ended 31 December 19X8, the opening and closing creditors, debtors and stocks were:

	1.1.X8 £	31.12.X8 £
Creditors	11,000	11,500
Debtors	12,000	11,800
Stock	7,000	10,000

Her mark-up is 20% on cost.

A summary of her business's bank account for the year ended 31 December 19X8 is as follows:

	£		£
Balance b/f 1.1.X8	12,500	Suppliers for purchases	114,000
Cash and cheques banked	121,000	Rent and rates	10,000
		Other expenses	4,000
		Balance c/f 31.12.X8	5,500

The opening and closing cash balances were:

	1.1.X8	31.12.X8
	£120	£150

Simone made the following payments out of the till during the year:

	£
Petrol	400
Stationery	200

She also drew money out of the till for her personal use, but she has not kept a record of the amounts drawn.

Required

Calculate the amount of drawings during the year.

Solution

(1) Calculation of purchases

Working creditors account

	£		£
Bank account	114,000	Balance b/f	11,000
Balance c/f	11,500	Purchases (balancing figure)	114,500
	125,500		125,500

(2)   Calculation of cost of sales

		£
Opening stock		7,000
Purchases (W1)		114,500
		121,500
Closing stock		(10,000)
		111,500

(3)   Calculation of sales

	£	%
Sales $\dfrac{120}{100}$	133,800 (5)	120 (3)
Cost of sales (W2)	111,500 (4)	100 (2)
Gross profit	22,300 (6)	20 (1)

(4)   Drawings

Working cash account

	£		£
Balance b/f	120	Petrol	400
Receipts (W5)	134,000	Stationery	200
		Bankings	121,000
		Drawings	12,370
		Balance c/f	150
	134,120		134,120

(5)   Debtors

Working debtors' account

	£		£
Balance b/f	12,000	Receipts (balancing figure)	134,000
Sales (W3)	133,800	Balance c/f	11,800
	145,800		145,800

QUESTIONS

1   Ignatius

Ignatius owns a small wholesale business and has come to you for assistance in the preparation of his accounts for the year ended 31 December 19X4.

For the year ended 31 December 19X4 no proper accounting records have been kept, but you establish the following information:

(1)   A summary of Ignatius's bank statements for the year to 31 December 19X4 is as follows:

	£		£
Opening balance	1,870	Payments to suppliers	59,660
Receipts from credit customers	12,525	Rent – one year	4,000
Cash banked	59,000	Rates – year beginning 1.4.X4	2,000
		Other administration costs	1,335
		Selling costs	1,940
		Equipment – bought 1.1.X4	800
			69,735
		Closing balance	3,660
	73,395		73,395

(2)   Credit sales for the year, as shown by a summary of copy invoices, totalled £12,760.

(3)   No record has been kept by Ignatius of cash sales or his personal drawings, in cash. It is apparent, however, that all sales are on the basis of a $33^{1}/_{3}\%$ mark-up on cost.

(4)   Apart from drawings, cash payments during the year have been:

	£
Payments to suppliers	755
Sundry expenses	155
Wages	3,055

The balance of cash in hand at 31 December 19X4 is estimated at £20, and it is known that £12 was in hand at the beginning of the year.

(5)   At the year-end, closing stock, valued at cost, was £5,375 (31 December 19X3 £4,570) and creditors for goods bought for resale amounted to £4,655.

(6)   At 31 December 19X3 creditors for goods bought for resale amounted to £3,845.

Required

Calculate the figures for sales and drawings.

2   Fish

Fish was a sole trader in a retail business, all sales being made for cash. His draft balance sheet on Friday, 30 June 19X7 was as follows:

	£	£		£
Capital account		4,500	Fixtures and fittings	1,400
Current account		500	Stock, at cost	3,600
Creditors: Trade	680		Balance at bank	980
Expenses	340		Cash in hand	40
		1,020		
		6,020		6,020

Exactly eight weeks later, on the night of Friday, 25 August 19X7, a fire occurred which destroyed all his stock, fixtures and fittings, financial books, records and papers, with the exception of the file of unpaid invoices and the cash box containing the unbanked cash that he had taken home with him.

His fire insurance policy included cover of his stock, at cost, not exceeding £5,000 and fixtures and fittings at an agreed value of £1,350. He had not insured against loss of profit.

The cash in hand on 30 June 19X7 and all takings up to the close of business on 25 August 19X7 had been banked with the exception of:

1   £12 per week paid as wages;
2   £15 per week that he had withdrawn for personal expenses; and
3   £60 in the cash box taken home with him.

All payments for goods and business expenses, other than wages, were made by cheque.

The selling price of his goods was obtained by adding 30% to the cost price.

An analysis of his bank statement for the eight weeks ended 25 August 19X7 showed the following receipts and payments:

	£
Receipts	
Cash banked	2,884
Payments	
Creditors for goods supplied	1,400
Expenses	460

The total of unpaid invoices on 25 August 19X7 amounted to:

	£
Goods	560
Expenses	140

Required

Prepare a statement setting out his claim for loss of stock.

Reconstruct the cash and bank accounts, the trade creditors' control account and the expense creditors' control account.

3   R Smith

R Smith, having converted the ground floor of his house into a retail shop, started to trade there on 1 October 19X0. The cost of the conversion was £2,500 and of fixtures and fittings £300. To finance this outlay, Smith opened a separate business account at his bank to which he transferred £500 from his private account and arranged overdraft facilities up to £3,000 under a guarantee from a friend, H Jones, who deposited securities with the bank as collateral. In consideration, Smith agreed to pay Jones 5% of the net profit of the first year's trading.

Apart from the bank statements, the only records Smith kept were files of statements from suppliers, paid cheques and unpaid invoices for goods purchased, together with a notebook in which he recorded a few sales to special customers who had credit accounts and paid by cheque. Cash from cash sales was paid into the till out of which he paid certain expenses, banking the balance at the end of each week apart from keeping a small balance as a float. He paid all suppliers of goods by cheque.

Smith paid all the expenses of the house out of his private account and used part of the dwelling portion as an office. It was agreed with Jones that for this he should be credited with the following in respect of the year: rent and rates £100, heat and light £50 and stationery and postage £26.

An analysis of the bank statements for the year ended 30 September 19X1 was as follows:

Receipts	£	*Payments*	£
Paid to open account	500	Cash for till	20
Suppliers, price allowance	10	Conversion of premises	2,500
Special customers	382	Fixtures and fittings	300
Weekly bankings	3,769	Suppliers, for purchases	3,728
Balance, 30 September 19X1	2,037	Insurance of stock	40
		Bank charges and interest	110
	6,698		6,698

Smith estimates that during the year the following were paid out of the till before making the weekly bankings: wages and national insurance £400, sundry shop expenses £50 and drawings £600; Jones agrees these figures. Depreciation is to be charged at 2% on the conversion cost and 5% on fixtures and fittings.

You ascertain that on 30 September 19X1:

(1)   Cheques totalling £30 from special customers, paid into the bank on 30 September 19X1, had not been credited by the bank.

(2)   The amount paid for insurance included the premium of £20 for the year ending 30 September 19X2.

(3)   Stock, correctly taken at cost, was £360.

(4)   The balance in the till was £15 including a post-dated cheque for £5 cashed for a customer.

(5)   Suppliers' unpaid invoices amounted to £403 and there was owing £8 for wages, £2 for national insurance and £6 for shop expenses.

(6)   Special customers owed £172.

Required

Prepare Smith's balance sheet at 30 September 19X1 and his trading and profit and loss account for the year ended on that date after allowing for Jones's guarantee commission.

4   Kevin

On 1 January 19X0 Kevin purchased a business which sold sports equipment.   The total purchase price was £96,000, made up as follows:

	£
Freehold premises	70,000
Fixtures and fittings	3,000
Goodwill	10,000
Stock	13,000
	96,000

Kevin registered for value added tax on 1 January 19X0. Unfortunately he is not very good at accounting.   He has made no VAT returns and his only accounting records are his bank statement (he used his personal account for the business) and details kept of payments made from the till.

Bank account summary for year ended 31 December 19X0

	£		£
Balance at 1 January 19X0		Purchase of business	96,000
(from Kevin)	120,000	Purchases of stock	40,000
Bankings from the till	35,000	Staff wages	5,200
Gift from Auntie Mabel	300	Electricity	200
Winnings from a bet	200	Drawings	4,500
		Rates for 3 months to 31 March 19X0	50
		Rates for y/e 31 March 19X1	400
		Hire of display equipment (incl. VAT)	90
		Balance at 31 December 19X0	9,060
	155,500		155,500

Payments from the till during the year ended 31 December 19X0

	£
Drawings	600
Wages	550
Cash purchases	2,000
Sundry business expenses (including VAT)	200

At 31 December 19X0 cash in hand was £100 and stock was valued at a cost of £15,000 (net of VAT).

Trade debtors at 31 December 19X0 were £300 and trade creditors were £40. All sales were chargeable to VAT at 17.5% and purchases included VAT at 17.5%. The following amounts were outstanding at the year-end:

Electricity	£20	(excluding VAT)
Hire of display equipment	£10	(excluding VAT)

Depreciation of fixtures and fittings is to be provided for at 10% pa and goodwill is to be written off over ten years.

Required

Prepare Kevin's trading and profit and loss account for the year ended 31 December 19X0 and a balance sheet at that date.

5   Pinker

Pinker Ltd is a small company engaged in the business of selling footballs. The business is run from a shop which is rented for £800 a year. During the year ended 30 September 19X3, the bookkeeper kept very poor records and some information was lost. However, the balances at 30 September 19X2 were as follows:

	£		£
Authorised, issued and fully		Van at cost less depreciation	1,600
paid £1 Ordinary shares	3,000	Stock at cost	2,000
Profit and loss account	2,750	Debtors	1,680
Creditors – Trade	1,400	Prepayment – rent	300
– Sundry	36	Cash in hand	83
		Cash at bank	1,523
	7,186		7,186

An examination of Pinker Ltd's books for the year revealed the following.

(1)   Amounts banked

	£
Loan from Trotter (1.1.X3)	500
Sale of old stock	1,200
Other	21,417
	23,117

(2)   The loan carries interest at the rate of 12% per annum. Trotter had been paid £40 from the till as part payment of the interest on his loan.

(3)   Cheques paid out

	£
Purchase of footballs	16,204
Wages	2,122
Rent	750
Motor expenses	1,214
Van	2,000
Repairs	522
Sundry expenses	613
	23,425

(4)   It was ascertained that the following additional amounts were paid out of the till before the bankings were made.

	£
Wages	516
Motor expenses	83
Sundry expenses	75
	674

(5)   The following closing balances were ascertained:

	£
Cash	37
Stock at cost	1,910
Creditors – Trade	1,341
– Sundry	47

(6)   Pinker Ltd makes a uniform gross profit margin of 40% on all footballs sold except those purchased from Upjohn, a new supplier, on which the margin is 15%. During the year £3,700 worth of footballs were purchased from Upjohn of which £470 were in closing stock.

(7)   The sale of old stock was of some of the balls which had been in stock at the beginning of the year. These were sold at 20% less than the normal selling price. All sales receipts were paid into the till.

(8)   During the year a new van was purchased for £3,400 and the old van was taken in part exchange. Depreciation of 20% on written down value is to be charged, a full year in the year of purchase and none in the year of sale.

(9)   Pinker Ltd owes £71 for wages and £113 for motor expenses.

Required

Prepare the company's trading and profit and loss account for the year ended 30 September 19X3 and a balance sheet at that date.

6   Carlton Moorland   (AAT CA J93)

Bassingham Ltd purchase most of their supplies of office equipment and stationery from Carlton Moorland, a sole trader who retails those products. Over the years you have got to know him quite well and often help with giving advice regarding his accounts.

On New Year's Eve, the night of 31 December 1992, a fire occurred which destroyed all his fixtures and fittings, his stock and his books of account. Fortunately he had the foresight (or good fortune) to take his cash tin and files of unpaid invoices home for the holiday period.

His fire insurance policy with the Sunbird Insurance Company covered the value of his stock (at cost) up to a maximum of £50,000 and his fixtures and fittings at an agreed valuation of £12,500.

His immediate problem is knowing how much to claim for his damaged stock.

He finds the following information at home for you to use:

(a)   Draft balance sheet as at 31 October 1992

	£
Fixtures and fittings	14,000
Stock (at cost)	36,000
Debtors	3,630
Bank	9,800
Cash	400
	63,830
Capital	53,420
Creditors (for purchases)	6,800
Creditors (for expenses)	3,610
	63,830

(b)   There was £600 in the cash tin on 31 December 1992.

(c) The file of unpaid invoices revealed:

Invoices for credit sales	£3,810
Invoices from creditors for purchases	£5,600
Invoices from creditors for expenses	£1,400

(d) The copy of the bank statement obtained from the bank for the two-month period 1 November 1992 to 31 December 1992 revealed the following summarised transactions:

Cash banked	£18,816
Cheques banked	£12,210

Cheque payments:	
to creditors for purchases	£14,000
to creditors for expenses	£4,600

All of the cash banked comprised cash sales.

All of the cheques banked comprised those received from trade debtors except for one cheque from a supplier of purchases which was a refund of £195 for an overpayment.

(e) Carlton remembered that he took cash discounts of £124 and £215 when paying two invoices for purchases.

(f) Wages of £120 per week were drawn out of cash before banking, as were £150 per week of personal drawings. November and December 1992 both contained four weeks.

(g) Carlton operates a strict mark-up of 30% of cost on all goods sold.

(h) Carlton depreciates fixed assets by a full year in the year of purchase, but not at all in the year of sale.

Assessment tasks

Task 1

Show in detail your calculation for Carlton's claim for loss of stock.

Task 2

Prepare the ledger account for fixtures and fittings, showing the position after the insurance claim has been made on 1 January 1993.

7   Sarah Harvey   (AAT CA J94)

You belong to a badminton club at the local leisure centre and always have a drink with one of your friends, Sarah Harvey, in the coffee shop after a game. Sarah is the owner of a small florist's business and has been trading for a year as Fancy Flowers. She has never kept proper books of account and has asked you to calculate her profit for the first year of trading which ended on 31 May 1994.

On 31 May, you carried out a stocktake which revealed the following situation:

	Cost	Mark-up
Pot plants	£280	100%
Roses	£240	75%
Tulips	£160	75%
Sprays	£340	100%
Plant food	£80	50%
Vases	£520	100%

A quarter of the pot plants were rather withered and Sarah thought she would have to throw them away. She thought a further quarter would have to be sold at cost price.

The roses were of a very high quality and Sarah thought she could probably sell them at a mark-up of 100%.

One of the sprays, costing £80, had been prepared for a customer who had never collected. This would have to be thrown away.

A box of ten vases, selling price £6 per vase, was badly damaged and would have to be thrown away.

You also elicit the following information:

(1)   All sales of the business are cash sales.

(2)   A summary of the bank statements revealed the following:

	£
Cash paid into the bank	31,420
Cheque payments:	
To plant and sundries wholesalers	24,180
Rent	5,000
Business rates	420
Advertising	385
Insurance	390
Electricity	780
Sundry expenses	560
Interest charged by bank	84

(3)   All the cash paid into the bank resulted from cash sales, except for an initial £5,000 invested by Sarah as start-up capital in the business.

(4)   Before paying the cash sales into the bank, Sarah withdrew cash for the following purposes:

Wages for self	14,200
Sundry expenses	345

She also retained £60 change in a cash tin after paying the remaining cash into the bank.

(5)   From her file of purchase invoices, Sarah discovered that the following were unpaid:

	£
Purchase of cut flowers for May	850
Purchase of roses (28 May)	345
Electricity (quarter ended 30 April)	360
Advertising charges for May	45

(6)   She pays rent of £1,000 per quarter in advance.

(7)   She regularly takes home about £10 worth of flowers (at selling price) each week.

Assessment tasks

Task 1

Prepare a valuation of closing stock.

Task 2

Calculate the profit for the first year of trading for Fancy Flowers.

Task 3

Calculate the balance on capital account for Sarah at the end of the first year of trading.

Task 4

Comment briefly on the situation revealed.

Show all your workings.

8   Somaira Rahman   **(AAT CA D94)**

On 1 October 1992, a friend of yours, Somaira Rahman, started a small business selling electrical goods through the street markets of South West London and to other businesses. She has now been approached by the Inland Revenue for details of the profit she has earned through the first two years of the business.

Somaira has never kept proper accounting records and has asked you to prepare draft statements of income from the financial information she has available as follows:

	1 October 1992	*Financial information at* *30 September 1993*	*30 September 1994*
	£	£	£
Trade debtors		2,100	5,250
Trade creditors		68,600	74,820
Overhead expenses prepaid		640	210
Overhead expenses accrued		760	190
Business premises (cost)		48,000	48,000
Motor van (at valuation)	18,000	15,000	12,000
Stock of goods (cost)	42,000	56,000	63,400
Cash		820	650
Balance at bank	16,000	41,600	29,490
Loan from TR Rahman	60,000	50,000	50,000

Notes

(1)   Somaira started the business on 1 October 1992 with a loan from her uncle. She provided the remainder of the start-up capital from her own resources. Her uncle provided the loan free of interest for the first year, but at 8% per annum thereafter. The interest for the second year of the business has still not been paid. Somaira was able to repay £10,000 of this loan on 1 September 1993.

(2)   The business premises were bought on 1 June 1993. Somaira paid 50% of the cost from her private bank account, the remainder being provided by a bank mortgage. The interest is paid monthly by direct debit.

(3)   On 1 August 1994 Somaira bought a new motor car for private use for £16,400.

(4)   Somaira uses money from sales receipts to finance her shopping bills of £275 per week.

        All the receipts during the year ended 30 September 1994 were sales receipts, except for £8,220 which represented private investment income.

(5)   She analysed the payments from her bank account during the year ended 30 September 1994 as follows:

Payments to trade creditors	£138,400
Overhead expenses	£7,440
Motor expenses (van)	£12,420
Motor expenses (non-business use)	£1,640
Mortgage interest payments	£2,400
New motor car	£16,400

Assessment tasks

Task 1

Prepare a calculation of the Capital a/c balance at 30 September 1993.

Task 2

Prepare a calculation of the net profit or loss for the year ended 30 September 1993.

Task 3

Prepare a detailed calculation of the net profit or loss of the business for the year ended 30 September 1994.

Task 4

Prepare a calculation of the balance on Somaira's Capital a/c at 30 September 1994.

Show all your workings.

SUMMARY

The 'cash book' method for incomplete records:

●   Prepare cash and bank account as necessary and discover what is missing.

●   Work through debtors' and creditors' ledger control accounts.

Value added tax – registration and administration

OBJECTIVES

At the end of this session you should understand and appreciate that:

- submissions are made in accordance with currently operative VAT laws and regulations;

- discussions with VAT inspectors are conducted openly and constructively to promote the efficiency of the VAT accounting system;

- VAT documentation is correctly filed.

INTRODUCTION

Value added tax (VAT) is a European tax – it applies throughout the European Community (EC).

We are going to look at VAT within the United Kingdom only. The United Kingdom includes England and Wales, Scotland and Northern Ireland (but not the Channel Islands).

VAT is a tax paid by consumers. Businesses who make *taxable supplies* collect the tax from their customers. Those businesses (*taxable persons*) have to assess the amount of tax payable on goods and services provided (*output tax*). They pay it over on a regular basis to HM Customs and Excise.

The definition of taxable supplies is wider than just sales. It includes goods taken from the business for personal use.

As the businesses themselves are not being taxed, they are allowed to reclaim tax on their own expenditure *(input VAT)*. The input VAT is deducted from the output VAT and the difference is paid each quarter to HM Customs & Excise.

Place of supply

A supply must take place within the United Kingdom to be a taxable supply under United Kingdom VAT law. The rules are different for supplies of goods and services.

Generally, if a business makes a supply of goods from stocks held in the United Kingdom, then the supply takes place in the United Kingdom. If the business must install the goods at the customer's premises, then the supply takes place at those premises.

When supplying services, the place of supply is the place where the supplier belongs, eg. where a supplier has fixed business premises.

Time of supply

Most businesses account for input and output VAT according to the dates that they issue and receive invoices. Some businesses use different systems, but these are beyond the scope of the *Standards* for Unit 8.

REGISTRATION

Compulsory registration

Anyone in business whose taxable supplies exceed a certain annual limit must register. This includes sole traders, partnerships and limited companies. Penalties for failing to register can be severe.

A business must register if:

• at the end of any month the value of taxable supplies in the past year has exceeded the annual limit of £46,000; or

• at any time there are reasonable grounds for believing that the value of taxable supplies to be made in the next 30 days will exceed the annual limit of £46,000; or

• their acquisitions from other EC member states are more than £46,000 in the calendar year

Voluntary registration

A business may volunteer to register for VAT. HM Customs and Excise may refuse registration if the applicant is unable to show that supplies are being made in the course of business.

More than one business

It is the person not the business which is required to register. So, if a person is carrying on several businesses, only a single registration is required and the turnovers of all businesses carried on by that person must be considered together when considering registration limits.

Here is an illustration of the idea of the *taxable person*.

Robert Parker has three businesses: a hairdressing business (taxable turnover £19,000 per annum), a printing business (taxable turnover £15,000 per annum) and he also deals in second-hand cars (taxable turnover £14,000 per annum).

The VAT registration limit applies to the total taxable turnover of *all* the business interests of a *taxable person*. In this case each business venture is below the limit, but in total they exceed the limit. Robert Parker would have to register for VAT.

Let us now assume that the hairdressing business is a partnership with Peter Green. The partnership would be treated as a different *taxable person* to Robert Parker trading alone. Both taxable persons (Robert Parker and the partnership) would avoid registration.

Group registration

Companies under common control may apply for group registration. Each VAT group of companies appoints one company to account for all the group's VAT. (Inter-company supplies are disregarded.)

Deregistration

A taxable person may deregister if the value of his taxable supplies (net of VAT) are expected to be less than £44,000 in the following 12 months. If the taxable person changes – for example, when a sole trader incorporates – then the registration of the sole trader will be cancelled.

On deregistration, a final VAT form (VAT 193) is completed and VAT is chargeable on stocks and capital assets on which input tax was originally claimed because the registered trader is effectively making a taxable supply. If the trade is transferred as a going concern to another taxable person, then VAT is not normally charged on such a transfer.

TYPES OF SUPPLY

There are three types of supply: standard-rated (with the reduced rate for domestic fuel and power), zero-rated and exempt. These are examples of zero-rated and exempt items.

Zero-rated	*Exempt*
• Water and certain types of food	• Land (including rent on property)
• Books and newspapers	• Insurance
• Drugs and medicines	• Postal services
• Charities	• Betting, gaming and lotteries
• Children's clothing and footwear	• Finance (eg. making loans)
	• Non profit-making education
	• Health services provided by doctors and dentists

Subject to one exception, all supplies that are not zero-rated or exempt are standard-rated. The exception is that VAT is only charged at 8% on the supply of fuel and power used for domestic purposes. The standard rate is currently 17.5%. The turnover limits for registration mentioned above include both zero-rated and standard-rated supplies. They do *not* include exempt supplies.

A person who deals only in exempt supplies cannot register for VAT and therefore cannot recover any input tax charged, whereas a person who makes zero-rated supplies can be registered and input tax can be reclaimed.

It is also important to identify items that are outside the scope of VAT. This includes items such as:

- business rates
- vehicle licences
- salaries and wages
- trade union subscriptions

PARTIAL EXEMPTION

A taxable person who makes both taxable and exempt supplies is referred to as 'partially exempt'. For this purpose, zero-rated supplies are treated as taxable. The problem which arises from partial exemption is that taxable supplies entitle the supplier to a credit for input tax, exempt supplies do not. It is therefore necessary to identify an acceptable method of apportioning input tax between taxable and exempt supplies.

VAT can only be reclaimed if it is incurred in making taxable supplies.

To calculate the input tax attributable to an exempt supply:

- Identify a person's input tax.

- Calculate the extent to which that input tax relates to input supplies which are wholly used or to be used by that person in making taxable supplies – this amount of input tax is reclaimable in full.

- Calculate the extent to which the input tax relates to input supplies which are wholly used or to be used by that person in making exempt supplies – this amount of input tax is disallowed in full.

- Calculate the disallowable proportion of any remaining input tax.

  The formula normally used for calculating the remaining input tax not reclaimable is :

  $$\frac{\text{Value of exempt supplies}}{\text{Value of total supplies}} \times \text{Value of remaining input tax}$$

For convenience, the disallowable input tax will normally be added to the cost of sales but may be apportioned back over the items giving rise to the disallowable input tax.

De minimis limits

The partial exemption rules do not apply if the exempt input tax in the accounting period does not exceed *both* of the following:

- £625 per month on average
- 50% of total input tax

ADMINISTRATION

The main source of law on VAT is the VAT Act 1994.

HM Customs and Excise is the government department that is responsible for administering VAT in the United Kingdom. The VAT Act 1994 gives it the power to do so. VAT offices across the country are responsible for the local administration of VAT within a particular geographical area.

Officers from the local VAT office deal with registration, visit taxpayers to check returns and deal with routine enquiries. They are also responsible for enforcing the tax.

Taxpayers send their returns and payments to the VAT Central Unit at Southend-on-Sea that keeps central records.

Customs and Excise have certain powers that help them administer the tax. They have the power to examine records, inspect premises, make assessments for underpaid tax and raise penalties for breaches of VAT law. Penalties may be made for (amongst other things) failing to register for VAT, failing to make returns or failing to make payments on time. They also decide whether or not supplies are liable to VAT.

The decisions of Customs and Excise are not legally binding.

There are inevitably disputes between the taxpayer and Customs and Excise. Customs and Excise have their own administrative procedures to deal with disputes. In certain cases the taxpayer may appeal to a VAT tribunal. The taxpayer may appeal against the decision of a VAT tribunal to the High Court (on a point of law only). Beyond that appeals may go to the Court of Appeal and then to the House of Lords. The ultimate legal authority on VAT is the European Court of Justice.

RECORDS

The form of records must allow Customs and Excise to check VAT returns adequately. Generally, the business must keep records of:

- all taxable and exempt supplies made in the course of business
- all taxable supplies received in the course of business
- a summary of the total output tax and input tax for each tax period – the VAT account.

The business must keep records to prove the figures shown on the VAT returns for the previous six years. These records might include the following:

- orders and delivery notes
- relevant business correspondence
- appointment and job books
- purchases and sales books
- cash books and other account books
- purchase invoices and copy sales invoices
- recordings of daily takings, including till rolls
- annual accounts
- import and export documents
- bank statements and paying-in slips
- VAT accounts
- any credit notes issued or received

A business can keep its records on microfilm. The business must tell Customs and Excise. It must be possible to inspect the records.

Any business that maintains its records on computer must tell Customs and Excise. The system must comply with VAT regulations.

Some businesses send or receive invoices by electronic means. Again they must tell Customs and Excise and check that they are complying with regulations.

A business must keep all of its records for six years.

REFERENCE SOURCES

The best sources of information are the notices and leaflets issued by Customs and Excise. The main source is *Notice 700: The VAT Guide.* You may use this guide during your devolved assessment and it will be a useful source of information and ideas.

DEFINITIONS

Supply of goods	the passing of exclusive ownership of goods to another person
Supply of services	doing something, other than supplying goods, for a consideration
Output tax	tax collected from customers and clients
Input tax	tax paid to suppliers of goods and services
Zero-rated	Specific items listed in the VAT Act 1994
Exempt	Specific items listed in the VAT Act 1994
Standard-rated	Items which are not zero-rated, exempt or outside of the scope of VAT

SUMMARY

The main points covered in this session were about registration and types of supply.

You should be aware of the basic facts that a supply must take place within the UK to be a taxable supply under UK law; that registration is compulsory for anyone in business where the taxable supplies exceed £46,000 a year; that generally the date of issue and receipt of invoice is when VAT is accounted for; and that there are zero, exempt and standard rated supplies.

We outlined the documents which must be kept to allow the Customs and Excise to check the VAT returns and mentioned that these must be kept for six years.

In order for you to achieve the objectives for this session, you must be able to discuss the currently operative VAT laws and regulations and must know which records are needed for VAT documentation.

Value added tax – invoicing and tax points

OBJECTIVES

At the end of this session you should be able to ensure the following:

■ relevant inputs and outputs are correctly identified and calculated;

■ submissions are made in accordance with currently operative VAT laws and regulations.

INVOICES

All businesses that are registered for VAT must collect tax on taxable supplies. They must also show certain information on invoices issued. There is no standard format for invoices. The exact design is the choice of the business, but it must show the following details (unless the invoice is a *less detailed tax invoice* that you will see later):

• identifying number

• date of supply (or *tax point* – see below) and the date of issue of the invoice

• supplier's name and address and registration number

• name and address of person to whom the goods or services are supplied

• type of supply

  – sale
  – hire-purchase, credit sale, conditional sale or similar transaction
  – loan
  – exchange
  – hire, lease or rental
  – process (making goods using the customer's own materials)
  – sale on commission (eg. by an estate agent)
  – supply on sale or return

• description of the goods or services

• quantity of goods or extent of services; the rate of tax and amount payable (in sterling) excluding VAT for each separate description

• total amount payable (excluding VAT) in sterling

• rate of any cash discount offered (these are also called *settlement discounts*)

- separate rate and amount of VAT charged for each rate of VAT

- total amount of VAT chargeable.

Here is an example of a tax invoice (see below).

MICRO TRAINING GROUP LTD **Unit 34** **Castlewell Trading Estate** **Manchester** **M12 5RF**					

To: JF Jenkins & Co 65 Green Street Manchester M12 4ED	Sales invoice number: 35 VAT registered number: 234 5566 87 Tax point: 12 September 19X2

SALE

Quantity	Description and price	Amount exc VAT	VAT rate	VAT net
6	Programmable calculators FR34 at £24.76	148.56	17.5%	
12	Programmable calculators GT60 at £36.80	441.60	17.5%	
		590.16		101.21
	Delivery	23.45	17.5%	4.02
Terms: Cash discount of 2% if paid within 10 days		613.61		105.23
	VAT	105.23		
	TOTAL	718.84		

Note: VAT and discounts

Note how the VAT is always calculated on the lowest amount that the customer may pay. You must assume that the customer will take the discount.

LESS DETAILED TAX INVOICES

Retailers do not have to issue a VAT invoice every time they make a sale. This would make trading impossible.

Retailers must, however, issue a tax invoice when requested by a taxable person. If the total amount of this supply (including VAT) does not exceed £100.00, a retailer may issue a *less detailed tax invoice*. The supplier only needs to show the following details on the invoice:

- supplier's name and address
- supplier's VAT registration number
- date of supply
- description sufficient to identify the goods or services
- amount payable (including VAT)
- rate of VAT

These invoices must only include items with the *same rate* of VAT. They must not include zero-rated or exempt items.

Although this invoice shows less detail, it is still a valid *tax invoice*.

All retailers must keep a record of their daily gross takings so that VAT can be calculated on the total of cash takings, not individual invoices. This means that the retailer will need to keep a careful note of any money taken for own use.

TAX POINTS

The tax point is the date on which the liability for output tax arises. Most taxable persons make a VAT return each quarter. The return must include all supplies whose tax points fall within that quarter.

The 'basic tax point' is the date of delivery of goods or completion/performance of services

Where an invoice is issued or payment received before this date, the earliest date becomes the 'actual tax point'. If a supplier issues an invoice within 14 days after the basic tax point, this becomes the actual tax point and is used as the tax point for the tax return, unless payment has been received earlier, in which case the payment date is the tax point.

The advantage of this system is that the tax return will tie in with the accounting records, in particular the books of prime entry.

Deposits received in advance

Any deposits received in advance create a basic tax point. The business must account for the VAT element. For instance a £50.00 deposit received in advance is inclusive of VAT. To calculate the VAT element, use the VAT fraction as follows.

$$£50 \times \frac{7}{47} = £7.44$$

CREDIT NOTES

When issuing a credit note the supplier does not have to adjust the VAT charge (by law). Both the supplier and the customer must agree to this. Otherwise the supplier must adjust the VAT charge and issue a credit note.

The credit note must show:

- the identifying number and date of issue
- the supplier's name, address and registration number
- the customer's name and address
- the reason for the credit (eg. goods returned)
- a description of the goods or services for which the credit is being allowed
- the quantity and mount credited for each description
- the total amount credited, excluding VAT
- the rate and amount of VAT credited.

The number and date of the original tax invoice should also appear on the credit note.

If the supplier issues the credit note without making a VAT adjustment the credit note must say: 'This is not a credit note for VAT'.

A supplier is not allowed to issue a credit note to recover VAT on bad debts. See section on bad debts for detailed procedures.

QUESTION

1 Retailers and wholesalers

How would the records of a retailer differ from those of a wholesaler?

SUMMARY

All businesses that are registered for VAT must collect tax on taxable supplies and in this session we concentrated on the details that must be included on the invoice.

Less detailed invoices were discussed and you should be able to use something like a receipt from a shop as an example and list the details required. You are also required to know what happens when credit notes are issued and also when deposits are received in advance.

The objectives that you should have achieved for this session were related to the last session in terms of the VAT laws and regulations, along with some further requirements and also the calculations necessary for the relevant inputs and outputs.

Value added tax – VAT returns

OBJECTIVES

At the end of this session you should be able to do the following:

■ complete VAT returns from the appropriate sources and ensure that they are submitted within the statutory time limits;

■ identify the relevant inputs and outputs and enter them correctly on VAT returns;

■ complete VAT returns in accordance with currently operative VAT laws and regulations.

COMPLETING THE RETURN

The tax period for VAT is three months or one month for taxpayers who choose to make monthly returns (normally taxpayers who receive regular refunds). The taxpayer must complete a *VAT return* (a VAT 100 form) at the end of each quarter. The return summarises all the transactions for the period. *See below*.

Traders who do not make monthly returns but have a total liability exceeding £2,000,000 over 12 months must make payments on account during the quarter.

The taxpayer must make the return within *one month* of the end of the tax period. The taxable person must send the amount due at the same time (ie. output tax collected less input tax deducted). Payment may be by cheque (made payable to HM Customs and Excise and crossed) or by credit transfer.

OUTPUT TAX

Output tax is tax due on sales and any other taxable income. This includes:

● petrol used for private motoring by employees (using scale charges)

● goods taken for private use (VAT is accounted for on the market value of such goods)

● sales to staff

● sales of business assets

● any imported services listed in the VAT Guide, Appendix G

**H M Customs
and Excise**

Value Added Tax Return

For the period

to

For Official Use

Your VAT Office telephone number is 071-928 3344

Registration Number | Period

You could be liable to a financial penalty if your completed return and all the VAT payable are not received by the due date.

Due date:

For Official Use

| REMEMBER |

You must Include VAT due on EC transactions in boxes 2 & 3 if they occur on or after 1.1.93.

If you are using Retail Scheme B1, D or J, please remember to carry out your annual adjustment at the appropriate time.

Before you fill in this form please read the notes on the back and the VAT Leaflet *"Filling in your VAT return"*. Complete all boxes clearly in ink, writing 'none' where necessary. Don't put a dash or leave any box blank. If there are no pence write **"00"** in the pence column. **Do not** enter more than one amount in any box.

			£	p
For official use	VAT due in this period on **sales** and other outputs	**1**		
	VAT reclaimed in this period on **acquisitions** from other **EC Member States**	**2**		
	Total VAT due **(the sum of boxes 1 and 2)**	**3**		
	VAT reclaimed in this period on purchases on purchases and other inputs (including acquisitions from the EC)	**4**		
	Net VAT to be paid to Customs or reclaimed by you **(Difference between boxes 3 and 4)**	**5**		
	Total value of **sales** and all other outputs excluding any VAT. **Include your box 8 figure**	**6**		00
	Total value of **purchases** and all other inputs excluding any VAT. **Include your box 9 figure**	**7**		00
	Total value of all **Supplies** of goods and related services, excluding any VAT, to other **EC Member States**	**8**		00
	Total value of all **acquisitions** of goods and related services, excluding any VAT, from other **EC Member States**	**9**		00

Retail schemes. If you have used any of the schemes in the period covered by this return please enter the appropriate letter(s) in this box.

If you are enclosing a payment please tick this box.	DECLARATION : You, or someone on your behalf, must sign below.

I, ... declare that the
(Full name of signatory in BLOCK LETTERS)

information given above is true and complete.

Signature .... Date .... 19 ....

A false declaration can result in prosecution.

CD 2859/N9(02/91)

F 3790(JANUARY 1992)CD 2859/R/N9(02/91)

B

VAT 100

Notes

These notes and the VAT Leaflet *Filling in your VAT Return* will help you fill in this form. You may also need to refer to other VAT notices and leaflets.

If you need help or advice please contact your local VAT office, their telephone number is shown over the page.

If you are using the cash accounting scheme, the amounts of VAT due and deductible are based on payments you receive and make, and not on invoices you receive and send out.

If you put negative figures in boxes 1 to 4, put them in brackets.

Amounts not declared correctly on previous returns

1.   If any of your previous returns declared too much or too little VAT which has not yet been accounted for you can correct the position using boxes 1 and 4 for net amounts of £1000 or less.

2.   Where the net amount is over £1000 promptly notify your local VAT office. Do not include the amount on this return.

If you do not follow these instructions you could be liable to financial penalty.

How to pay the VAT due

Cross all cheques and postal orders "AC Payee Only" and make them payable to "HM Customs and Excise". In your own interest do not send notes, coins, or uncrossed postal orders through the post.

If you wish to pay by credit transfer ask your local VAT office. The printed booklets of credit transfer slips will then be sent to you.

Please write your VAT registration number on the back of all cheques and credit transfer slips.

Where to send this return

You must ensure that the completed form and any VAT payable are received by the 'due date' (shown over the page) by:

**The Controller
VAT Central Unit
HM Customs and Excise
21 Victoria Avenue
Southend-on-Sea X
SS99 1AA**

Box 1

You must show the VAT due on all goods and services you supplied in this period.

Box 2

Show the VAT due (but not paid) on all goods and related services you acquired in this period from other EC Member States.

Box 3

Show the total amount of the VAT due ie the sum of boxes 1 and 2. This is your total Output tax.

Box 4

Show the amount of VAT deductible on any business purchases including acquisitions of goods and related services from other EC Member States. This is your **Input tax**.

Box 5

If this amount is under £1, you need not send any payment, nor will any repayment be made to you, but you must still fill in this form and send it to the VAT Central Unit.

Boxes 6 and 7

In box 6 show the value excluding VAT for your total outputs (supplies of goods and services). Include zero rated, exempt outputs and EC supplies from box 8.

In box 7 show the value excluding VAT of all your inputs (purchases of goods and services). Include zero rated, exempt inputs and EC acquisitions from box 9.

Boxes 8 and 9

EC TRADE ONLY

Use these boxes if you have supplied goods to or acquired goods from another EC Member State. Include related services such as transport costs where these form part of the invoice or contract price. The figures should exclude VAT.

The other EC states are: Belgium, Denmark, France, Germany, Greece, Holland, Ireland, Italy, Luxembourg, Portugal and Spain.

You must tell your local VAT office about any changes in your business circumstances (including changes of address).

CD 2859/R/N9(02/91)

Printed in the U.K. for H.M.S.O. 11/91 Dd.8324457 C46000 38806 G4123

INPUT TAX

A business cannot reclaim all of its input tax, ie. input tax on the following:

- purchases of motor cars (where the purchaser is neither a car dealer nor leasing business)
- business entertaining expenses
- non-business expenditure
- directors' accommodation
- purchases of 'luxury' items for business promotion (eg. aeroplane, boat, racehorse)
- purchase of goods accounted for under a second hand scheme (eg. motor cars)

To reclaim input tax the business must hold proper tax invoices as follows.

- For items over £100.00, a full tax invoice.
- For items under £100.00, a less detailed tax invoice (if a retailer) or a full tax invoice.

EXPORTS AND IMPORTS

The destination principle

Generally, goods exported from the United Kingdom are zero-rated (ie. there is no tax charged on them, even if there normally would be).

Goods that are imported from outside the EC have to have customs duty paid on them when they enter the country. Goods that would be taxed at the standard rate of VAT if supplied in the United Kingdom are also subject to VAT. The tax is collected in the same way as customs duties. The amount payable is based on their value including duty. This applies to all goods whether or not they are for business use. The aim of the charge is to treat foreign goods in the same way as home-produced goods.

If imported goods *are* for business use and the business uses them to make taxable supplies, it can reclaim the VAT paid.

This system is obviously the reverse of the normal system and is called the *destination principle*.

The EC System

It is not necessary to make an import declaration on an acquisition of goods from another member state (with certain exceptions). A person registered for VAT in the UK must account for VAT at the usual rate on any goods or services he receives from the EC. This then becomes recoverable input VAT in the usual way.

Certain services

A business must pay tax on certain services that it receives from overseas suppliers. These services are *reverse charge services* and include professional services, advertising, hire of goods and royalties. Reverse charge services are taxable supplies for the registration limits.

Payment of VAT

VAT on imports (from outside the EC) can be paid in one of three ways:

- *On the spot* when the imports enter the country

- By the *standing deposit system*. The importer (or the agent) maintains an account with Customs and Excise. Customs and Excise debit VAT payable on imports against this account.

- By the *deferred payment system*. The importer provides security to Customs and Excise to cover the maximum amount of VAT (and duty) which may arise in one month. This is usually a bank guarantee At the end of the month Customs and Excise calculates the total payable and collects this by *direct debit* from the importer's bank account.

Documents and forms

Intrastat is the new system for collecting statistics on the trade in goods between member states. Boxes 2, 4, 8 and 9 on the VAT return are used to collect such data.

The correct documents are very important to importers and exporters.

If the company trades (sales or purchase) with any company in another EC country, they must obtain VAT registration numbers and country codes from all their VAT registered customers and suppliers in other EC member states.

If the total EC supplies are less than £11,500 per annum then the company will need to send a list of the EC member state customers' VAT registration numbers to Customs and Excise each year.

For companies whose total EC supplies are over £11,500 there is a requirement to produce the EC Sales List (ESL) quarterly. This also applies to UK companies whose turnover is more than £145,000 per annum.

If a UK company's sales to non-registered customers, in any one member state, in one year, is likely to exceed that country's threshold then the company must register for VAT in the country or countries concerned. If this is the case, the VAT number in that country will have to be printed on invoices to non-VAT registered customers in those countries.

Exporters must have documents that *prove* that goods have been exported. Invoices to foreign addresses, sales orders and general correspondence are not enough.

The business must obtain proof within *three months* of the goods leaving the country.

If a business wishes to reclaim VAT paid on imports, it must have the correct document. This is *Form C79,* a monthly certificate that Customs and Excise send directly to the importer.

BAD DEBTS

Suppliers cannot issue credit notes to recover VAT on bad debts.

The business must make an adjustment through the VAT return. The business can reclaim VAT already paid over if:

- output tax was paid on the original supply;

- six months have elapsed between the date of supply and the date of the VAT return; and

- the debt has been written off as a bad debt in the accounting records.

If the business receives a repayment of the debt later, it must make an adjustment to the VAT relief claimed.

PENALTIES

Late notification

If a trader trades in excess of the registration limits without informing HM Customs & Excise, a penalty is levied for failing to register by the proper date.

This penalty is a proportion of the net tax due from the date registration should have taken place. The proportion percentage varies as follows:

Period of failure to register	*Percentage of tax*
9 months or less	5%
Over 9 months, but not over 18 months	10%
Over 18 months	15%

A minimum penalty of £50 exists. If the trader can show a reasonable excuse for not registering, the penalty may be mitigated.

Default surcharge

A default occurs when a trader submits his VAT return late or submits the return on time but pays the VAT late. On default, HM Customs & Excise serve a default liability notice on the taxpayer which identifies a surcharge period which runs from the date of the notice until the anniversary of the end of the period for which the taxpayer is in default.

If a second default occurs in the surcharge periods the surcharge period is further extended until the anniversary of the end of the period to which the new default relates.

If VAT is paid late in a surcharge period, a surcharge is payable as follows:

Default involving late payment of VAT in the surcharge period	*Surcharge, % of outstanding VAT*
1st	2%
2nd	5%
3rd	10%
4th and above	15%

(The minimum charge is £30.)

Misdeclaration penalties

Making returns which understate the trader's VAT liability incurs a penalty of 15% of the lost tax. Errors of up to £2,000 can be rectified on the usual quarter-end VAT 100 return.

Default interest

Interest is charged on VAT due on an assessment from HM Customs & Excise. Interest runs from the date the VAT should have been paid (up to a maximum of three years).

Repayment supplement

A repayment supplement is paid by HM Customs & Excise where payments of VAT occur and, although the original tax was paid on time, HM Customs & Excise did not refund the excess within 30 days of its receipt.

COMPLETING THE VAT RETURN

VAT account

The main source of information needed for the VAT return is the VAT account. See example below.

VAT ACCOUNT – EXAMPLE

1 April 19Z5 to 30 June 19Z5

VAT deductible – input tax		VAT payable – output tax	
VAT on purchases		VAT on sales	
April	X	April	X
May	X	May	X
June	X	June	X
VAT on imports	X		
Adjustments of previous errors			
(if £2,000 or less)			
Net underclaim	X	Net overclaim	X
Bad debt relief	X		
Other adjustments			
		Partial exemption	X
Capital goods	X	Capital goods	
		Own use	X
Less: Credit notes received	X	Less: Credit notes issued	X
Total tax deductible	X	Total tax payable	X
		Less total tax deductible	X
		Payable to Customs and Excise	X

A worked example

Thompson Brothers Ltd
1 April 19Z5 to 30 June 19Z5

VAT deductible – input tax		VAT payable – output tax	
VAT on purchases		VAT on sales	
April	525	April	875
May	350	May	1,750
June	350	June	88

Other adjustments			
Less: Credit notes received	15	Less: Credit notes issued	108
Total tax deductible	1,210	Total tax payable	2,605
		Less total tax deductible	1,210
		Payable to Customs and Excise	1,395

These details would be entered on the VAT returns as follows.

H M Customs and Excise

Value Added Tax Return

For the period
01-04-X5 to 30-06-X5

010 666 1589 15 W022

THOMPSON BROTHERS LTD
THE GLADE
FOX'S BANK LANE
WHISTON
L35 3ST

Your VAT Office telephone number is 071-928 3344

For Official Use

Registration Number	Period
010 666 1589 15	30.06.X5

You could be liable to a financial penalty if your completed return and all the VAT payable are not received by the due date.

Due date: 31-07-X5

For Official Use

REMEMBER

You must Include VAT due on EC transactions in boxes 2 & 3 if they occur on or after 1.1.93.

If you are using Retail Scheme B1, D or J, please remember to carry out your annual adjustment at the appropriate time.

Before you fill in this form please read the notes on the back and the VAT Leaflet *"Filling in your VAT return"*. Complete all boxes clearly in ink, writing 'none' where necessary. Don't put a dash or leave any box blank. If there are no pence write **"00"** in the pence column. **Do not** enter more than one amount in any box.

For official use			£	p
	VAT due in this period on **sales** and other outputs	**1**	2,605	
	VAT reclaimed in this period on **acquisitions** from other **EC Member States**	**2**	1,210	
	Total VAT due (**the sum of boxes 1 and 2**)	**3**	1,395	
	VAT reclaimed in this period on purchases on purchases and other inputs (including acquisitions from the EC)	**4**	14,885	
	Net VAT to be paid to Customs or reclaimed by you **(Difference between boxes 3 and 4)**	**5**	6,914	
	Total value of **sales** and all other outputs excluding any VAT. **Include your box 8 figure**	**6**		00
	Total value of **purchases** and all other inputs excluding any VAT. **Include your box 9 figure**	**7**		00
	Total value of all **Supplies** of goods and related services, excluding any VAT, to other **EC Member States**	**8**		00
	Total value of all **acquisitions** of goods and related services, excluding any VAT, from other **EC Member States**	**9**		00

Retail schemes. If you have used any of the schemes in the period covered by this return please enter the appropriate letter(s) in this box.

If you are enclosing a payment please tick this box.

DECLARATION : You, or someone on your behalf, must sign below.

I, JOE THOMPSON .... declare that the
(Full name of signatory in BLOCK LETTERS)

information given above is true and complete.

Signature ... J Thompson ...... Date 19 JULY 19 X5

A false declaration can result in prosecution.

B

CD 2859/N9(02/91)   F 3790(JANUARY 1992)CD 2859/R/N9(02/91)

VAT 100

QUESTIONS

1   Panther

You are preparing the VAT return for Panther Alarms Ltd and you must first identify the sources of information for the VAT account.

Suggest the best sources of information for the following figures:

(a)   Sales
(b)   Credit notes issued
(c)   Purchases
(d)   Credit notes received
(e)   Capital goods sold
(f)   Capital goods purchased
(g)   Goods taken from business for own use
(h)   Bad debt relief

2   Mr Brown

Mr Brown, a self-employed builder, has telephoned your firm with some queries regarding his VAT. Please draft the main body of the letter in reply explaining what documents he must keep, and for how long, to comply with the regulations. Also he wants to know whether he can reclaim the VAT on the deposit he has paid for his new business car.

SUMMARY

In this session we looked at how to complete a VAT return form quarterly for HM Customs and Excise. We identified input and output tax and listed the items where a business cannot claim all of the input tax. We also looked at businesses which import and export.

The main objective for this session was to feel confident about completing a VAT return, identifying the relevant inputs and outputs and entering them correctly.

Review of Module Two

You have now completed the second and final module of the Study Pack.

In this module, you have covered the following:

- accounting concepts and principles and accounting standards

- the preparation of accounts from incomplete records

- preparing VAT returns

This module has concentrated on Element 5.2 *Prepare accounts from incomplete records* and Unit 8 *Prepare VAT returns*. You should now have all the knowledge and understanding that you need to meet the competences required for both Unit 5 and Unit 8.

The ability to prepare accounts from incomplete records tests your understanding of double-entry and accounting techniques. It is essential that you practise all the techniques used (including the use of control accounts and cash books) and that you are familiar with the calculation of gross profit percentages, mark-ups and cost structures.

Assessments will test your numerical accounting skills but you should remember that communication skills are equally important. You must be able to explain accounting principles and concepts in such a way that a non-accountant can understand them; your ability to do this will be tested in the Central Assessment. Attempting practice questions should help you to be aware of the practical implications of accounting principles and accounting concepts. You need to understand these aspects of your studies rather than merely learning by rote.

Answers

SESSION 1

1   G Brown

Trading and profit and loss account for the year ended 31 May 19X6

		£	£	£
Sales				96,450
Less:	Cost of goods sold			
	Opening stock		23,500	
	Purchases	73,180		
Less:	Returns outwards	(1,105)		
Add:	Carriage inwards	560		
			72,635	
			96,135	
Less:	Closing stock		(25,350)	
Cost of goods sold				(70,785)
Gross profit				25,665
Less:	Expenses			
	Carriage outwards		1,850	
	Wages and salaries		11,250	
	Rent and rates		6,050	
	Communication expenses		352	
	Insurance		820	
	Sundry expenses		318	
				(20,640)
Net profit				5,025

G Brown
Balance sheet as at 31 May 19X6

	Cost £	£	Net book value £
Assets employed			
Fixed assets			
Buildings	25,000		25,000
Fixtures	3,500		3,500
Motor vehicles	12,000		12,000
	40,500		40,500
Current assets			
Stock		25,350	
Debtors		14,320	
Cash at bank		3,500	
Cash in hand		150	
		43,320	
Less current liabilities			
Creditors		12,295	
Net working capital			31,025
			71,525
Financed by			
Capital		65,000	
Add: Profit for the period	5,025		
Less: Drawings	(8,500)	(3,475)	
			61,525
Long-term liabilities (**Note**)			
Loan – C Green			10,000
			71,525

Note

G Brown's business as at 31 May had assets worth £71,525. These assets were financed by capital from two sources. The first was the usual capital provided by the owner, G Brown. The second source of capital was in the form of a loan of £10,000 from C Green.

Loan capital (capital provided by anyone other than the owner) is always recorded under the heading of **long-term liabilities**, which may be found beneath the capital section in the balance sheet (alternatively they may be deducted from the net assets section).

2   Jason Sarmiento

MEMORANDUM

To: Jason Sarmiento   **Date:**

From:

Subject: Adaptation of the accounting system to cope with the diversification of the business

___

I have been considering the way in which we will have to adapt our accounting system to include manufacturing and selling of both futons and sofabeds.

It will be necessary to increase the number of trading accounts to allow for the analysis into two products: eg. Sales a/c (futons) and Sales a/c (sofabeds). The same will apply to the materials a/c, Production Wages a/c and Stock a/c. It may be better to provide analysis columns within the accounts.

A system will also have to be in place to analyse purchase invoices for materials into the two categories and, if the assembler is to work on both products, a time-recording system to allow for the apportionment of production wages will be needed.

A system may be developed to apportion some of the overheads between the two products, if required.

3   Abdul Mohim

MEMORANDUM

To: Abdul Mohim

From:

Subject: Profitability comparisons   **Date:** 3 December

___

It should be possible to set up our computerised system to compare the profitability of the four categories of product.

From the computer system's point of view it would mean four sales accounts, four purchases accounts, four stock accounts – one for each category of product. It may also be possible to analyse some of the overheads between products, but I doubt this.

It will also be necessary to re-draft our trading, profit and loss account.

From a practical point of view, it is essential that we are clear which products we include in each category. It may be a good idea to devote different areas of the warehouse to different categories of product.

Finally, it is essential that everyone is aware of the new system since all sales and purchases will in future have to be analysed into the four categories and not be treated globally.

SESSION 2

1   (8/12 × £6,000) = £4,000

2

Insurance

	£		£
Balance b/f	400	Profit and loss account	1,300
Cash	1,200	Balance c/f	300
	1,600		1,600

The prepayment is the amount carried forward.

3

Rent and rates expense

	£		£
Balance b/f	20	Balance b/f	100
Cash	840	Profit and loss account	850
Balance c/f	120	Balance c/f	30
	980		980

4   (a)   **Note:** This question is concerned with rent receivable (ie. income).

Rent receivable

	£		£
Trading and profit and loss a/c	500	Cash	1,000
Balance c/f	500		
	1,000		1,000
		Balance b/f	500

(b)

Rent receivable

	£		£
Trading and profit and loss a/c	400	Balance c/f	400
	400		400
Balance b/f	400		

5   Payment received in advance. Treated as a current liability in the end of year accounts. In 1994 it will be part of income.

6 (a) Yes

(b) Based on one third of last year's second quarter bill, uprated by any increase of this year's first quarter bill over last

7 (a) Dr Personal a/c
Cr Sundry Income a/c (or any other sensible account name)

On payment:

Dr Bank
Cr Personal a/c

(b) A sundry debtor

- revenue in the Profit and Loss a/c
- current asset in the Balance Sheet

8 Accruals and prepayments

MEMORANDUM

To: Mary Bassingham

From:

Subject: Accruals and prepayments   **Date:** 9 June 1993

This proposal is not allowed. The accruals (matching) concept, enshrined in SSAP2 requires that the revenues and costs relating to a period are matched with one another within the profit and loss account.

From the revenue point of view, this represents the revenue earned (normally invoices issued) *not* the cash received.

Therefore, from a cost point of view, we require the cost used *not* the cash paid.

If cash paid out were subtracted from cash received, the profitability would be distorted, probably very significantly. For instance, the cost of an expensive new fixed asset which would be of service for many years would be part of the year's payment. Similarly, money borrowed as a long-term loan would be part of the receipts. There are many other examples where receipts do not represent earnings and payments do not represent costs incurred in relation to that year's operations.

9   Wally

Rent payable account

	£		£
Cash (3 quarters at £1,500)	4,500	Trading and profit and loss a/c	6,000
Accrued expense c/f	1,500		
	6,000		6,000
		Balance b/f	1,500

Rent receivable account

	£		£
Balance b/f (amount due from Tony)	450	Balance b/f (amount prepaid by Gregory)	300
Trading and profit and loss a/c	3,000	Cash – Tony	900
Balance c/f	450	Cash – Tony	450
		Cash – Tony	450
		Cash – Tony	900
		Cash – Gregory	600
		Balance c/f	300
	3,900		3,900
Balance b/f (amount due from Gregory)	300	Balance b/f (amount prepaid by Tony)	1,500

10   Hayward

Rent receivable

	£		£
Balance b/f	17,100	Balance b/f	10,350
Trading and profit and loss a/c	120,600	Cash received	114,750
Balance c/f	7,650	Balance c/f	20,250
	145,350		145,350
Balance b/f	20,250	Balance b/f	7,650

Interest payable

	£		£
Balance b/f	1,750	Balance b/f	4,900
Cash paid	28,700	Trading and profit and loss a/c	26,250
Balance c/f	3,500	Balance c/f	2,800
	33,950		33,950
Balance b/f	2,800	Balance b/f	3,500

11 A Metro

Motor tax and insurance

		£			£
Balance b/f		570	Trading and profit and loss		
Cash:	1 April	420	account (W2)		2,205
	1 May	1,770	Balance c/f (W1)		835
	1 July	280			
		3,040			3,040
Balance b/f		835			

Workings

(1) Prepayment at the end of the year

	£
Motor tax on 6 vans paid 1 April 19X0 3/12 × £420	105
Insurance on 10 vans paid 1 May 19X0 4/12 × £1,770	590
Motor tax on 4 vans paid 1 July 19X0 6/12 × £280	140
	835

(2) Profit and loss charge for the year

There is no need to calculate this as it is the balancing figure, but it could be calculated as:

	£
Prepayment	570
Motor tax 9/12 × £420	315
Insurance 8/12 × £1,770	1,180
Motor tax 6/12 × £280	140
	2,205

12 Maisey Hemmery

(a)

Electricity account

	£		£
Cash	150	Balance b/f	40
Balance c/f	60	Trading and profit and loss a/c	
		(150 − 40) + (1/4 × £240)	170
	210		210
		Balance b/f (1/4 × £240)	60

(b)
Rates account

	£		£
Balance b/f	100	Trading and profit and loss a/c	400
Cash	400	Balance c/f	100
	——		——
	500		500
	——		——
Balance b/f	100		

(c)
Bank interest account

	£		£
Cash	20	Balance b/f	20
Cash	25	Trading and profit and loss a/c	130
Cash	30		
Cash	35		
Balance c/f	40		
	——		——
	150		150
	——		——
		Balance b/f	40

(d)
Ground rent account

	£		£
Balance c/f	115	Trading and profit and loss a/c	30
		Balance c/f	85
	——		——
	115		115
	——		——
Balance b/f	85		

(e)
Assistant's wages account

	£		£
Cash	500	Balance b/f	60
Balance c/f	30	Trading and profit and loss a/c	470
	——		——
	530		530
	——		——
		Balance b/f	30

SESSION 3

1 **(a)** To allow for bad debts which the company expects to suffer during the succeeding year, but which cannot yet be attributed to a specific debtor.

    (b) Deducted from debtors balance. To accurately reflect the 'true' position in line with the prudence concept (ie. some debtors will not pay).

2   A retail shop has no debtors, all sales being either cash sales or cash with order.

3   Dr   Customer a/c (and Total Debtors a/c)
    Cr   Bad Debts a/c (or Bad Debts Recovered a/c)
    Dr   Bank a/c
    Cr   Customer a/c (and Total Debtors a/c).

4   **Mr Green**

Debtors' accounts

X Ltd account

	£		£
1.1.X6 Balance b/f	150	31.12.X6 Bad debts expense a/c	150
	150		150

PQ & Co

	£		£
31.12.X6 Balance b/f	50	31.12.X6 Bad debts expense a/c	50
	50		50

Provision for doubtful debts account

	£		£
31.12.X6 Balance c/f	350	1.1.X6 Balance b/f	300
		31.12.X6 Bad debts expense a/c	50
	350		350

Note: Balance carried forward at 31 December is:

	£
A & Co	150
Mr Z	200
	350

Bad debts expense account

	£		£
31.12.X6 PQ & Co	50	31.12.X6 Trading and profit	
31.12.X6 X Ltd	150	and loss account	250
31.12.X6 Provision for doubtful debts	50		
	250		250

5 DD Co

Provision for doubtful debts account

	£		£
Bad debts expense	80	Balance b/f	1,680
Balance c/f	1,600		
	1,680		1,680

Note: The provision required at 31 December 19X5 is calculated by taking 5% of the total debtors at 31 December 19X5 (ie. 5% × £32,000 = £1,600). As there is already a provision of £1,680, there will be a release of the provision of £80.

Bad debts expense account

	£		£
Debtors	1,950	Provision for doubtful debts	80
		Trading and profit and loss a/c	1,870
	1,950		1,950

6 Geoff

Provision for doubtful debts account

	£		£
Balance c/f 10% × 140,000	14,000	Balance b/f	10,000
		Bad debts a/c	4,000
	14,000		14,000

Bad debts expense

	£		£
Provision for doubtful debts	4,000	Profit and loss account	5,000
Bad debts written off	1,000		
	5,000		5,000

Note: Since the bad debt balance appears in the trial balance, debtors must already have been adjusted.

7   Peter

Provision for doubtful debts account

	£		£
Bad debts account	98	Balance b/f	1,490
Balance c/f			
Specific	800		
General 1% × (61,000 –			
1,000 – 800)	592		
	1,490		1,490

Bad debts expense

	£		£
Bad debts written off	1,000	Provision for doubtful debts	98
		Profit and loss account	902
	1,000		1,000

8 **Jason Sarmiento**

MEMORANDUM

To: Jason Sarmiento

From:

Subject: Bad debt, doubtful debt and provision	**Date:**

In an attempt to clarify the difference between bad and doubtful debts and to explain the position regarding provisions, I have prepared the following outlines:

Bad debts:

– Those debts that we have decided are totally uncollectable (eg. a bankrupt debtor).

Doubtful debts:

– Specific doubtful debts are those debts that we think will become uncollectable.

– General doubtful debts are where we know that a percentage of debtors become bad debts but we cannot identify the specific debts.

Provision:

– An example of the prudence concept where allowance is made for a possible future loss. Thus the debtor's balance is reduced by the doubtful debts which we predict.

From the evidence available, it appears that Futon Enterprises has few long-term debtors and little experience of bad debts. Therefore, a general provision for doubtful debts would seem to be unnecessary. Specific long-term debtors may be identifiable as doubtful debts so a provision could possibly be allowed for those (eg. more than six months overdue).

SESSION 4

1

	£
Revised market value	100
Less: Additional cost	36
Net realisable value	64

Net realisable value is less than historic cost of £96, so £64 should be the valuation. This will result in neither profit nor loss in the next accounting period when the futons are sold. Total stock value reduced by £32.

2 (a) Purchases a/c

(b) Dr Purchases a/c
Cr Office expenses a/c

---

3   (a)   Closing stock valuation would have to be reduced by (£3 × 4) = £12, stock being valued at cost or net realisable value, whichever is the lower (in this case, market value).

              (b)   This would reduce profit by £12

4   No accounting entries have to be made since no transaction (in this case a sale) has yet occurred. It is merely the location of the stock which is altered; its ownership is unchanged.

5   **Edgar**

Total tons purchased	234
Sales	168
Closing stock	66

              (a)   FIFO

Assuming that the oldest stocks are always sold first, the closing stock will be valued at:

Tons	Date of purchase	Unit price £	£
24	10 December	50.00	1,200
28	29 November	37.50	1,050
14	15 October	35.20	493
66			2,743

              (b)   LIFO

Assuming that at each date of sale the latest stocks are sold, the goods sold on 10 October will have been purchased:

49 on 30 September
42 on 12 August
9 on 1 July

100

The goods sold on 31 December will have been purchased:

24 on 10 December
28 on 29 November
16 on 15 October

68

The closing stock will be valued at:

Tons	Date of purchase	Unit price £	£
19 (35 – 16)	15 October	35.20	669
47 (56 – 9)	1 July	20.50	963
66			1,632

6 Sally

Closing stock is an asset in the balance sheet and is deducted from cost of sales (and hence added to profit) in the profit and loss account. An increase of stock from £8,500 to £9,200 would therefore increase assets and profit by £700 (= £9,200 – £8,500).

7 Karen

Stock is valued at the lower of cost and net realisable value (costs to be incurred in selling stock are deducted from selling price in computing NRV).

	Cost £	Price less commission £	Lower of cost and NRV £
A	1,200	1,425	1,200
B	6,200	5,795	5,795
C	920	884	884
			7,879

8 John

Stock account

	£		£
31.12.X6 Trading and profit and loss account	20,000	31.12.X6 Balance c/f	20,000
	20,000		20,000
1.1.X7 Balance b/f	20,000	31.12.X7 Balance c/f	20,000
31.12.X7 Trading and profit and loss account (closing stock)	38,000	1.1.X7 Trading and profit and loss account (opening stock)	38,000
	58,000		58,000
1.1.X8 Balance b/f	38,000		

SESSION 5

1   Rugg

Extended trial balance at 31 December 19X0

	Trial balance Dr £	Trial balance Cr £	Adjustments Dr £	Adjustments Cr £	P & L account Dr £	P & L account Cr £	Balance sheet Dr £	Balance sheet Cr £
Capital 1 January		2,377						2,377
Rent	500		100		600			
Stock 1 January	510				510			
Rates	240			90	150			
Insurance	120				120			
Wages	1,634			120	1,514			
Debtors	672			37			635	
Sales		15,542				15,542		
Repairs	635		27		662			
Purchases	9,876		72	63	9,885			
Discounts		129				129		
Drawings	1,200		63				1,383	
			120					
Petty cash	5						5	
Bank balance	763						763	
Vehicles	1,740						1,740	
Fixtures	829						829	
Depreciation provision – Vehicles		435		435				870
– Fixtures		166		166				332
Travel	192				192			
Creditors		700						700
Sundry expenses	433			27)	334			
				72)				
c/f	19,349	19,349	382	1,010	13,967	15,671	5,355	4,279

Cont'd . . .

Extended trial balance at 31 December 19X0 (continued)

	Trial balance Dr £	Trial balance Cr £	Adjustments Dr £	Adjustments Cr £	P & L account Dr £	P & L account Cr £	Balance sheet Dr £	Balance sheet Cr £
b/f	19,349	19,349	382	1,010	13,967	15,671	5,355	4,279
Depreciation expense – Vehicles			435		435			
– Fixtures			166		166			
Stock 31 December – Balance sheet			647				647	
– P & L account				647		647		
Bad debts expense			37		37			
Accruals				100				100
Prepayments			90				90	
					14,605			
Profit for the year					1,713			1,713
	19,349	19,349	1,757	1,757	16,318	16,318	6,092	6,092

2 Hick

Extended trial balance at 31 December 19X6

	Trial balance Dr £	Trial balance Cr £	Adjustments Dr £	Adjustments Cr £	P & L account Dr £	P & L account Cr £	Balance sheet Dr £	Balance sheet Cr £
Fittings	7,300						7,300	
Provision for depreciation 1.1.X6		2,500		400				2,900
Leasehold	30,000						30,000	
Provision for depreciation 1.1.X6		6,000		1,000				7,000
Stock 1 January 19X6	15,000		21,000	21,000	15,000	21,000	21,000	
Debtors	10,000						9,500	
Provision for doubtful debts 1.1.X6		800	515	500				285
Cash in hand	50						50	
Cash at bank	1,250						1,250	
Creditors		18,000						18,000
Capital		19,050						19,050
Drawings	4,750		1,200				5,950	
Purchases	80,000			1,200	78,800			
Sales		120,000				120,000		
Wages	12,000			200	11,800			
Advertising	4,000		200		4,200			
Rates	1,800			360	1,440			
Charges	200				200			
Depreciation – Fittings			400		400			
Depreciation – Lease			1,000		1,000			
Bad debts expense			500	515		15		
Prepayments			360				360	
					112,840			
Net profit					28,175			28,175
	166,350	166,350	25,175	25,175	141,015	141,015	75,410	75,410

3 Michael

(a) Extended trial balance at 31 December 19X0

	Trial balance Dr £	Trial balance Cr £	Adjustments Dr £	Adjustments Cr £	P & L account Dr £	P & L account Cr £	Balance sheet Dr £	Balance sheet Cr £
Capital account		30,000						30,000
Freehold factory	20,000						20,000	
Plant and machinery	4,800						4,800	
Cars	2,600						2,600	
Depreciation								
Factory		1,920		320				2,240
Plant and machinery		1,600		480				2,080
Cars		1,200		650				1,850
Stock	8,900		10,800	10,800	8,900	10,800	10,800	
Debtors	3,600			60			3,540	
Creditors		4,200						4,200
Provision for doubtful debts		280	60					220
Purchases	36,600				36,600			
Wages and salaries	19,800			3,000	16,800			
Rates and insurance	1,510			260	1,250			
Sundry expenses	1,500		120		1,620			
Motor expenses	400		600		1,000			
Sales		72,000				72,000		
Bank balance	11,490						11,490	
c/f	111,200	111,200	11,580	15,570	66,170	82,800	53,230	40,590

Continued on next page

	Trial balance		Adjustments		P & L account		Balance sheet	
	Dr £	Cr £	Dr £	Cr £	Dr £	Cr £	Dr £	Cr £
b/f	111,200	111,200	11,580	15,570	66,170	82,800	53,230	40,590
Bad debts expense			60	60				
Drawings			2,400				2,400	
Depreciation								
Factory			320		320			
Plant and machinery			480		480			
Cars			650		650			
Accruals				120				120
Prepayments			260				260	
					67,620	82,800	55,890	40,710
Net profit					15,180			15,180
	111,200	111,200	15,750	15,750	82,800	82,800	55,890	55,890

(b)   **Trading and profit and loss account for the year ended 31 December 19X0**

	£	£
Sales		72,000
Stock 1 January 19X0	8,900	
Purchases	36,600	
	45,500	
Less: Stock 31 December 19X0	(10,800)	
Cost of goods sold		(34,700)
Gross profit		37,300
Salaries and wages	16,800	
Rates and insurance	1,250	
Motor expenses	1,000	
Depreciation	1,450	
Sundry expenses	1,620	
		(22,120)
Net profit		15,180

Balance sheet at 31 December 19X0

	Cost £	Depreciation £	£
Fixed assets			
Freehold factory	20,000	2,240	17,760
Plant, etc.	4,800	2,080	2,720
Cars	2,600	1,850	750
	27,400	6,170	21,230
Current assets			
Stocks at cost		10,800	
Debtors, less provision and			
prepayments		3,580	
Bank balance		11,490	
		25,870	
Current liabilities			
Trade creditors	4,200		
Accrued charges	120		
		4,320	
			21,550
			42,780

Financed by

	£
Proprietor's interest	
Capital 1 January 19X0	30,000
Profit	15,180
	45,180
Less: Drawings	(2,400)
	42,780

SESSION 6

1   Colin

Correct entry was to **credit** purchases returns account with £8,260. To correct, Cr purchases returns with £8,260 + £8,620 = £16,880. Dr goes to suspense account, as the original entry will have created a suspense account balance by putting the accounts out of balance.

2   Chris

	£
Balance per bank statement (overdrawn)	(1,400)
Unpresented cheques	(800)
Uncleared lodgements	500
	(1,700)
Charges not entered in cash book	(40)
Balance per cash book	1,660

In preparing the TB the following entries have been omitted:

Dr	Bank charges	40	
Cr	Cash (800 – 500)		300

Each of these missing entries will affect the suspense account, so the net effect is:

Dr	Suspense	260

The full journal entry is therefore:

Dr	Bank charges	40	
	Suspense	260	
Cr	Cash		300

3   GA

The corrections would be:

			Dr £	Cr £
1	**Debit** Debtors		10	
	Credit Suspense account			10

being correction of undercast in debtor's account.

			Dr £	Cr £
2	**Debit** Carriage on sales		4	
	Credit Carriage on purchases			4

being correction of wrong posting.

			Dr £	Cr £
3	**Debit** Creditors		17	
	Credit Suspense account			17

being correction of omitted entry.

			Dr £	Cr £
4	**Debit** Drawings		35	
	Credit Sundry expenses			35

being payment for private expenses.

			Dr £	Cr £
5	**Debit** Postage and telephone		9	
	Credit Suspense account			9

being correction of transposition error.

Suspense account (not required)

	£		£
Difference per trial balance	36	Debtors	10
		Creditors	17
		Postage	9
	36		36

Trial balance after adjustments

	Dr £	Cr £
Petty cash	20	
Capital		1,596
Drawings	1,435	
Sales		20,607
Purchases	15,486	
Purchases returns		210
Stock at 1 January 19X4	2,107	
Fixtures and fittings	710	
Sundry debtors	1,829	
Sundry creditors		2,061
Carriage on purchases	105	
Carriage on sales	188	
Rent and rates	460	
Light and heat	75	
Postage and telephone	100	
Sundry expenses	155	
Cash at bank	1,804	
	24,474	24,474

4   Sylvia Smith

MEMORANDUM

To: Sylvia Smith

From:

Subject: Suspense accounts   **Date:** 3 December

In a manual system a suspense account has two uses.

Firstly, you are not quite correct when you say that the nominal ledger account for posting should always be known. There may be some doubt where to post a particular transaction, so, to try to keep the accounts in balance and up to date, a transaction may be posted to Suspense a/c pending future decision.

However, the more usual use of a Suspense a/c is when a trial balance is taken out. If the trial balance does not balance, which is quite possible in a manual system, but not in a computer system, the amount of the imbalance is normally entered into the Suspense a/c. As errors in the double-entry postings are discovered, these are corrected with entries being made to Suspense a/c where appropriate. After correction of all the errors, the balance on Suspense a/c should have disappeared.

5   Kidditoys

JOURNAL ENTRIES	Dr £	Cr £
(i) Dr Suspense a/c	1,908	
Cr T Ditton a/c (purchase ledger)		1,908
Being correction of misposting of purchases. Goods purchased from T Ditton originally debited to supplier		
(iii) Dr Suspense a/c	50	
Cr Shop fittings (cost) a/c		3,240
Dr Shop fittings (provision for dep'n) a/c	1,944	
Dr Loss of sale of fixed assets	1,246	
Dr Shop fittings (cost) a/c	9,620	
Cr Kingston Displays Ltd a/c (purchase ledger)		9,620
Being disposal of old shop fittings and purchase of replacements		
(iii) Dr Drawings a/c	24,000	
Cr Wages a/c		24,000
Being transfer of 'wages' of owner to Drawings a/c		
(iv) Dr E Molesey a/c (purchase ledger)	3	
Cr Discount received a/c		3
Being discount received from E Molesey after accidental underpayment		
(v) Dr Drawings a/c	640	
Cr. Sales a/c		545
Cr VAT a/c		95
Being withdrawal of stock for own use		
(vi) Dr Bank current a/c	9	
Cr Interest received a/c		9
Being interest received on current account for November		

KIDDITOYS – EXTENDED TRIAL BALANCE

	Ledger Balances Dr £	Ledger Balances Cr £	Adjustments Dr £	Adjustments Cr £	Profit and Loss a/c Dr £	Profit and Loss a/c Cr £	Balance Sheet Balances Dr £	Balance Sheet Balances Cr £
Sales		392,727						
Sales returns	1,214							
Purchases	208,217							
Purchase returns		643						
Stock	32,165		21,060	21,060				
Wages	26,000							
Rent	27,300			2,100				
Rates	8,460			2,080				
Light and heat	2,425		212					
Office expenses	3,162							
Selling expenses	14,112							
Motor expenses	14,728							
Sundry expenses	6,560							
Motor vans (cost)	12,640							
Motor vans (provision for depreciation)		2,528		2,528				
Shop fittings (cost)	9,620							
Shop fittings (provision for depreciation)				962				
Office equipment (cost)	4,250							
Office equipment (provision for depreciation)		2,550		850				
Cash	100							
Bank current account	4,429							
Bank investment account	68,340							
Interest received		3,289						
Capital		22,145						
VAT		6,515						
Purchase ledger total		29,588						
Loss on sale of fixed assets	1,246							
Kingston Displays Ltd		9,620						
Drawings	24,640							
Discount received		3						
Depreciation (motor vans)			2,528					
Depreciation (shop fittings)			962					
Depreciation (office equipment)			850					
Prepayments			2,100 / 2,080					
Accruals				212				
	469,608	469,608	29,792	29,792				

SESSION 7

1   Warren, Hall and Oates

(a)   The appropriation scheme is as follows:

(1)   The partners are allowed interest on capitals at 13% per annum.

(2)   Salaries are to be appropriated to the partners as follows:

Warren	£6,000
Hall	£7,000
Oates	£7,000

(3)   The balance of profits is to be shared in the ratio 4:3:1 respectively, ie:

Warren	4/8
Hall	3/8
Oates	1/8

(4)   No interest is to be charged on drawings.

(b)   The net profit for the year was £60,002. This can be calculated by adding up the amounts appropriated to each of the partners as follows.

	Warren £	Hall £	Oates £	Total £
Interest on capital	5,200	4,940	4,550	14,690
Salary	6,000	7,000	7,000	20,000
Share of balance	12,656	9,492	3,164	25,312
	23,856	21,432	14,714	60,002

(c)   The net profit of £60,002 would have been divided equally between the three partners, ie. £20,000.67 to each partner.

(d)   (i)

	Warren £	Hall £	Oates £	Total £
Interest on capital	5,200	4,940	4,550	14,690
Salary	6,000	7,000	7,000	20,000
Share of balance	20,155	15,116	5,039	40,310
	31,355	27,056	16,589	75,000

(ii)   The preferential appropriation (ie. interest on capitals and salaries) would still have been allowed in full. These, however, total £34,690. There is therefore a negative balance of £4,690 (£30,000 less than £34,690) which would be charged to the partners in their profit-sharing ratio, thus:

	Warren £	Hall £	Oates £	Total £
Interest on capital	5,200	4,940	4,550	14,690
Salary	6,000	7,000	7,000	20,000
Share of balance	(2,345)	(1,759)	(586)	(4,690)
	8,855	10,181	10,964	30,000

2 Alf, Ben, Connie and Dora

(a)   (i)   Each partner's share of profits will be £14,000, that is:

$$\frac{£56,000}{4}$$

(ii)   Each partner's share of profits will be :

			£
Alf	(4/10th of £56,000)	=	22,400
Ben	(3/10th of £56,000)	=	16,800
Connie	(2/10th of £56,000)	=	11,200
Dora	(1/10th of £56,000)	=	5,600
			56,000

(iii)   Each partner's share of profits will be:

	Alf £	Ben £	Connie £	Dora £	Total £
Interest on capital	4,500	3,000	2,000	1,500	11,000
Share of balance	18,000	13,500	9,000	4,500	45,000
	22,500	16,500	11,000	6,000	56,000

(iv)   Here the profit of £56,000 will be shared thus:

	Alf £	Ben £	Connie £	Dora £	Total £
Interest on capital	4,500	3,000	2,000	1,500	11,000
Salary	–	–	5,000	5,000	10,000
Share of balance	14,000	10,500	7,000	3,500	35,000
	18,500	13,500	14,000	10,000	56,000

(b)

Appropriation account
for the year ended 31 October 19X5

Net profit					£56,000

Appropriated thus:

	Alf £	Ben £	Connie £	Dora £	Total £
Interest on capital	4,500	3,000	2,000	1,500	11,000
Salary	–	–	5,000	5,000	10,000
Share of balance	14,000	10,500	7,000	3,500	35,000
	18,500	13,500	14,000	10,000	56,000

(c)

Alf – Current account

19X4		£	19X4		£
	Drawings	18,000	1 Nov	Balance b/f	104
19X5			19X5		
31 Oct	Balance c/f	604	31 Oct	Interest on capital	4,500
			31 Oct	Salary	–
			31 Oct	Share of profits	14,000
		18,604			18,604

Ben – Current account

19X4		£	19X4		£
	Drawings	13,300	1 Nov	Balance b/f	270
19X5			19X5		
31 Oct	Balance c/f	470	31 Oct	Interest on capital	3,000
			31 Oct	Salary	–
			31 Oct	Share of profits	10,500
		13,770			13,770

Connie – Current account

19X4		£	19X4		£
	Drawings	14,500	1 Nov	Balance b/f	614
19X5			19X5		
31 Oct	Balance c/f	114	31 Oct	Interest on capital	2,000
			31 Oct	Salary	5,000
			31 Oct	Share of profits	7,000
		14,614			14,614

Dora – Current account

19X4		£	19X4		£
	Drawings	10,200	1 Nov	Balance b/f	317
19X5			19X5		
31 Oct	Balance c/f	117	31 Oct	Interest on capital	1,500
			31 Oct	Salary	5,000
			31 Oct	Share of profits	3,500
		10,317			10,317

3   Futon Enterprises

FUTON ENTERPRISES

JOURNAL ENTRIES	Dr £	Cr £
(i) Delivery vans (cost)	12,400	
Suspense		10,000
Delivery vans (cost)		12,000
Delivery vans (depreciation provision)	7,884	
Loss on disposal of delivery van	1,716	
Being purchase of delivery van and disposal of similar in part-exchange		
(ii) Furniture and fittings (cost)	240	
Production wages		240
Being time spent by assembler on improving fixed asset		
Note: Consideration will be given to candidates who consider the amount to be immaterial.		
(iii) Dr Drawings	168	
Cr Sales ledger total		168
Being the withdrawal of two futons by S Crane for own use		
Note: The personal account in the sales ledger will also have to be credited.		
(A figure of £197.40 which includes VAT at 17.5% is also acceptable.)		

FUTON ENTERPRISES – EXTENDED TRIAL BALANCE

	Ledger Balances		Adjustments		Profit and Loss a/c		Balance Sheet Balances	
	Dr £	Cr £	Dr £	Cr £	Dr £	Cr £	Dr £	Cr £
Delivery vans (cost)	12,400						12,400	
Delivery vans (depreciation provision)				3,720				3,720
Assembling machinery (cost)	3,650						3,650	
Assembling machinery (depreciation provision)		1,095		365				1,460
Furniture and fittings (cost)	11,030						11,030	
Furniture and fittings (depreciation provision)		5,730		2,206				7,936
Raw materials (stock)	1,320		1,526	1,526	1,320	1,526	1,526	
Finished goods (stock)	1,440		1,104	1,104	1,440	1,104	1,104	
Sales ledger total	1,692			168*			1,524	
Bank		320						320
Cash	50						50	
Purchase ledger total		4,265						4,265
Sales		120,240				120,240		
Materials	35,465				35,465			
Production wages	12,240				12,240			
Driver's wages	11,785				11,785			
Salaries	22,460				22,460			
Employer's NI	4,365				4,365			
Motor expenses	2,160			114	2,046			
Rent	3,930			786	3,144			
Sundry expenses	3,480		60		3,540			
VAT		1,220						1,220
Inland Revenue		1,365						1,365
Drawings	12,568						12,568	
Capital		7,516						7,516
Depreciation delivery vans	1,716				1,716			
Depreciation assembling machinery			3,720		3,720			
Depreciation furniture and fittings			365		365			
Accruals			2,206		2,206			
Prepayments			114				114	
Mercury Insurance Co			786				786	
Bad debts			168*		168			
Profit				60	16,890			16,890
	141,751	141,751	10,049	10,049	122,870	122,870	44,752	44,752

* A figure of £197.40 which includes VAT at 17.5% is also acceptable.

4   Punch

Manufacturing account for the year ended 31 March 19X1

	£	£
Raw materials consumed		
Opening stock	12,725	
Purchases	82,550	
	95,275	
Less: Closing stock	(9,650)	
		85,625
Factory wages		64,750
Prime cost		150,375
Factory overheads		
Rent (W4) (70%)	20,038	
Repairs to buildings (80%)	4,400	
Depreciation – Plant and machinery (W1)	3,650	
– Buildings (80%)	720	
Electricity and power (W2)	12,373	
		41,181
Opening WIP	18,000	
Closing WIP	(21,000)	
		(3,000)
Factory cost of goods produced		188,556

Trading and profit and loss account for the year ended 31 March 19X1

		£	£
Sales			362,720
Less:	Cost of goods sold		
	Opening stock	20,500	
	Transfers from factory	188,556	
		209,056	
Closing stock		(24,500)	
			(184,556)
Gross profit			178,164
Less:	Selling and distribution expenses		
	Wages	26,920	
	Selling expenses (22,000 + 60% × 240)	22,144	
	Bad and doubtful debts (700 + 354) (W3)	1,054	
	Depreciation of motor vans	4,950	
	Sales manager's commission (W5)	20,516	
			(75,584)
Less:	Administration expenses		
	Wages	24,360	
	Electricity and power (W2)	6,187	
	Rent (30%) (W4)	8,587	
	Repairs to buildings (20%)	1,100	
	Depreciation buildings (20%)	180	
	Sundry (850 + 5,900 + 40% × 240)	6,846	
			(47,260)
Net profit			55,320

Balance sheet as at 31 March 19X1

	Cost £	Depreciation £	£
Fixed assets			
Freehold land and buildings	45,000	3,600	41,400
Plant and machinery	36,500	8,150	28,350
Motor vans	19,800	8,650	11,150
	101,300	20,400	80,900
Current assets			
Stocks – Raw materials		9,650	
– WIP		21,000	
– Finished goods		24,500	
Debtors (W3) (38,270 – 1,914)		36,356	
Cash in hand		45	
		91,551	
Current liabilities			
Bank overdraft		6,320	
Creditors		42,230	
Accruals			
[960 + 240 + 850 + 6,625 (W4) + 20,516 (W5)]		29,191	
		77,741	
			13,810
Net current assets			94,710

Represented by:

	£
Capital @ 1.4.X0	39,390
Profit for the year	55,320
	94,710

Workings

(1)   Depreciation – Land and buildings $= 2\% \times 45{,}000 = 900$
                 – Plant and machinery $= 10\% \times 36{,}500 = 3{,}650$
                 – Motor vehicles $= 25\% \times 19{,}800 = 4{,}950$

(2)   Electricity and power

	£
Per question	17,600
Accruals	960
	18,560
Factory (²/₃)	12,373
Admin. (¹/₃)	6,187

(3)   Debtors

	£
Per question	38,970
Less: Bad debt provision	(700)
	38,270

	£
Provision: $5\% \times 38{,}270$	1,914
Opening provision	1,560
Increase	354

(4)   Rent

Charge for the year $= 22{,}000 + {}^{3}\!/_{12} \times 26{,}500$
                     $= 22{,}000 + 6{,}625$
                     $= 28{,}625$

Factory (70%)	=	20,038
Admin. (30%)	=	8,587

(5)   Sales manager's commission

	£
Gross profit	178,164
Less: Expenses (26,920 + 22,144 + 1,054 + 4,950)	(55,068)
	123,096 (120%)
Commission (20%)	(20,516)
	102,580

SESSION 8

1   **Transit Ltd**

(a)   **Profit and loss account for the year ended 31 March 19X8**

	£	£
Turnover		206,500
Cost of sales (W1)		(134,050)
Gross profit		72,450
Less: Distribution costs (10,000 + 500 van depreciation)	10,500	
Administrative expenses (7,650 + 25,000)	32,650	
		(43,150)
		29,300
Profit on sale of van (W2)		190
Investment income		340
Rental income		3,600
		33,430
Less: Interest payable		
Bank interest	162	
Debenture interest	1,050	
		(1,212)
Profit before taxation		32,218
Corporation tax		(12,700)
Profit after taxation		19,518
Dividends		
Interim	1,260	
Final – proposed	4,200	
		(5,460)
Retained profits for the year		14,058
Profit and loss account 1 April 19X7		17,852
Profit and loss account 31 March 19X8		31,910

(b)

Balance sheet at 31 March 19X8

	Cost £	Depreciation £	£
Fixed assets			
Leasehold properties	75,000	–	75,000
Motor vans	2,400	960	1,440
	77,400	960	76,440
Current assets			
Stock at the lower of cost or net realisable value		16,700	
Debtors		31,000	
Investments		6,750	
		54,450	
Less: Creditors: Amounts falling due within one year			
Creditors	24,350		
Corporation tax	12,700		
Proposed dividend	4,200		
Bank overdraft	730		
		(41,980)	
Net current assets			12,470
Total assets less current liabilities			88,910
Less: Creditors: amounts falling due after more than one year			
7% Debentures			(15,000)
			73,910

Representing

Share capital	
Ordinary shares of £1 each	42,000
Reserves	
Profit and loss account	31,910
Shareholders' funds	73,910

Workings

(1)   *Cost of sales*

	£
Stock 31 March 19X7	12,000
Purchases	138,750
	150,750
Stock 31 March 19X8	(16,700)
	134,050

(2)   *Profit on sale of van*

	£
Cost	900
Depreciation to 31.3.X8 (3 years)	(540)
	360
Proceeds	550
Profit	190

2   Pirbright Precision Ltd

(a)

Suspense account

	£		£
Incorrect stock in trial balance (9,880 – 8,220)	1,660	Commission not posted	1,385
		Difference, to be added back to admin. expenses	275
	1,660		1,660

(b)   **Profit and loss account for the year ended 31 March 19X4**

		£	£
Sales			102,142
Cost of sales (W1)			(65,091)
			37,051
Less:	Distribution costs (2,610 + 1,385 + 230)	4,225	
	Administrative expenses (W4)	30,621	
			(34,846)
Net profit before tax			2,205
Less:	Taxation (10,400 + 160)		(10,560)
Net loss after tax			(8,355)
Profit and loss account balance at 1 April 19X3			7,613
Adverse balance carried forward at 31 March 19X4			(742)

Balance sheet at 31 March 19X4

	£	£
Fixed assets (W3) at net book value		
Fixtures and fittings		294
Motor vehicles		7,554
Plant and machinery		5,537
Premises		10,560
		23,945
Current assets		
Stock (9,880 – 500)	9,380	
Debtors and prepayments	12,390	
Bank (715 – 187)	528	
	22,298	
Creditors: Amounts falling due within one year		
Creditors and accruals (W5)	7,585	
Taxation (due 1 January 19X5)	10,400	
	17,985	
		4,313
		28,258
Creditors: Amounts due after one year		
Debentures		(4,000)
		24,258

Share capital	20,000
Share premium account	5,000
Profit and loss account	(742)
	24,258

Workings

(1)   Cost of sales

	£
Opening stock (as adjusted)	8,220
Purchases (66,751 – 500)	66,251
	74,471
Closing stock (9,880 – 500)	(9,380)
	65,091

(2)   Disposals of fixtures and fittings

	£
Cost	1,000
Less: Accumulated depreciation (20% × 1 year)	(200)
Net book value	800
Sales proceeds	400
Loss on disposal	400

(3)   Fixed assets and depreciation

	F & F £	MV £	P & M £	Premises £
Cost balance b/f	2,280	17,284	16,327	12,000
Add back: Sale proceeds	400			
Less: Disposal (W2)	(1,000)			
	1,680	17,284	16,327	12,000
Depreciation				
Balance b/f	1,250	7,212	9,557	1,200
Disposals (W2)	(200)			
Charge for year				
20% × 1,680	336			
25% × (17,284–7,212)		2,518		
10% × (16,327–4,000)			1,233	
2% × 12,000				240
	1,386	9,730	10,790	1,440
Net book value	294	7,554	5,537	10,560

(4)   Administrative expenses

	£
Per question	8,474
Trial balance difference	275
	8,749
Loss on disposal	400
Depreciation (W3)	
Fixtures	336
Motor vehicles	2,518
Plant	1,233
Premises	240
Wages and salaries	18,518
Bank charges	187
	32,181
Less: Taxation paid	(1,560)
	30,621

(5)   Creditors and accruals

	£
Per question	7,855
Commission due	230
	8,085
Sale or return	(500)
	7,585

Answers

3   Bassingham Ltd

TRIAL BALANCE AS AT 31 MARCH 1993

	£	£
	Dr	Cr
Purchases a/c	157,712	
Sales a/c		326,845
Salaries a/c	59,200	
Rent & Rates a/c	32,800	
Motor expenses a/c	3,840	
Light & Heat a/c	972	
Office expenses a/c	22,485	
Interest on loan a/c	1,800	
Stock a/c	27,200	
Provision for doubtful debts a/c		2,240
Fittings & Equipment (cost) a/c	31,400	
Fittings & Equipment (acc. dep'n) a/c		12,350
Motor vehicles (cost) a/c	24,200	
Motor vehicles (acc. dep'n) a/c		12,100
Share capital a/c		2,000
Loan a/c		20,000
Profit & Loss a/c		34,402
Debtors	76,040	
Creditors		28,032
Bank a/c	230	
Cash a/c	180	
Suspense a/c		90
	438,059	438,059

JOURNAL ENTRIES	Dr £	Cr £
(i) Suspense a/c	90	
R Swinderly a/c		90
Being correction of mispost of credit purchase		
(ii) Sales a/c	360	
T Brough a/c		360
Being correction of posting of a sale-or-return in error		
(iii) Fixtures and equipment	3,860	
Office expenses		3,860
Being correction of an error of principle		
(iv) Sales a/c	4,250	
Motor vehicle (cost) a/c		12,100
Motor vehicle (acc. dep'n) a/c	6,050	
Loss on sale of motor vehicle a/c	1,800	
Being correction of error in posting of sale of fixed asset		

EXTENDED TRIAL BALANCE 31 MARCH 1993

	Ledger		Adjustments		Profit and Loss a/c		Balance Sheet Balances	
	Dr	Cr	Dr	Cr	Dr	Cr	Dr	Cr
	£	£	£	£	£	£	£	£
Purchases a/c	157,712				157,712			
Sales a/c		322,235				322,235		
Salaries a/c	59,200				59,200			
Rent & Rates a/c	32,800				32,800			
Motor expenses a/c	3,840				3,840			
Light & Heat a/c	972				972			
Office expenses a/c	18,625				18,625			
Interest on loan a/c	1,800		600		2,400			
Stock a/c	27,200		38,120 240	38,360	27,200	38,360	38,360	
Provision for doubtful debts a/c		2,240	729					1,511
Fittings & Equipment (cost) a/c	35,260						35,260	
Fittings & Equipment (acc. dep'n) a/c		12,350		7,052				19,402
Motor vehicles (cost) a/c	12,100						12,100	
Motor vehicles (acc. dep'n) a/c		6,050		3,025				9,075
Share capital a/c		2,000						2,000
Loan a/c		20,000						20,000
Profit & Loss a/c		34,402						34,402
Sales ledger balances	75,680		173	303			75,550	
Purchase ledger balances		28,122						28,122
Bank a/c	230			256				26
Cash a/c	180						180	
Loss on sale of motor vehicle a/c	1,800				1,800			
Dep'n (fittings & equipment) a/c			7,052		7,052			
Dep'n (motor vehicles) a/c			3,025		3,025			
Bank charges			83		83			
Bad debts			303		303			
Decrease in provision for doubtful debts				729		729		
Accruals				600				600
Profit					46,312			46,312
	427,399	427,399	50,325	50,325	361,324	361,324	161,450	161,450

4   Country Crafts Ltd

JOURNAL ENTRIES	Dr £	Cr £
(i) Motor vans (cost) a/c	22,600	
Motor vans (cost) a/c		16,200
Motor vans (provision for dep'n) a/c	12,150	
Suspense a/c		17,600
Profit on sale of fixed asset a/c		950
Being for sale of motor van H247AFE in part-exchange for motor van L673NFU		
(iii) Suspense a/c	3,900	
Motor cars (cost) a/c		9,200
Motor car (provision for dep'n) a/c	4,600	
Profit on sale of fixed asset a/c	700	
Being sale of motor car J168TFE		
(iii) Sales a/c	250	
Sundry sales a/c		250
Being transfer of income from loan of field for car boot sale from Sales a/c to a Sundry Sales a/c.		

COUNTRY CRAFTS LTD – EXTENDED TRIAL BALANCE

	Ledger Balances		Adjustments		Profit and Loss		Balance Sheet Balances	
	Dr	Cr	Dr	Cr	Dr	Cr	Dr	Cr
	£	£	£	£	£	£	£	£
Motor vans (cost)	42,400						42,400	
Motor cars (cost)	9,200						9,200	
Office furniture (cost)	4,850						4,850	
Computer equipment (cost)	16,830						16,830	
Motor vans (PD)		4,950		10,600				15,550
Motor cars (PD)		4,600		2,300				6,900
Office furniture (PD)		1,940		485				2,425
Computer equipment (PD)				5,610				5,610
Stock	24,730				24,730	31,600	31,600	
Debtors control	144,280						144,280	
Bank		610		43				653
Cash	50		43	43			50	
Creditors control		113,660						113,660
Sales		282,240				282,240		
Purchases	152,140			1,150	150,990			
Rent	12,480			4,992	7,488			
Heat and light	1,840		210		2,050			
Wages and salaries	75,400				75,400			
Office expenses	7,900		43		7,943			
Motor expenses	14,890				14,890			
Dep'n (motor vans)			10,600		10,600			
Dep'n (motor cars)			2,300		2,300			
Dep'n (office furniture)			485		485			
Dep'n (computer equipment)			5,610		5,610			
Share capital		50,000						50,000
Profit and loss		35,850						35,850
VAT		12,640						12,640
Profit on sale of fixed asset		250				250		
Sundry sales		250				250		
Raven Moon Insurance Co			950				950	
c/f	506,990	506,990	20,241	25,223	302,486	314,340	250,160	243,288

	Ledger Balances		Adjustments		Profit and Loss		Balance Sheet Balances	
	Dr	Cr	Dr	Cr	Dr	Cr	Dr	Cr
	£	£	£	£	£	£	£	£
b/f	506,990	506,990	20,241	25,223	302,486	314,340	250,160	243,288
Stock loss			200		200			
Increase in provision for doubtful debts a/c			7,214		7,214			
Provision for doubtful debts a/c				7,214				7,214
Prepayments			4,992				4,992	
Accruals				210				210
Profit					4,440			4,440
	506,990	506,990	32,647	32,647	314,340	314,340	255,152	255,152

SESSION 9

1   Mary Bassingham

(a)   **MEMORANDUM**

To: Mary Bassingham

From:

Subject: Depreciation policy   **Date:** 9 June 1993

There appears to be a good case for reviewing and changing the company's depreciation policy. Although this would be against the concept of consistency, depreciation policy can be changed if the new policy is thought to give a fairer representation of the financial position of the business which this clearly does.

This would entail creating separate accounts (at cost and accumulated depreciation) for office fittings (and furniture?) and for office equipment and analysing the existing combined figures accordingly. The remaining unamortised cost of each category would then be written off over its remaining useful life.

(b)   **MEMORANDUM**

To: Mary Bassingham

From:

Subject: Accounting Standards   **Date:** 9 June 1993

In answer to your enquiry, both are right. According to SSAP12 'the allocation of depreciation to accounting periods involves the exercise of judgement by management in the light of technical, commercial and accounting considerations'. Thus the specific depreciation method can vary from company to company, though the general principle of spreading an asset's cost over its useful life will remain the same.

Similarly land and buildings can be revalued upwards to reflect their market value and give a truer picture of the company's financial position. However, revalued assets should themselves be depreciated.

Standards then do aim to allow comparisons between companies' accounts, but try to include a semblance of reality and to allow companies to use different methods or policies to achieve the same accounting principle.

2   James McBride

                        MEMORANDUM

To: James McBride

From:

Subject: Accounting concepts   **Date:** 3 December

There are, as you say, a number of accounting concepts and at times these concepts appear to conflict. The reason for this is that the names used to describe the concepts have rather imprecise definitions. However, the accounting standards do accept that there are conflicts between accounting concepts. For example, SSAP2 states that the accruals concept should be applied provided that, where there are inconsistencies with the prudence concept, the latter prevails.

To take your specific examples. SSAP9 insists that stock should be valued at the lower of historic cost and net realisable value. This is clearly prudent, not letting the value of stocks rise, but allowing their value to fall if net realisable value falls when a loss is already evident even before the sale. (The rise in value will be realised when a sale takes place.) Thus, stocks will not necessarily be valued at an 'objective' value, but at a prudent value.

Consistency is achieved by being prudent at all times.

3 Cash accounting

MEMORANDUM

To: Jason Sarmiento

From:

Subject: Introduction of cash accounting system   **Date:**

Although it may be desirable to revert to a system of cash accounting, this is simply not allowed by the rules of basic accounting.

The concept of matching states that revenues and expenses for a period must be matched when determining profit. Revenue does not represent cash received from sales, but sales made and, similarly, expenses do not relate to payments made, but to resources used.

Therefore, we need to measure the gas used as charged on the gas bills, not the gas paid.

In the same way, the cost of a fixed asset must be spread over its useful life, using the system of depreciation, and not written off on its initial purchase.

I should point out that, since our existing system operates properly according to the above rules, it would probably cause problems if we did introduce a cash accounting system, so it would be preferable to retain our current accounting system.

4 Sophie Stewart

(a)   Monday 5 December 1994

Sophie,

It is good that you have foreseen these potential problems since, operating a cash with order system, these situations are bound to occur sooner or later. I will deal with each statement separately:

(i)   The sales should not be recorded until you have fulfilled the order, therefore the correct entry should be:

        Dr   Bank a/c
        Cr   Personal a/c of customer

    The customer is technically a creditor of the business and you may wish to create a separate ledger for these payment in advance customers.

    Upon delivery of the goods you would simply:

        Dr   Personal a/c of customer
        Cr   Sales a/c
        Cr   VAT a/c

(ii)   The situation here is slightly different in that you have to decide whether to refund the payment or merely send the customer a credit note for further purchases. The key point to remember is that all receipts and payments of cash should be recorded.

You may also have the situation where only a part-order can be supplied.

The accounting treatment is straightforward. If payment is returned, no transaction has occurred, therefore no entry is required. If payment for a part-order has to be returned it may be necessary to:

Dr   Bank (whole payment)
Cr   Bank (payment returned)

If payment is retained and a credit note sent, then the treatment would be as in (i) above.

I hope this explains the situation clearly.

(b)   Monday 5 December 1994

Sophie,

Accounts are prepared according to a framework, which in your case comprises Accounting Standards and Accounting Concepts. What we call SSAP9 (Statement of Standard Accounting Practice No. 9) controls the way stocks must be valued for financial accounting purposes.

The rule is simple: stocks must be valued at the lower of cost or net realisable value (market value).

Thus, in your first example, the stock must be valued at cost price, otherwise profits would be anticipated. In the second example, if the market value falls below cost price, the stock must be valued at market value accounting for the anticipated loss.

This method is being consistent in that the concept of prudence is being followed in both cases.

However, this role applies only to your financial accounts. If you want to value your stock at sales price, you can, as a separate management accounting report for your own use.

I hope this helps.

SESSION 10

1   Clarence

Step 1

Calculate the figure for purchases.

Creditors' control account

	£		£
Cash	9,000	Balance b/f	2,100
Balance c/f	2,600	Purchases (balancing figure)	9,500
	11,600		11,600
		Balance b/f	2,600

Note that we are constructing the control account, and producing the balancing figure which represents the purchases made during the year.

Remember the double-entry involved here. The cash of £9,000 will be a credit in the cash account. The purchases (£9,500) will be debited to the purchases account and transferred to the trading profit and loss account at the year-end:

Purchases account

	£		£
Creditors' control account	9,500	Trading and profit and loss a/c	9,500

Step 2

Now compute the cost of sales.

	£
Opening stock	1,800
Purchases	9,500
	11,300
Less: Closing stock	(1,600)
Cost of sales	9,700

Step 3

Now you can work out the cost structure and sales.

(a)   Work out the cost structure.

The mark-up is arrived at by reference to the cost of sales. Thus, cost of sales is 100%, the mark-up is 20% and therefore the sales are 120%:

	%
Sales (balancing figure)	120
Less: Gross profit	20
Cost of sales	100

(b)   Sales $= \dfrac{120}{100} \times$ Cost of sales

$= \dfrac{120}{100} \times £9,700$

$= £11,640$

2   Alistair

	£
Opening stock	2,000
Purchases	18,000
Less: Closing stock	(4,000)
Cost of sales	16,000

	%	£
Sales	100	21,333
Cost of sales	(75)	(16,000)
Gross profit	25	5,333

3   Anita Ltd

	£	£	%
Sales		19,476	100
Cost of sales			
Opening stock	3,025		
Purchases	12,108		
Closing stock	(1,500)		
		(13,633)	(70)
Gross profit		5,843	30

SESSION 11

1   Andrew

		%
Sales (20,150 + 5,960)	26,110	140
Mark-up	7,460	40
Cost of sales	18,650	100
Purchases (21,120 + 2,340)	23,460	
Stock (23,460 – 18,650)	4,810	

2   Desdemona

Step 1

Calculate the figures for the purchases and sales using control accounts.

Debtors' control account

	£		£
Balance b/f 1.1.X4	310	Cash	7,420
Sales (balancing figure)	7,110		
	7,420		7,420

Creditors' control account

	£		£
Cash	4,600	Balance b/f 1.1.X4	850
Balance c/f 31.12.X4	760	Purchases (balancing figure)	4,510
	5,360		5,360
		Balance b/f	760

Step 2

The gross profit is calculated by constructing the trading account:

	£	£
Sales		7,110
Opening stock	1,200	
Add: Purchases	4,510	
	5,710	
Less: Closing stock	(900)	
Cost of sales		(4,810)
Gross profit		2,300

Therefore gross profit expressed as:

(a)   a percentage of sales $= \dfrac{2.300}{7.110} \times 100 = 32.3\%$

(b)   a percentage of cost $= \dfrac{2.300}{4.810} = 47.8\%$

SESSION 12

1   Ignatius

Step 1

Using all the information in points (1) and (4) of the question, the following cash account results:

Working cash account

	£		£
Balance 1.1.X4	12	Payments to suppliers	755
Receipts from cash customers	?	Other costs	155
		Balance 31.12.X4	20
		Wages	3,055
		Cash banked	59,000
		Drawings	?
	?		?

Once again, there are two unknowns, receipts from cash customers (ie. cash sales) and drawings.

Step 2: Stop and think.

This question is similar to the example in the text and you should be able to see your way through. The steps are briefly outlined below and then calculated in detail.

(i)   Opening and closing creditors together with the payments to suppliers will lead to purchases.

(ii)   Purchases together with opening and closing stocks will lead to cost of sales.

(iii) Cost of sales together with the mark-up on cost will lead to total sales.

(iv)   Total sales less sales on credit will give cash sales.

(v)   Cash sales entered in the cash book will lead to drawings.

These are now examined in detail.

Step 3: Calculate purchases.

Creditors' control account

	£		£
Cash – payments to suppliers	755	Creditors 1.1.X4	3,845
Bank – payments to suppliers	59,660	Purchases (balancing figure)	61,225
Creditors 31.12.X4	4,655		
	65,070		65,070

Step 4: Calculate cost of sales.

	£
Opening stock 1.1.X4	4,570
Purchases	61,225
	65,795
Stock 31.12.X4	(5,375)
Cost of sales	60,420

Step 5: Calculate sales.

Cost structure

Cost	=	100%
Mark-up	=	$33^1/_3\%$
Therefore sales	=	$133^1/_3\%$

$$\text{Sales} = \frac{\text{Cost of sales}}{100} \times 133^1/_3\% = \frac{60.420}{100} \times 133^1/_3\% = £80,560$$

These sales are cash and credit.

	£
Credit sales (per question)	12,760
Total sales	80,560
Therefore, cash sales	67,800

Step 6: Calculate drawings.

Enter the cash sales in the cash account. This will give drawings as a balancing figure. The cash account is reproduced here.

Cash account

	£		£
Balance 1.1.X4	12	Payments to suppliers	755
Receipts from cash sales	67,800	Other costs	155
		Wages	3,055
		Cash banked	59,000
		Drawings (balancing figure)	4,827
		Balance 31.12.X5	20
	67,812		67,812

2   **Fish**

Claim for loss of stock destroyed by fire on 25 August 1987

	£	£
Stock at cost, 30 June 19X7		3,600
Purchases for the eight weeks to 25 August 19X7 (W2)		1,280
		4,880
Sales for eight weeks to 25 August 19X7 (W1)	3,120	
Gross profit: $\frac{30}{130} \times £3,120$	720	
Cost of sales		(2,400)
Total claim for loss of stock		2,480

Workings

(1)
Combined cash and bank summary
for the period 1 July 19X7 to 25 August 19X7

	Cash £	Bank £		Cash £	Bank £
Balance b/f	40	980	Creditors for goods		
Cash banked		2,884	supplied		1,400
Cash sales	3,120		Expenses		460
(balancing figure)			Wages (8 × £12)	96	
			Drawings (8 × £15)	120	
			Cash banked	2,884	
			Balances c/f	60	2,004
	3,160	3,864		3,160	3,864

(2)

Trade creditors' control account

	£		£
Bank	1,400	Balance b/f	680
Balance c/f	560	Purchases (balancing figure)	1,280
	1,960		1,960

(3)

Expense creditors' control account

	£		£
Bank	460	Balance b/f	340
Balance c/f	140	Expenses (balancing figure)	260
	600		600

3   R Smith

Balance sheet at 30 September 19X1

	Cost £	Dep'n £	£
Fixed assets			
Premises	2,500	50	2,450
Fixtures and fittings	300	15	285
	2,800	65	2,735
Current assets			
Stocks		360	
Debtors		177	
Prepayment		20	
Cash in hand		10	
		567	
Less: Current liabilities			
Creditors	403		
Accrued charges	16		
Jones – commission	40		
Bank overdraft	2,007		
		2,466	
			(1,899)
			836

	£
Proprietor's funds	
Opening capital	500
Capital introduced	176
Net profit for year	760
	1,436
Less: Drawings	(600)
	836

Trading and profit and loss account for the year ended 30 September 19X1

	£	£
Sales: Cash (W1)		4,814
Credit (W2)		584
		5,398
Cost of goods sold		
Purchases (W3)	4,121	
Less: Closing stock	360	
		(3,761)
Gross profit		1,637
Wages and National Insurance	410	
Rent and rates	100	
Heat and light	50	
Insurance	20	
Stationery and postage	26	
Sundry expenses	56	
Bank charges and interest	110	
Depreciation	65	
		(837)
Net profit before commission		800
Commission		(40)
Net profit		760

Workings

(1)
Cash account

	£		£
Bank – contra	20	Wages and national insurance	400
Cash sales	4,814	Sundry shop expenses	50
		Drawings	600
		Bank – contra	3,769
		Balance c/f (including debtor £5)	15
	4,834		4,834

(2)
Debtors' control account

	£		£
Sales	584	Cash	382
		Cash	30
		Balance c/f	172
	584		584

(3)
Creditors' control account

	£		£
Cash	3,728	Cash	10
Balance c/f	403	Purchases	4,121
	4,131		4,131

(4)
Capital account

	£		£
Drawings	600	Cash	500
Balance c/f	836	Rent and rates	100
		Heat and light	50
		Stationery and postage	26
		Net profit for year	760
	1,436		1,436

4   Kevin

Trading and profit and loss account for the year ended 31 December 19X0

		£	£
Sales (W2)			32,979
Less:	Cost of sales		
	Opening stock	13,000	
	Purchases (W3)	35,779	
		48,779	
	Closing stock	(15,000)	
			(33,779)
			(800)

		£	£
Less:	Wages (5,200 + 550)	5,750	
	Rates (300 + 50)	350	
	Electricity $(200 + 20) \times \dfrac{200}{235}$	187	
	Hire of equipment $(90 + 10) \times \dfrac{200}{235}$	85	
	Sundry expenses $200 \times \dfrac{200}{235}$	170	
	Amortisation: Goodwill	1,000	
	Depreciation: Fixtures and fittings	300	
			(7,842)
Net loss			(8,642)

Balance sheet at 31 December 19X0

	£	£
Fixed assets		
Goodwill (10,000 – 1,000)		9,000
Freehold land and buildings		70,000
Fixtures and fittings (3,000 – 300)		2,700
		81,700
Current assets		
Stock	15,000	
Debtors	300	
Prepayment – rates	100	
VAT (W4)	568	
Cash at bank	9,060	
Cash in hand	100	
	25,128	
Current liabilities		
Trade creditors	40	
Accruals – electricity	20	
– hire purchase	10	
	70	
		25,058
		106,758

Financed by:

	£
Proprietor's funds	
Capital introduced (120,000 + 300 + 200)	120,500
Less: Loss for the year	(8,642)
Less: Drawings (4,500 + 600)	(5,100)
	106,758

Workings

(1)

Cash account

	£		£
Takings (balancing figure)	38,450	Bankings	35,000
		Purchases	2,000
		Wages	550
		Sundries	200
		Drawings	600
		Balance c/f	100
	38,450		38,450

(2)

Debtors' control account

	£		£
Sales (balancing figure)	32,979	Takings (W2)	38,450
VAT $\left(\dfrac{35}{235} \times 38,750\right)$	5,771	Balance c/f	300
	38,750		38,750

(3)

Creditors' control account

	£		£
Payments (40,000 + 2,000)	42,000	Purchases (balancing figure)	35,779
Balance c/f	40	VAT (35/235 × 42,040)	6,261
	42,040		42,040

(4)

VAT control account

	£		£
Input VAT on purchases (W3)	6,261	Output VAT (W2)	5,771
Input VAT on sundries $\dfrac{35}{235} \times 200$	30		
Input VAT on hire charges $\dfrac{35}{235} \times 100$	15	Balance c/f	568
Input VAT on electricity $\dfrac{35}{235} \times 220$	33		
	6,339		6,339

5   Pinker

Trading and profit and loss account for the year ended 30 September 19X3

	£	£
Sales (W4)		25,175
Opening stock	2,000	
Purchases (W3)	16,145	
	18,145	
Closing stock	1,910	
		(16,235)
Gross profit		8,940
Wages (2,122 + 71 + 516)	2,709	
Rent	800	
Motor expenses (1,214 + 113 + 83)	1,410	
Van depreciation (W6)	680	
Loss on sale of van (W6)	200	
Repairs	522	
Sundry (−36 + 613 + 47 + 75)	699	
Interest on loan (500 × 12% × 9/12)	45	
		(7,065)
Net profit		1,875
Profit and loss account b/f		2,750
Profit and loss account c/f		4,625

Balance sheet at 30 September 19X3

	Cost £	Depreciation £	£
Fixed assets			
Van	3,400	680	2,720
Current assets			
Stock		1,910	
Debtors (W5)		3,570	
Rent prepaid (W8)		250	
Cash at bank (1,523 + 23,117 − 23,425)		1,215	
Cash in hand		37	
		6,982	
Current liabilities			
Creditors (W7)		1,577	
			5,405
Loan – Trotter			(500)
			7,625
Share capital £1 ordinary shares			3,000
Profit and loss account			4,625
			7,625

Workings

(1)   **Cash account**

	£		£
Balance b/f	83	Bankings	
Takings (balancing figure)	23,285	Old stock	1,200
		Other	21,417
		Loan interest	40
		Wages	516
		Motor expenses	83
		Sundry expenses	75
		Balance c/f	37
	23,368		23,368

(2)

Cost structure	Normal %	Old stock %	Upjohn %
Sales	100	80	100
Cost of sales	60	60	85
Gross profit	40	20	15

(3)   Cost of sales

    (a)   Total

	£
Opening stock	2,000
Purchases (−1,400 + 16,204 + 1,341)	16,145
	18,145
Closing stock	1,910
	16,235

    (b)   Old stock

1,200 × 60/80	900

    (c)   Upjohn

3,700 − 470	3,230

    (d)   Other

16,235 − 900 − 3,230	12,105

(4)   Sales

	£
Old stock	1,200
Upjohn 3,230 × 100/85	3,800
Other 12,105 × 100/60	20,175
	25,175

(5)

Debtors' control account

	£		£
Balance b/f	1,680	Cash received (W1)	23,285
Sales (W4)	25,175	Balance c/f (balancing figure)	3,570
	26,855		26,855

(6)   Van

	£
Book value b/f	1,600
Proceeds – part exchange allowance (3,400 – 2,000)	1,400
Loss on sale	200
Depreciation 3,400 × 20%	680

(7)   Creditors

	£
Trade	1,341
Sundry expenses	47
Wages	71
Motor expenses	113
Loan interest (45 – 40)	5
	1,577

(8)   Rent prepaid

Rent account

	£		£
Balance b/f	300	Profit and loss account	800
Cash paid	750	Balance c/f (balancing figure)	250
	1,050		1,050

6   Carlton Moorland

(a)   Calculation of cash sales:

	£
Cash banked	18,816
Wages (120 × 8)	960
Drawings (150 × 8)	1,200
Increase in cash balance	200
	21,176

Calculation of credit sales:

Cash received	12,015
Increase in debtors	180
	12,195

Calculation of total sales:

Cash sales	21,176
Credit sales	12,195
	33,371
At cost price	25,670

Calculation of purchases:

Cash paid	14,000
Discount taken	339
	14,339
Refund	(195)
Decrease in creditors	(1,200)
	12,944

Calculation of closing stock:

Opening stock	36,000
Purchases	12,944
	48,944
Sales at cost	(25,670)
Closing stock	23,274

(b)

Fixtures & Fitting a/c

		£				£
31.10.93	Balance b/f	14,000	1.1.93	Sunbird Insurance Co		12,500
			1.1.93	Loss of fixtures and fittings		1,500
		14,000				14,000

7   Sarah Harvey

Task 1

Closing stock valuation	£
Pot plants	210
Roses	240
Tulips	160
Sprays	260
Plant food	80
Vases	490
	1,440

Task 2

Calculation of sales	£
Cash paid into bank	31,420
Less: Start-up capital	(5,000)
	26,420
Wages	14,200
Sundry expenses	345
Cash tin	60
Drawings	520
	41,545

Calculation of purchases	£
Cheque payments	24,180
Invoices due:	850
	345
	25,375

Calculation of profit	£	£
Sales		41,545
Purchases	25,375	
Less: Closing stock	(1,440)	
Cost of sales		(23,935)
Gross profit		17,610
Rent	4,000	
Business rates	420	
Advertising (385 + 45)	430	
Insurance	390	
Electricity (780 + 120 + 360)	1,260	
Sundry expenses (560 + 345)	905	
Interest charged	84	
		7,489
Net profit		10,121

Note: Drawings shown as an expense in calculating profit is acceptable.

Task 3

Capital a/c	£
Capital paid in	5,000
Net profit	10,121
	15,121
Drawings (wages)	(14,200)
Drawings (flowers)	(520)
Capital (closing balance)	401

Proof: Calculation of net assets:

	£		£
Stock	1,440	Creditors (purchases)	1,195
Prepaid rent	1,000	Creditors (electricity)	360
Cash	60	Creditors (advertising)	45
		Accrued electricity	120
		Bank overdraft	379
			2,099
		Net assets	401
	2,500		2,500

Note: The proof is not required.

Task 4

Sarah is drawing almost half as much again as she is making in profit. Consequently, her capital account is extremely low and is less than bank and creditors' accounts combined. The business is solvent, but only just. Great care will have to be taken and restraint shown in drawings, unless more capital can be introduced. The bank may be concerned about the overdraft and it is uncertain as to how creditors will be paid.

8   Somaira Rahman

Task 1

Calculation of capital a/c balance at 30 September 1993

		£	£
Assets:	Debtors	2,100	
	Prepayments	640	
	Premises	48,000	
	Motor van	15,000	
	Stock	56,000	
	Cash	820	
	Bank	41,600	
			164,160
Liabilities:	Creditors	68,600	
	Accruals	760	
	Loan	50,000	
	Mortgage	24,000	
			(143,360)
Capital			20,800

Task 2

Calculation of net profit for year ended 30 September 1993

Calculation of capital a/c at 1 October 1992:

		£	£
Assets:	Van	18,000	
	Stock	42,000	
	Bank	16,000	
			76,000
Liability:	Loan		(60,000)
Capital			16,000

Calculation of net profit:

Opening capital	16,000
Capital introduced	24,000
	40,000
Net loss	(4,900)
	35,100
Drawings (275 × 52)	(14,300)
Closing capital	20,800

Task 3

To calculate sales revenue:

	£
Total payments made from bank account	178,700
Less: Reduction in bank balances	(12,110)
	166,590
Less: Investment income	(8,220)
Sales receipts paid into bank	158,370
Add: Drawings (£275 × 52)	14,300
	172,670
Less: Reduction in cash balance	(170)
	172,500
Increase in debtors	3,150
	175,650

To calculate purchases:

	£
Total payments to trade creditors	138,400
Increase in trade creditors	6,220
	144,620

Calculation of profit:

	£	£
Sales revenue		175,650
Opening stock	56,000	
Purchases	144,620	
	200,620	
Less: Closing stock	(63,400)	
		(137,220)
Gross profit		38,430
Overhead expenses (7,440 + 430 – 570)	7,300	
Motor expenses	12,420	
Loan interest	4,000	
Mortgage interest	2,400	
Depreciation of van	3,000	
		(29,120)
Net profit		9,310

Other approaches may be used in the calculation of net profit, but the detail above should be shown.

Task 4

Capital a/c at 30 September 1994:

		£	£
Opening capital			20,800
Net profit			9,310
Capital introduced			8,220
			38,330
Drawings:	Regular	14,300	
	Car	16,400	
	Motor expenses	1,640	
			(32,340)
Closing capital			5,990

SESSION 14

1 Retailers and wholesalers

A retailer, unlike a wholesaler, cannot be expected to cover every sale with an invoice. The retailer calculates his tax on his cash takings, not the totals of individual invoices.

Modern cash tills can be very sophisticated and the retailer will be required to keep the daily ring-up, the 'Z' reading. Without a cash register the daily gross takings must be recorded. The nature of mainly cash receipts means that the retailer must make a careful note of any money taken from the till for own use.

SESSION 15

1   Panther

The two basic records needed are the sales day book and purchase day book for the sales and purchases.

For cash sales and purchases the cash book should be analysed.

Information about credit notes received and issued should be in the purchase returns and sales returns day books.

The capital goods purchased and sold will probably be in a separate assets account under plant and machinery unless the company maintains analysed purchase and sales day books which include asset purchases and disposals.

The goods taken for own use should be recorded in the sales day book and the drawings account.

The bad debt relief is generally found in the bad and doubtful debts account.

2   Mr Brown

Address

Date

Dear Mr Brown

In reply to your recent telephone enquiry to this office I have been asked to advise you on two areas regarding VAT.

Firstly, you must keep your business records for six years. In your case these records will include:

- –   orders and delivery notes
- –   cash book, bank statements and paying in books
- –   purchase invoices and copy sales invoices
- –   annual accounts, including trading and profit and loss account.
- –   your VAT accounts
- –   credit notes issued or received
- –   any business correspondence.

Secondly, as you are neither a car-dealer nor a car-leasing business, you cannot reclaim VAT charged on the purchase of a car even if it is used wholly for business purposes. Normally you could claim VAT back on goods which are supplied to your business and for which you have paid a deposit.

Yours sincerely

Practice simulations (Panther Alarms Ltd)

INTRODUCTION FOR SIMULATIONS 1 AND 2

Both these simulations are connected with the accounts of Panther Alarms Ltd. The first simulation is in four parts and covers the performance criteria assessed under Unit 5 *Preparing financial accounts*. The second simulation covers the performance criteria assessed under Unit 8 *Preparing VAT returns*.

Business name	Panther Alarms Ltd
Location	Cambridge
Nature of business	Wholesale of car alarms

The company was incorporated on 1 February 19X3 and started trading on 1 April 19X3.

DATA

Personnel

The company's personnel are as follows:

Managing director	James Wheeler
Sales director	Peter Armstrong
Purchasing director	Trevor Jones

Fixed assets

The company is situated in a unit on a new industrial estate. The company was able to buy the freehold on 15 February 19X3.

Most of the building consists of warehouse space. Part of the warehouse is let to another business, Taylor and Preston Autospares.

The company owns all of its assets. These are computers, cars, office equipment, office furniture and warehouse fittings.

Customers

All customers are other businesses who are allowed credit terms. The terms of trade are currently 30 days credit from the date of invoice. The directors are considering introducing settlement discounts.

Most of the customers are car dealerships.

The major customers are:

Abraham Motors Ltd
Graham Brothers
Fox and Walker

Suppliers

The main suppliers are:

> Dexter and Hills Ltd
> Garwood James
> Heath and Blake
> Trumann Manufacturing Ltd

None of the suppliers offer settlement discounts.

Products

The company sells and fits alarms suitable for cars and vans. It specialises in fitting alarms to new cars. The company has tended to concentrate on the luxury end of the market. Models tend to be updated quickly and the company tries to limit the risk of obsolete stock by keeping stock levels to a minimum.

Sources of finance

The shareholders are James Wheeler, Peter Armstrong and Trevor Jones, who have all worked in the car alarm trade for many years and who founded the business. They are also the directors.

Their shareholdings are as follows:

	£1 ordinary shares	%
James Wheeler	50,000	50
Peter Armstrong	30,000	30
Trevor Jones	20,000	20
	100,000	100

The company's major source of finance is a bank loan from Southern Bank plc.

Accounting systems

You have recently been appointed in a full-time capacity. Cath Brennan will continue to maintain the ledgers, but you will be responsible for the nominal ledger, wages and salaries, fixed assets, VAT and preparing the year-end accounts. All systems are currently manual.

Computer systems

The company has two PCs which run a number of software programs. These are:

(a)   payroll program;
(b)   spreadsheet program;
(c)   database program;
(d)   stock control program.

The company hopes to install an integrated ledger programme (debtors', creditors' and nominal) during 19X4.

YOUR ASSIGNMENT

You will carry out a number of projects for the year ended 31 March 19X4, including:

1	Reviewing income and expenditure accounts and preparing accruals and prepayments
2	Valuing stock and identifying bad and doubtful debts
3	Preparing an extended trial balance
4	Preparing accounts from incomplete records
5	Preparing the VAT return

NOMINAL LEDGER

In the first case study, you prepared a list of suggested nominal ledger codes. Attached is the finalised list of nominal ledger codes (which you will use from now on) and copies of the nominal ledger accounts showing the draft balances as at 31 March 19X4 (after posting cash and credit transactions).

Nominal ledger codes

Income

A001	Sales	Category 1
A002		Category 2
A003		Category 3
A010	Rental income	
A020	Interest income	

Purchases

B001	Purchases	Category 1
B002		Category 2
B003		Category 3
B010	Carriage inwards	
B020	Carriage outwards	

Expenses

C001	Rates
C002	Motor expenses
C003	Motor insurance and road tax
C004	General insurance
C005	Computer hardware maintenance
C006	Premises repairs and maintenance
C007	Heat and light
C008	Refuse collection
C009	Office cleaning
C010	Photocopier charges
C011	Coffee and sundries
C012	Stationery
C013	Telephone
C014	Legal and professional
C015	Travel
C016	Subsistence
C017	Entertainment disallowed

C100   General expenses
C101   Wages and salaries
C102   Pension costs (employer's contributions)
C103   Employer's NICs
C104   NIC on cars
C201   Depreciation   Freehold buildings
C202   Plant and machinery
C203   Fixtures and fittings
C301   Accountancy and audit
C302   Magazine subscriptions
C401   Interest payable
C402   Bank charges

Assets

D101   Cost   Land and buildings
D102   Office furniture
D103   Office equipment
D104   Warehouse fittings
D10   Motor vans
D106   Cars
D107   Computer equipment
D201   Depreciation   Land and buildings
D202   Office furniture
D203   Office equipment
D204   Warehouse fittings
D205   Motor vans
D206   Cars
D207   Computer equipment

E100   Stock (opening)
E200   Debtors' ledger control account
E201   Sundry debtors
E300   Other debtors
E401   Cash at bank
E402   Cash in hand

Liabilities

F100   Bank overdraft
F200   Creditors' ledger control account
F201   VAT control
F202   PAYE control
F203   Pensions control
F300   Wages control account
F400   Loan account

Capital and reserves

G100   Share capital
G101   Share premium
G200   Profit and loss account

Miscellaneous

X101   Disposals

Nominal ledger accounts

Sales 1			A001
£			£
		31.3.X4 Balance b/f	115,678

Sales 2			A002
£			£
		31.3.X4 Balance b/f	354,201

Sales 3			A003
£			£
		31.3.X4 Balance b/f	158,211

Rental income			A010
£			£
		31.3.X4 Balance b/f	1,500

Interest income			A020
£			£
		31.3.X4 Balance b/f	136

Purchases 1			B001
£			£
31.3.X4 Balance b/f	87,915		

Purchases 2			B002
£			£
31.3.X4 Balance b/f	251,480		

Purchases 3			B003
£			£
31.3.X4 Balance b/f	132,905		

Carriage inwards			B010
£			£
31.3.X4 Balance b/f	1,395		

Carriage outwards   B020

	£		£
31.3.X4 Balance b/f	2,399		

Rates   C001

	£		£
31.3.X4 Balance b/f	1,030		

Pre

Motor expenses   C002

	£		£
31.3.X4 Balance b/f	593		

Motor insurance/road tax   C003

	£		£
31.3.X4 Balance b/f	2,020		

Pre

General insurance   C004

	£		£
31.3.X4 Balance b/f	6,214		

Pre

Computer hardware maintenance   C005

	£		£
31.3.X4 Balance b/f	476		

Premises repairs and maintenance   C006

	£		£
31.3.X4 Balance b/f	312		

Heat and light   C007

	£		£
31.3.X4 Balance b/f	1,541		

Acc

Refuse collection   C008

	£		£
31.3.X4 Balance b/f	220		

Acc.

Office cleaning   C009

	£		£
31.3.X4 Balance b/f	511		

Alc

Photocopier charges   C010

	£		£
31.3.X4 Balance b/f	216		

Pre

Coffee and sundries   C011

	£		£
31.3.X4 Balance b/f	78		

Stationery   C012

	£		£
31.3.X4 Balance b/f	328		

Telephone   C013

	£		£
31.3.X4 Balance b/f	1,127		

Pre/All

Legal and professional   C014

	£		£
31.3.X4 Balance b/f	812		

Travel   C015

	£		£
31.3.X4 Balance b/f	314		

Subsistence   C016

	£		£
31.3.X4 Balance b/f	790		

Entertainment disallowed   C017

	£		£
31.3.X4 Balance b/f	268		

General expenses   C100

	£		£
31.3.X4 Balance b/f	115		

Wages and salaries   C101

	£		£
31.3.X4 Balance b/f	153,910		

Pension costs (employer)   C102

	£		£
31.3.X4 Balance b/f	5,843		

Employer's NICs   C103

	£		£
31.3.X4 Balance b/f	10,560		

NICs on cars   C104

	£		£

Depreciation – Freehold buildings   C201

	£		£

Depreciation – Plant and machinery   C202

	£		£

Depreciation – Fixtures and fittings   C203

	£		£

Accountancy and audit   C301

	£		£
31.3.X4 Balance b/f	829		

Magazine subscriptions   C302

	£		£
31.3.X4 Balance b/f	48		

Pre Pay

Interest payable   C401

	£		£
31.3.X4 Balance b/f	414		

A Accrual

Bank charges   C402

	£		£
31.3.X4 Balance b/f	391		

Cost – Land and buildings   D101

	£		£
31.3.X4 Balance b/f	250,118		

Cost – Office furniture   D102

	£		£
31.3.X4 Balance b/f	52,759		

Cost – Office equipment   D103

	£		£
31.3.X4 Balance b/f	25,224		

Cost – Warehouse fittings   D104

	£		£
31.3.X4 Balance b/f	77,623		

Cost – Motor vans   D105

	£		£
31.3.X4 Balance b/f	8,511		

Cost – Cars   D106

	£		£
31.3.X4 Balance b/f	50,602		

Cost – Computer equipment   D107

	£		£
31.3.X4 Balance b/f	5,117		

Depreciation – Land and buildings   D201

	£		£

Depreciation – Office furniture   D202

	£		£

Depreciation – Office equipment   D203

	£		£

Depreciation – Warehouse fittings   D204

	£		£

Depreciation – Motor vans   D205

	£		£

Depreciation – Cars   D206

	£		£

Depreciation – Computer equipment   D207

	£		£

Stock   E100

	£		£

Debtors' ledger control   E200

	£		£
31.3.X4 Balance b/f	52,359		

Sundry debtors   E201

	£		£
31.3.X4 Balance b/f	80		

Other debtors   E300

	£		£

Cash at bank   E401

	£		£

Cash in hand   E402

	£		£
31.3.X4 Balance b/f	150		

Bank overdraft   F100

	£		£
		31.3.X4 Balance b/f	3,020

Creditors' ledger control   F200

	£		£
		31.3.X4 Balance b/f	24,561

VAT control   F201

	£		£
		31.3.X4 Balance b/f	5,445

PAYE control   F202

	£		£
		31.3.X4 Balance b/f	3,800

Pensions control   F203

	£		£
		31.3.X4 Balance b/f	1,700

Wages and salaries control — F300

£		£

Loan — F400

£		£
	31.3.X4 Balance b/f	400,000

Share capital — G100

£		£
	31.3.X4 Balance b/f	100,000

Share premium — G101

£		£
	31.3.X4 Balance b/f	10,000

Profit and loss — G200

£		£

Disposals — X101

£		£
	31.3.X4 Balance b/f	9,345

SIMULATION 1

PART 1: ACCRUALS AND PREPAYMENTS

Introduction

All cash expenditure has been recorded in the nominal ledger to the end of March, but it has not been adjusted for accruals and prepayments.

Do not adjust the nominal ledger accounts until Part 3.

Tasks

Identifying accruals and prepayments

Review the nominal ledger accounts and identify which accounts are likely to include a prepayment and those which are likely to require an accrual.

Give reasons for your choices.

Reviewing purchases

Cath Brennan has analysed the outstanding GRNs at the end of the year and has produced a list.

She has also produced an analysis of purchase orders.

Use this information to estimate the value of the accrual needed for purchases at the year-end.

Reviewing expenses

You have now been presented with a list of certain payments and what they cover. (You selected the accounts and Cath Brennan prepared the analyses.) Using this information *estimate* the accruals or prepayments needed.

State any other information which you might need before deciding on the accrual or prepayment.

(Other accruals will be calculated by other methods.)

Reviewing other income

The tenants have paid their rent (£500 a quarter) up until 30 April 19X4. Calculate the adjustment which will be required.

All interest income has already been accounted for.

SIMULATION 1

Analyses

Goods received notes

Date	GRN No.	Supplier	Goods
28/3	456	Garwood James	10 × SP6788
29/3	457	Heath and Blake	20 × FR45
31/3	458	Treadgold (Imports)	10 × 8YHH
31/3	459	Garwood James	10 × SP6789

Purchase orders

Date	PO No.	Supplier	Goods	£ excl VAT
14/3	234	Treadgold (Imports)	15 × 6YHH	780.00
15/3	236	Garwood and James	20 × SP6789	1,120.00
			10 × SP6788	530.00
17/3	240	Heath and Blake	20 × FR45	1,360.00
17/3	241	Treadgold (Imports)	10 × 8YHH	680.00

Expenses to 31 March 19X4

Rates

	£
Initial payment to 31 March 19X3	115
Year 19X3/4	915
	1,030

Motor insurance and road tax

	£
Twelve-month cover 1 April 19X3	756
Renewal of insurance 1 April 19X4	824
Road tax – 1 April 19X3 ⎤	110
Road tax – 30 April 19X3 ⎬ for the ensuing 12 months	110
Road tax – 15 June 19X3 ⎦	220
	2,020

General insurance

	£
Buildings insurance – 12 months to 14 March 19X4	1,560
Buildings contents insurance – 12 months to 31 March 19X4	524
Consequential loss – 12 months to 30 June 19X4	995
Key man – 12 months to 31 January 19X5	603
Building insurance renewal – 12 months	1,899
Building contents renewal – 12 months	633
	6,214

Computer hardware maintenance

	£
Annual service contract to 30 June 19X4	359
Upgrade (seven months) from 1 December 19X3	117
	476

Heat and light

	£
Eastern Electric – quarter ended 30 April 19X3	120
Electricity recharge from previous owner	76
Eastern Gas – period ended 30 June 19X3	210
Eastern Electric – quarter ended 31 July 19X3	196
Eastern Gas – quarter ended 30 September 19X3	195
Eastern Electric – quarter ended 31 October 19X3	199
Eastern Gas – quarter ended 31 December 19X3	265
Eastern Electric – quarter ended 31 January 19X4	280
	1,541

Refuse collection

	£
November 19X3	55
December 19X3	55
January 19X4	55
February 19X4	55
	220

Telephone

	£
English Telecomm – quarter ended 15 June 19X3	112
English Telecomm – quarter ended 15 September 19X3	178
English Telecomm – quarter ended 15 November 19X3 (fax)	108
English Telecomm – quarter ended 15 December 19X3	296
English Telecomm – quarter ended 15 February 19X4 (fax)	121
English Telecomm – quarter ended 15 March 19X4	312
	1,127

Magazine subscriptions

	£
Car Specialist – 6 months to 31 August 19X4	12
What Car? – 12 months to 30 September 19X4	36
	48

PART 2: STOCK AND BAD AND DOUBTFUL DEBTS

Introduction

You are now going to perform some more year-end adjustments: stock and bad and doubtful debts.

Tasks

Stock valuation

A stock count took place on 31 March 19X4. There were five types of alarm in stock.

Cath Brennan has prepared a list of purchases for those stock lines.

What methods of stock valuation might you use? Prepare calculations for each method. Which method seems the most suitable for this type of stock?

Bad and doubtful debts

Here is the aged debtors' listing at 31 March 19X4. Peter Armstrong has also prepared some notes for you.

Which balances would you like to write off and which balances would you like to provide against? Give reasons for your decisions.

Analyses

Stock at 31 March 19X4

	Number held
FR45	25
SP6788	12
SP6789	11
8YHH	10
TY656	14

Purchases since start of trade

	Date	Number	Total cost (excl. VAT) £
FR45	29/3	20	1,360
	15/2	10	640
	31/10	30	1,860
	30/6	40	2,440
SP6788	28/3	10	530
	31/1	15	720
	30/10	5	240
SP6789	31/3	10	560
	15/1	5	275
8YHH	31/3	10	680
	31/1	10	670
TY656	21/7	20	1,150

The model TY656 alarms were bought on 21 July 19X3. Trevor Jones thinks he could sell them for £30 each.

Aged debtors' listing at 31 March 19X4

	Current £	30+ £	60+ £	90+ £
Abraham Motors Ltd	123	255	75	199
Davies MacGregor	332	367	125	350
Peter Mills Dealers	130		234	340
Quorn Dealers				1,456
Other accounts	28,678	18,450	1,245	
Totals	29,263	19,072	1,679	2,345

Abraham Motors have since cleared all amounts over 60 days old.

Davies MacGregor have cleared all amounts over 60 days old with the exception of £25 which they are still disputing.

Peter Mills Dealers are disputing the amounts over 60 days old. Peter Armstrong has letters which suggest they may pay 50% of the amounts outstanding.

Peter Armstrong has received a letter from the liquidator of Quorn Dealers. As unsecured creditors Panther Alarms are unlikely to receive any of the outstanding debt.

PART 3: EXTENDED TRIAL BALANCE

Tasks

Extracting a trial balance

Extract the balances from the nominal ledger accounts and list them on a sheet of analysis paper. Ensure that the trial balance does balance.

Posting adjustments

Following discussions with the directors you have agreed the following adjustments. Prepare the necessary journals and enter these on an extended trial balance.

(1)	Depreciation charge	*Fixed asset category*	£
	Buildings	Freehold buildings	3,612
	Office furniture	Fixtures and fittings (F&F)	4,221
	Office equipment	Plant and machinery (P&M)	5,045
	Warehouse fittings	F&F	6,210
	Motor vans	P&M	1,702
	Cars	P&M	8,181
	Computer equipment	P&M	1,838

(2)	Reclassification of revenue expenditure (originally posted to relevant fixed asset cost account)	
	Motor expenses (motor cars)	1,122
	Computer hardware maintenance	365

(3)	Amounts removed in respect of fixed asset disposals	
	Motor cars – cost	12,416
	Motor cars – accumulated depreciation	2,845
	Computer equipment – cost	165
	Computer equipment – accumulated depreciation	62

(4)	Bad debt write-off	1,456

(5)	Doubtful debt provision required (including a 2% general provision Note (1))	1,580

(6)	Stock valuation	4,021

Note (1)

Bad debt provision

	Total debt	Provision
Total debtors	52,359	
Write-off Quorn Dealers	(1,456)	
Davies MacGregor	(1,174)	25
Peter Mills Dealers	(704)	574
Other accounts	49,025	981
Total provision		1,580

Posting accruals and prepayments

Following discussions with the directors, you have agreed to post the following prepayments and accruals. Put these onto your extended trial balance.

	Prepayment	Accrual
Rental income (received in advance)		167
GRNI Purchases 1		1,360
Purchases 2		1,090
Purchases 3		680
Carriage inwards		78
Carriage outwards		73
Motor insurance and road tax	879	
General insurance	1,464	
Computer hardware maintenance	140	
Heat and light		452
Refuse collection		55
Photocopier charges		25
Stationery		32
Telephone		112
NICs on cars		1,560
Accountancy and audit		4,000
Magazine subscriptions	28	
Interest payable		76
Bank charges		192

Preparing the extended trial balance

Allocate each account to the profit and loss account or the balance sheet. Ensure that the extended trial balance does balance.

Closing the books

Return to the nominal ledger accounts and post the adjustments to the individual ledger accounts. Bring forward the opening balances for the next accounting period. Close off the profit and loss items to the profit and loss account.

PART 4: INCOMPLETE RECORDS

Introduction

The directors are thinking of buying Taylor and Preston Autospares, the business which lets part of Panther Alarms Ltd's warehouse. The directors have asked you to carry out an investigation into the business.

Taylor and Preston Autospares is a partnership started in 19X1 by Jim Taylor and Bob Preston. They sell tyres to retail customers and car dealerships. The directors feel this would be a complementary activity selling tyres to their existing customers.

The partnership has a bookkeeper who maintains the accounting records. Unfortunately he has been ill and the nominal ledger in particular is incomplete. He has provided you with a summary of the cash book which shows transactions through the bank account only. All records are manual.

The partnership's year-end is 31 December.

The partnership is registered for VAT. All supplies are standard-rated. They also offer a 2% settlement discount to credit customers who settle their invoice within 10 days.

The business's only assets are tyre fitting equipment, warehouse racking and office furniture. According to the records available the net book value of fixed assets at 31 December 19X2 was £20,650. There have been no additions or disposals during the year.

Assessment tasks

Task 1

Advise the directors on the best method of valuing stock.

Task 2

Prepare a draft trial balance as at 31 December 19X3 from the information provided.

Task 3

Calculate gross profit for the year ended 31 December 19X3. Assume that the final stock valuation is £5,443.

Task 4

What information would you need to complete the extended trial balance? Prepare a list to give the directors.

Valuation of stock

A stock count took place on 31 December 19X3. Stock was valued at £12,789, using selling prices. The business has not kept records of all of its purchases and a full FIFO valuation is not possible. In addition some of the original stock count sheets have been mislaid.

Trevor Jones has asked your advice on the stock valuation. He wonders if it has to be stated at cost or if selling price can be used. Suggest a possible method of valuation and describe how it could be carried out in practice. State any disadvantages of this method.

Opening balances

Here are the opening balances as at 1 January 19X3.

	£
Fixed assets	20,650
Trade debtors	15,678
Stock	9,566
Cash at bank (overdraft)	2,444
Cash in hand	345
Trade creditors	15,677
VAT control	3,566
PAYE control	641
Loan interest	560
Rent (prepayment)	167
Heat and light (accrual)	654
Telephone (accrual)	99
Loan	10,600
Partners' capital accounts	12,165

Summary of cash book

Receipts		*Payments*	
Bankings from till	50,778	HM Customs and Excise	13,677
Cheques received in post	150,677	Inland Revenue	5,141
Capital introduced	19,000	Payments to suppliers	97,198
		Wages and salaries	20,566
		Drawings	50,000
		Loan interest	950

Payments to suppliers

Purchases	91,455
Heat and light	3,566
Telephone	677
Rent	1,500

The bookkeeper has told you that although cheques received in the post are all from debtors, some receipts from debtors have also been recorded through the till. He also knows that some customers took a discount but he has not kept records of the amounts involved.

At 31 December 19X3 the till held £620. You have confirmed that no payments were made directly from the till.

Year-end debtors are £16,990 before making any adjustments for bad debts.

The bookkeeper has reviewed the VAT returns and the day books for the year and can confirm that sales (including VAT) were £204,542 and purchases (including VAT) were £89,789.

SIMULATION 2

Introduction

Today is 4 July 19X5. You are preparing the VAT return for the quarter ended 30 June 19X5. This is the first time you have prepared the VAT return for Panther Alarms Ltd. The accountants prepared the VAT returns in the past.

They have provided you with a pro forma for preparing the VAT account (*see below*).

During the quarter the following items were purchased:

		£	£	
Raw materials from Heath and Blake who have agreed a settlement discount of 2%			10,600	before VAT and discount
Raw materials from Garwood James			12,000	before VAT

1 May 19X5	Supervan Ltd		
	Motor van K70 EFT	12,500.00	
	VAT @ 17.5%	2,187.50	
		14,687.50	
	Vehicle excise duty	110.00	
			14,797.50

31 May 19X5	Intersport Ltd		
	BMW convertible K224 EFR	25,000.00	
	VAT @ 17.5%	4,375.00	
		29,375.00	
	Vehicle excise duty	110.00	
			29,485.00

4 June 19X5	Office equipment Ltd		
	2 filing cabinets @ £425 each	850.00	
	VAT @ 17.5%	148.75	
			998.75

The VAT due to the Customs and Excise Department on 31 March 19X5 amounting to £7,250 was paid on 21 April 19X5.

During the quarter ended 30 June 19X5 the turnover, before VAT, amounted to £50,120 and analysed for VAT purposes was as follows:

		Turnover £			
		April 19X5	May 19X5	June 19X5	Total
Taxable	Standard rate	15,200	14,250	16,250	45,700
	Zero rated	800	750	770	2,320
Non-taxable	Exempt	700	700	700	2,100
		16,700	15,700	17,720	50,120

Assessment tasks

Task 1

Prepare the purchases day book of Panther Alarms Ltd for the three months to end of June 19X5.

Note: Assume the company maintains an analytical purchase day book for the purpose of this exercise.

Task 2

Draw up a VAT control account.

Task 3

Prepare the account for HM Customs and Excise – VAT for the three months ended 30 June 19X5, using the form provided.

H M Customs and Excise

Value Added Tax Return

For the period
01-04-X5 to 30-06-X5

022 466 5726 13 WO1181

PANTHER ALARMS
WALDEN ROAD
CAMBRIDGE
CB14 8NJ

Your VAT Office telephone number is 071-928 3344

For Official Use

Registration Number	Period

You could be liable to a financial penalty if your completed return and all the VAT payable are not received by the due date.

Due date: 31-07-X5

For Official Use

REMEMBER

You must Include VAT due on EC transactions in boxes 2 & 3 if they occur on or after 1.1.93.

If you are using Retail Scheme B1, D or J, please remember to carry out your annual adjustment at the appropriate time.

Before you fill in this form please read the notes on the back and the VAT Leaflet *"Filling in your VAT return"*. Complete all boxes clearly in ink, writing 'none' where necessary. Don't put a dash or leave any box blank. If there are no pence write **"00"** in the pence column. **Do not** enter more than one amount in any box.

For official use		£	p
	VAT due in this period on **sales** and other outputs **1**		
	VAT reclaimed in this period on **acquisitions** from other **EC Member States** **2**		
	Total VAT due (**the sum of boxes 1 and 2**) **3**		
	VAT reclaimed in this period on purchases on purchases and other inputs (including acquisitions from the EC) **4**		
	Net VAT to be paid to Customs or reclaimed by you (**Difference between boxes 3 and 4**) **5**		
	Total value of **sales** and all other outputs excluding any VAT. **Include your box 8 figure** **6**		00
	Total value of **purchases** and all other inputs excluding any VAT. **Include your box 9 figure** **7**		00
	Total value of all **Supplies** of goods and related services, excluding any VAT, to other **EC Member States** **8**		00
	Total value of all **acquisitions** of goods and related services, excluding any VAT, from other **EC Member States** **9**		00

Retail schemes. If you have used any of the schemes in the period covered by this return please enter the appropriate letter(s) in this box.

If you are enclosing a payment please tick this box.	DECLARATION : You, or someone on your behalf, must sign below.
	I, ... declare that the
	(Full name of signatory in BLOCK LETTERS)
	information given above is true and complete.
	Signature .... Date .... 19 ....
	A false declaration can result in prosecution.

B

CD 2859/N9(02/91)   F 3790(JANUARY 1992)CD 2859/R/N9(02/91)

VAT 100

Practice central assessment

The practice central assessment is in three parts. Complete ALL tasks in EACH part.

Time allowed: 3 hours

SECTION 1

Data

(a)   The trial balance of B Banana as at 31 December 19X5 is reproduced below. The total of the debit balances did not equal the total of the credit balances and the difference was entered in a suspense account pending investigation.

Trial balance as at 31 December 19X5

	Dr £	Cr £
Sales		299,300
Purchases	145,800	
Carriage	1,880	
Salaries and wages	79,600	
Rent, rates and insurance	11,150	
Drawings	12,000	
Heating and lighting	2,150	
Carriage inwards	3,550	
Postage and stationery	4,210	
Advertising	8,880	
Bad debt expense	850	
Cash at bank	3,220	
Cash in hand	460	
Stock as at 1st January 19X5	17,090	
Debtors ledger control account	16,770	
Creditors ledger control account		14,030
Discounts allowed and received	2,400	1,350
Equipment – at cost	100,000	
Equipment – accumulated depreciation		40,000
Suspense account		1,011
Capital		54,319
	410,010	410,010

(b)   The investigation of the accounting records revealed the following errors:

(i)   The sales day book had been undercast by £1,000.

(ii)   Goods with a value of £340 returned to H Spore and Sons, a supplier, had been omitted from the goods returned book.

(iii)   Discount of £20 allowed to N Natt, a credit customer, had been correctly included in the cash book, but had not been posted to the debtors ledger control account or to the personal account of the customer in the sales ledger.

(iv)   The total of the purchase day book had been undercast by £50.

(v)   The discount received column in the cash book has been undercast by £41.

(c)   The following additional matters need to be taken into account:

(i)   Rent, rates and insurance includes £108 paid as a premium covering the year to 30 June 19X6. Nothing has been included as yet in prepaid expenses in respect of this.

(ii)   The last electricity bill paid by the business covered the three months ending 30 November 19X5. Nothing has been included for electricity estimated to have been used in December; this is estimated at £120.

(iii)   Unsold goods in stock as at 31 December 19X5 were valued at cost at £19,160.

(iv)   Depreciation is to be provided on equipment at 20% of cost.

Assessment tasks

Task 1

Prepare journal entries to correct the errors listed in (b). Narratives are required.

Task 2

Enter all the account balances, including those adjusted in Task 1 above, in the first two columns of the extended trial balance.

Task 3

Make appropriate entries in the adjustments column of the extended trial balance. Create additional accounts as required.

Task 4

Extend the figures into the extended trial balance columns for profit and loss account and balance sheet. Total all columns, transferring the balance of profit or loss as appropriate.

SECTION 2

Answer each of the following questions. Your answers should be complete, but as concise as possible.

1 A company held the following stock of computer software at 31 March 1993:

	Cost £	Market value £
Proprietary business software	9,080	14,640
Own-label business software	6,360	7,250
Games software	22,680	16,315

What should the valuation of closing stock have been on 31 March 1993? *(AAT CA J93)*

2 If a business rented out a flat above its premises for £80 per month and the tenants paid the rent a month in advance:

(a) In which account would the flat rent be recorded?

(b) How would the £80 rent paid in advance be shown in the balance sheet at the year-end? *(AAT CA J93)*

3 You have heard a rumour that one of your customers, who owes you £1,640, is about to go out of business. Should this debt be treated as a bad debt, a doubtful debt or should the rumour be ignored? Give reasons. *(AAT CA D93)*

4 If a company decided it needed a china coffee set to use to entertain potential customers, and it took a suitable one from the stock in the warehouse, how would you record this in the books of the company? *(AAT CA D93)*

5 Explain fully what the balance on VAT a/c represents. *(AAT CA D93)*

6 When cash sales are banked, which accounts would be debited and credited? *(AAT CA D94)*

7 If, in preparing the extended trial balance for a business, the business were found to be making a loss:

(a) Would the loss appear in the Dr or Cr column of the profit and loss account balances?

(b) How would the loss be dealt with in the balance sheet balances columns?
  (AAT CA D94)

8 You work as an accounting technician and have recently prepared accounts for the first year of trading of a new business. Mr Batty had always been an employee until he started his own business and he does not really understand accounts. Soon after showing him the draft accounts you receive the following memoranda.

(1) 'I see that you have included a heading of 'depreciation' in expenses. I do not recall spending anything on such an item. Please explain what this is. In addition, I purchased a van during the year and sold it for less than I paid for it. Why then do the accounts show a profit on the disposal of this van? Is it something to do with 'depreciation'?'

(2)   'I note that you have not used the figures from the stock schedules which I sent you in the accounts. I valued all my stock using the most recent price lists, since those are prices which I would have to pay to replace these stocks. I see that in the accounting policies note you state that stock is valued at the lower of cost and net realisable value. What does this mean?'

Write memoranda to Mr Batty in response to his queries.

SECTION 3   (AAT CA D93)

A friend of yours from Leicester, Kuldipa Potiwal, runs a small computer games retail and mail order business, but she does not keep proper accounting records. She has now been approached by the Inland Revenue for the details of the profit she has earned for the last year. She has provided you with the following bank account summary for the year ended 31 October 1993:

Bank account summary

	£
Balance at bank (1 November 1992)	
Bank overdraft	3,250
Receipts	
Cash paid in	56,000
Cheques from debtors	46,000
Investment income *Do not include.*	1,500
Rent received	2,500
Payments	
Payments to trade creditors	78,000
Rent and rates	6,400
Postage and packing costs	2,200
Motor expenses	5,050
Administration expenses	4,600

Additional information was provided as follows:

(1)   Kuldipa intends to sell all her computer games at cost plus 50%.

(2)   Before paying cash receipts into the bank, Kuldipa used some of the cash received to make a number of payments:

Wages of shop assistant and driver	£350 per week
Drawings	£220 per week
Administration expenses	£750 per annum

(3)   The investment income was interest on her private investment account.

(4)   Other balances were as follows:

	31 October 1992 £	31 October 1993 £
Delivery van (valuation)	17,500	12,500
Stock of games	12,200	13,750
Trade creditors	9,000	13,400
Trade debtors	6,000	7,200
Rates paid in advance	500	200
Rent receivable	–	250
Administration expenses owing	175	215

(5)   During the year a vanload of games being delivered to credit customers was stolen. The van was recovered, undamaged, but the games have not been recovered. The insurance company has agreed to pay for 50% of the stolen games, but payment has not yet been received.

Kuldipa Potiwal calculated from the copy delivery notes that the selling price value of the games stolen was £6,000.

(6)   At Christmas 1992 Kuldipa Potiwal gave games as presents to her young relatives. The selling price of these games was £480.

Task 1

Prepare a detailed calculation of the net profit of the business for the year ended 31 October 1993.

Task 2

Calculate the balance of Kuldipa's capital account at 31 October 1993.

Index

Publications Questionnaire

At Financial Training we are interested in knowing your views of our products. We would appreciate your assistance in helping us to maintain our high standards by completing this simple questionnaire.

1   Title of publication _____

2   Content

For each question, tick the box which most closely reflects your view.

	Excellent	Good	Satisfactory	Poor
Did the content cover the syllabus thoroughly?	☐	☐	☐	☐
Was the writing style clear and easy to understand?	☐	☐	☐	☐
Were the worked examples useful and relevant?	☐	☐	☐	☐
Were there sufficient diagrams, graphs and tables?	☐	☐	☐	☐
Were the exam style questions beneficial?	☐	☐	☐	☐
Were the answers to questions comprehensive?	☐	☐	☐	☐
Were the style and layout clear?	☐	☐	☐	☐

3   General

Please suggest any improvements that you feel would be beneficial:

_____

_____

_____

Have you noticed any errors in this publication? If so, please specify?

Page   Error

_____   _____

_____   _____

_____   _____

4   Further information

If you would like to receive information on other Financial Training products and courses, please supply your name and address:

_____

_____

Thank you for your co-operation.

Please return your completed questionnaire to: *Production Department*
Financial Training
136–142 Bramley Road, London W10 6SR